John Pentland Mahaffy

Prolegomena to Ancient History

John Pentland Mahaffy

Prolegomena to Ancient History

ISBN/EAN: 9783337014759

Printed in Europe, USA, Canada, Australia, Japan

Cover: Foto ©ninafisch / pixelio.de

More available books at **www.hansebooks.com**

[To face Title-page.

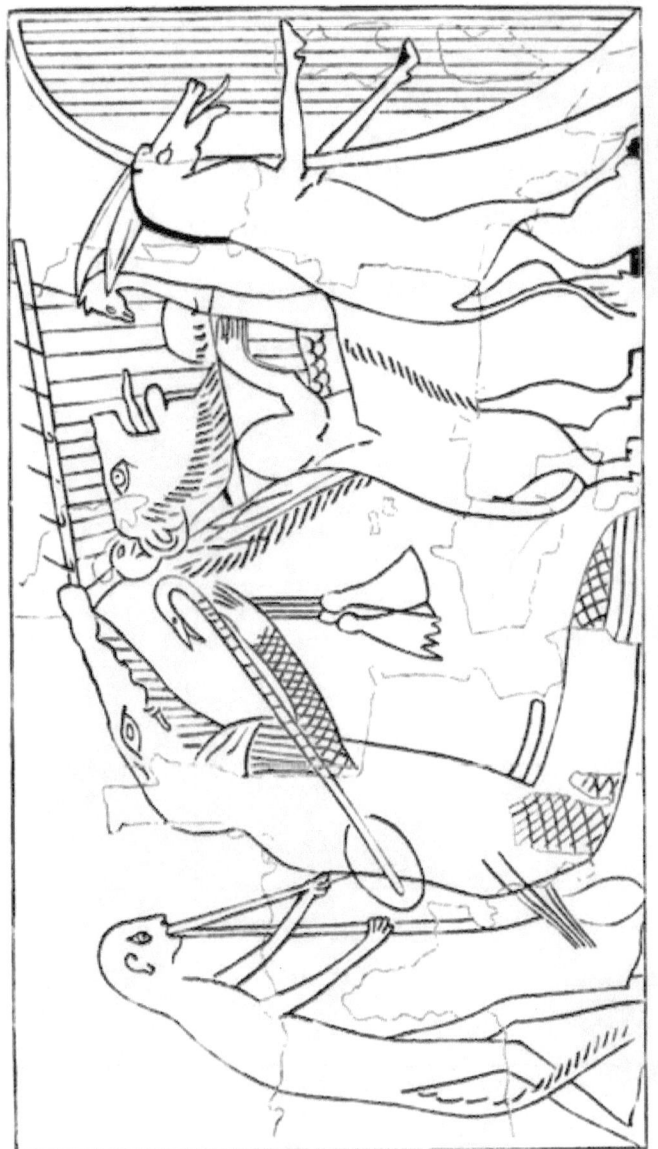

CARICATURE OF AN EGYPTIAN CONCERT.

(From the Turin Satiric Papyrus.)

Prolegomena to Ancient History,

CONTAINING

PART I.—THE INTERPRETATION OF LEGENDS AND INSCRIPTIONS.

PART II.—A SURVEY OF OLD EGYPTIAN LITERATURE.

BY

JOHN P. MAHAFFY, A.M., M.R.I.A.,

FELLOW AND TUTOR OF TRINITY COLLEGE,
AND
LECTURER IN ANCIENT HISTORY IN THE UNIVERSITY OF DUBLIN.

LONDON:
LONGMANS, GREEN, & CO.
1871.

TO

WILLIAM STOKES,

M.D., D.C.L., M.R.I.A., ETC.,

REGIUS PROFESSOR OF PHYSIC IN THE UNIVERSITY OF DUBLIN,

THIS VOLUME

IS

AFFECTIONATELY DEDICATED

PREFACE.

THE following Essays, compiled from a course of public Lectures in the University of Dublin, contain the facts which the audience desired to obtain in a permanent form. The omission of local allusions, and of colloquial address, will, I trust, make the book of wider application and of larger use, as it is intended to expound, briefly and yet accurately, some of the great discoveries made in our day concerning early civilisations. The Essays are not properly History, but *Prolegomena to History*, being mainly concerned in discussing the nature and the value of our evidences for human culture antecedent to that of Greece and Rome.

In the present day, the *ipse dixit* of a Professor, even in his own subject, may command assent from the general public, but cannot claim it from the youngest earnest inquirer, if he be independent and desires to think for himself. It was therefore to me a real cause of satisfaction, that not merely competent critics, but even the student readers of my former published Lectures, complained that there were no citations of the evidence from which I drew my pictures of primitive civilisations. The same intelligent doubts encountered me when undertaking my present duties. If hieroglyphical inscriptions were quoted, I was asked: are they really deciphered? If the statements of legends were received, it was objected, that legends might be pure fictions.

Nothing can be more encouraging to an honest teacher than to find this sound scepticism in his class. But it necessitates a prolonged and serious discussion of preliminary questions, and a complete digest of original authorities and of their evidence, before the descriptive teaching of historical facts can be approached. This thread, therefore, binds together the various subjects discussed in the volume. All the following Essays supply the reader with evidence either of real results in deciphering hitherto unknown languages, or of the credit to which primitive legends are entitled.

The latter question being *adhuc sub judice*, I

cannot expect to avoid criticism, especially as the attitude assumed is polemical, and opposed to the school now most popular in England. But I venture to think that the arguments brought together in the second Essay, especially the psychological points, have not yet been fully stated, and are worthy of the serious attention of Comparative Mythologers. I must record specially the assistance given me by Dr. Lottner in this part of the book.

Perhaps it was unwise to put forth in the outset an adverse judgment of Thukydides without going more fully into the evidence. He has so tormented and yet interested critical scholars with his pregnant grammatical anomalies, that they love him with that peculiar affection which a mother feels for the wayward but clever child that has cost her most trouble and anxiety. It may be necessary to state elsewhere ampler reasons for my conclusions on this point, which are no sudden thoughts, but the results of long, and I hope, mature consideration.

The Essays which concern Persian, Assyrian, and Egyptian records are not subject to the same criticism. The conclusions which they assert are no longer contested by any competent judge, but they are almost unknown to the larger part of the intelligent public. The few men who have mastered hieroglyphic or cuneiform writing are so busy with fresh discoveries, that they have neither time nor inclination to give the world any succinct general survey of the results already attained. Moreover, the discoverer is apt to lay so much stress on detail, and to turn aside so frequently from broad and plain arguments to special researches, that he may not be the best exponent, to the world at large, even of the discoveries to which he has himself largely contributed.

The best apology to these special scholars, who despise a merely historical account of their researches, is, that as *they* have not deigned to expound them sufficiently, others must do so. Considering the labour required to ascertain the sources and arrange the information on Egyptian and cuneiform writing, this short survey will be acceptable, not only to those who are entering upon such studies, but to a larger class, who desire to weigh fairly the value of recent discoveries in enlarging our knowledge of ancient History. So scattered, so difficult of access, are the various monographs and papers on Egyptology and Assyriology, that without the aid of a public Library, and of a public Library specially supplied with the Transactions and Proceedings of foreign societies, it is hardly possible to ascertain where they are and to obtain them. I have to thank the Board of Trinity College for allowing me to order all the special books required, and should have been well supplied but for the late war, which prevented my obtaining several important works from Paris during the siege.

I trust those English discoverers, who are second to none in Europe, will not suspect me of omitting to quote them fully from any want of due appreciation. It was rather because in this country their works are better known, and probably in the hands of all who are interested in such subjects, and also because the newest exposition was naturally the most complete, and therefore best suited to instruct the reader. Dr. Birch's original translations, for example, of many Egyptian documents, have been supplemented and completed in later versions by foreign scholars, who, while they followed his footsteps, have added from their own stores.

Had I been acquainted with any survey, even

tolerably complete, of old Egyptian literature, I should hardly have ventured to discuss it; but the sketches of Dr. Birch, of Baron Bunsen, and of M. Naville, are either so brief, or now so long published, that none of them can claim to bring the reader up to the present state of the subject. They are also unsatisfactory in not quoting extracts sufficient to give a distinct notion of the works described. I have therefore ventured to collect in the last and longest of these Essays most of the scattered information published up to the present time, and have sacrificed form and symmetry, in order to quote, as much as possible, from accurate translations of the documents themselves. Where my defective knowledge of the language prevented my testing these translations, I have taken pains to compare independent versions, and have used them where they agree. Historical documents were intentionally excluded, as being best discussed in connexion with the epoch and the men to which they refer—a large subject, and beyond the scope and compass of these Prolegomena. For the same reason I have marked events in Egyptian History by dynasties, in order to avoid the thorny subject of early Egyptian chronology. For the reader's convenience, however, I have appended to this Preface a table of *approximate* dates B. C. from M. Mariette's writings, which will serve as a general indication how to classify the dynasties.¹

But enough of excuses and explanations, lest the reader should compare me to the desponding Nikias, who would not commit his soldiers to the battle without delaying each of them, πατρόθεν τε ἐπονομάζων καὶ αὐτοὺς ὀνομαστὶ καὶ φυλήν, ἄλλα τε λέγων ὅσα ἐν τῷ τοιούτῳ ἤδη τοῦ καιροῦ ὄντες ἄνθρωποι οὐ πρὸς τὸ δοκεῖν τινι ἀρχαιολογεῖν φυλαξάμενοι εἴποιεν ἄν.

I must not, however, omit to thank my friends, Dr. Lottner, Mr. Tyrrell, and Mr. Leeper, for their valuable aid in correcting the proof sheets.

The Index is in some respects more complete than the text, as several important books, which reached me too late for quotation in the footnotes, have been there cited.

---

¹ Under the word *chronology* in the Index I have added the best authorities on the subject.

APPROXIMATE CHRONOLOGY

OF THE MOST REMARKABLE EGYPTIAN DYNASTIES.

NOTE.—Other chronologers lower the date of Menes considerably, but none below 3200 B.C. **Later researches are** distinctly tending rather to **increase than** diminish the antiquity of Egyptian civilisation. The differences cease about the invasion of the shepherds, from which point scholars generally keep within the same century in their dates, a limit accurate enough in such very high figures. Mr. Goodwin places Menes, circ. 4000 B.C.; the IVth dynasty, before 3200; the XIIth beginning with 2400; **his conclusions agree** with Lepsius and Brugsch pretty closely.

OLD EMPIRE.

DYNASTY.		DATE.
Ist. (Menes),	circ.	5000 B.C.
IInd. (Sent),	,,	4700 ,,
IIIrd. (1st part of Prisse papyrus),	,,	4450 ,,
IVth. (Pyramids),	,,	4200 ,,
Vth. (Ptah-hotep),	,,	3900 ,,

MIDDLE EMPIRE.

XIth. (Earliest specimen of Ritual),	,,	} 3050 ,,
XIIth. (Amenemha, &c.),	,,	
XIVth. (Invasion of shepherds),	,,	2400 ,,

NEW EMPIRE.

XVIIIth. (Amenophis, Tothmes, &c.),	,,	1700 ,,
XIXth. (Ramses II., Menephtah, and the Exodus),	,,	1450 ,,
XXth.	,,	1280 ,,
XXIst.	,,	1110 ,,
XXIInd. (Shishak and Rehoboam)	,,	980 ,,
XXVIth. (Psamtik I.), *certainly in*	,,	665 ,,
XXXIst. (Cambyses and Persians),	,,	340 ,,

ESSAYS,

&c. &c.

ESSAY I.

On the Methods of Writing and Teaching Ancient History—Herodotus and Thukydides.

"Quæ priores eloquentia percoluere, hæc rerum fide tradentur."
                                                        TACITUS.

ANCIENT History has ever been one of the chief objects of human curiosity and therefore of human learning. Men have differed widely in their theories and methods of writing and of teaching it, but no human beings above the rank of the lowest savages are ever careless about their ancestors or the past annals of their nation. The very principle of causality, the great agent that prompts every human inquiry, forbids us to rest content with the Now and the Here, and urges us to search for the hidden and the past. Some sort of ancient history therefore must exist, and has existed since the dawn of civilization. But history differs from history as much as the medicine-man from the modern histologist, the amulet and charm from the treatment of the enlightened physician. First come the floating legend and the simple tale, handed down by oral tradition, embellished with wonders and idealised by lofty motives. They are told by some aged crone or sightless bard, and received by simple hearers without doubt or criticism. Then there is a time when such things no longer command assent, when men want to know dates and generations and a rational sequence of events, and so there springs up beside the rich epic, which pictured human life and motives, the barren chronicle: instead of varied poetry men's minds are fed with bald and wretched prose, or prosy verse. Such, for example, was the style of the Greek historical writers who preceded Herodotus, which affects indeed greater accuracy than its beautiful predecessor, but abandons far more than it adds. Such a change can in no way be called an advance in knowledge, except in so far as it lays the foundation for better things. Then comes the day of pragmatical narrative, when not only are facts recorded, but motives and reflections added; and this is the first record that can properly be called history. There is yet a further step, before we reach critical history, which consists in the careful weighing of the evidence for our facts, and, consequently, for our theories.

Thukydides, for example, who is generally thought a critical historian, is not strictly such. He submits present events, it is true, to careful sifting, and rejects altogether any miraculous interference. But I believe that had Thukydides not been **a sceptic in** religion he would never have had so **high a** reputation. To historical scepticism he can lay no **claim.** On the legendary history of his country he *pragmatises* (as the Germans say), and accommodates motives which he thinks suitable **to the** recorded **events.** But his whole criticism affects the *motives* **of the heroes,** and not the stories alleged concerning **them.**[1] Thukydides, in fact, and the Athenian school to which he belonged, were so engrossed **with politics** and **with** political notions, that whenever they could attribute any **such origin to** an alleged fact, it became to them not **only** probable but **a** matter of history. There were political reasons for Minos and his naval power, political reasons for the armament under Agamemnon, **and,** therefore, these accounts were admitted into history. To allow any interference of the gods, to admit any chivalrous motives or **any unselfish passion as** an efficient cause in human affairs; above all, to believe that any woman could influence politics or change the history of **a nation,** these were the ideas rejected by Thukydides and his school with scorn. **It was under** this theory that he reviewed the past history of his country. From Herodotus, **with** whom **he** intentionally contrasts **him-**

---

[1] Thus, for example, he alludes to the story of the murder of Itys (II. c. 29) as an historical fact.

self, he really differs only in omitting from his estimate of causes the action of gods and of women, as well as of benevolence and of self-denial.

To ignore and to neglect, along with popular superstitions, these prominent facts in human nature, is the capital defect of the history of Thukydides.

Just as it is possible to write a chronological skeleton of a period of history, which gives all the events in their order, without any logical sequence or coherence, so it is equally possible to give a *political* skeleton of a period, in which the action of the great general causes at the basis of historical changes is given, but the action of individuals and their special assistance or hindrance to the general laws of history, are either omitted or undervalued. Such a political outline is, like the chronological one, imperfect, just as a skeleton is an imperfect representation of a man with flesh and blood. But the political skeleton is not only imperfect, it becomes actually false, if the writer intends it for a complete image of the period which he desires to represent. From this point of view I consider the history of Thukydides not merely defective, but, to some extent, false, as compared with Herodotus, whose work is like a mirror, reflecting to us all that he had seen and heard.

Although, therefore, Thukydides certainly sifted his materials, and may therefore in one sense be called a critical historian, from another he cannot lay claim to the title; for he selected his materials with a view to a foregone conclusion; he made them fit a preconceived theory. To use the expression of Sir G. C. Lewis, he is a "complete historical sophist."[1] But it is justly to his credit that he does so merely by *omission*. He neither invents nor (so far as we know) distorts facts, and in this differs widely from the other great political theorist of antiquity who preached his doctrines by writing a history. Tacitus both relates unfounded gossip, which he meant his readers to believe, and assigns motives, in themselves absurd, and often contradictory to each other, to make out a case against the Roman imperial system.[2]

---

[1] Applied, in his Letters, p. 348, to a well-known living historian.

[2] This habit is by no means extinct. Even the most brilliant German historians seem tainted with the impropriety of displaying their political opinions through a thin veil of history. Of course, the French anti-Imperialists afford the most obtrusive example of the same defect. The infamous injustice of Tacitus has been exposed with extraordinary care by L. Freitag, in his essay entitled "*Tiberius und Tacitus.*" A careful perusal of this book will fill the reader with wonder at the cleverness, and indignation at the grossness, of the libel. According to Tacitus' own statements thirty-nine persons were executed during the twenty-three years of Tiberius's reign. Of these only seventeen were executed for treason. Twelve of them are conceded guilty by Tacitus. The remaining five were put to death against the Emperor's will by the Senate. Almost all the other twenty-two persons executed were themselves *delatores*

What, then, is a critical historian? He is a man who not only acts with perfect honesty and impartiality, in stating *all* the evidence which can be procured, but who is competent to weigh the exact value of the evidence of every witness produced. He must take nothing on trust, but must show accurately the source not only of his own, but of his witnesses' information. From such a point of view we can hardly point out a really critical historian before the present century. But among our own writers Mr. Hallam is a critical historian, and Sir G. C. Lewis and Bishop Thirlwall; so also is M. Albert Rillier.[1]

The reader will observe with surprise that I have not mentioned the names of the greatest modern historians in this list. The omission was made advisedly. For though an historian is bound to do all that these men have done in sifting the evidence for their evidence, and weighing it critically—though he is also bound not to do what Tacitus and the modern quasi-historians in France have done, who make history a mere arena for supporting a pre-conceived political theory—after all these conditions are fulfilled, there yet remains the distinctive quality of a *great* historian—the formation of an historical theory based upon his facts, and the sober balancing of probable evidence, and of uncontradicted though

---

[1] Author of the "*Origines de la Confederation Suisse.*"

unsubstantiated tradition. History is not a mere Report upon evidence, nor a mere judicial inquiry, as the lawyers would have us believe. Blue Books, such as the works of G. C. Lewis, and of many of the Germans, are the materials for history, and not history itself.

After all the materials are collected, there remains the appreciation of them, a far more subtile process, and beyond the scope of ordinary inquirers. This appreciation, or historic sense, is a quality inborn in some men, just as a faculty of *diagnosis* is natural to a great physician. It is of course trained, improved, and corrected by study and experience, but no ordinary man will ever create it within himself by such means; and as the faculty is a sort of instinct, so the conclusions to which it leads cannot always be explained to the ordinary juryman or lawyer, who cross-examines the historian from his lower standpoint. This is always the difficulty of the expert, when brought into contact with the vulgar. The most ordinary example is that of a physician in a court of law, where the common *nisi prius* devices are often sufficient to overthrow all his authority. How can he transfer his power of diagnosis to the judge and jury? How can he give a reason for his instinct? And yet, if he cannot explain himself, how is his evidence to be of value in a court of law, where everything is to be explained?

The appreciation, therefore, of delicate evidence

is one of the distinctive features of a great historian as such. By this faculty conclusions are felt long before the evidence for them is such as can be definitely stated; and it is by keeping such a goal before our eyes, that the greatest discoveries will ever be accomplished.

The very setting up however of such a mental goal implies more than the mere sifting of evidence; it implies a definite theory formed upon that evidence, a theory which underlies all the details, and gives consistency to the huge mass of otherwise unconnected particulars. Without some such theory that enlists his sympathies, that adds passion to his judgment, and unity to his researches, the most acute and painstaking inquirer will only be a Commissioner, and not an Historian. Such have been two of the patient writers to whom I have already alluded. They had every quality save what is vaguely called genius. In history, genius appears to me to mean this strong stamp with which the writer's mind marks all his materials—this frame into which he is able to fit all his figures. If the frame be formed, and inadequate to include all the facts, he is a *doctrinaire*, whose work will be interesting and often very suggestive; but yet he will not be a great historian. A remarkable specimen of such a mind is Bishop Warburton, whose *Divine Legation of Moses* is probably the most remarkable attempt in our language to bring myriad facts within the compass of an inadequate and irrelevant theory. The highly interesting *Histoire des Perses*, lately published by the Comte de Gobineau, is another less extreme specimen, full of genius and eminently suggestive; yet from an historical point of view exceedingly unsound.[1] But when the theory is really adequate to the facts, then there results one of the great books that mould the thoughts of many generations.

Consider the history of Herodotus. He wrote on one definite theory, perhaps on more than one. But the effects of the Divine *Nemesis* on the empires of men gave him a fixed principle from which he viewed the history of the world before his time. Many and various as are his digressions and anecdotes, this one great idea raises them from an invertebrate, so to speak, to a vertebrate organism; and although the conception is in itself objectionable, and even slightly Swinburnian, and prompts him to give an excessive attention to tales of wonder and of superstition, yet it has also undeniable advantages. Being an essentially theological, and not

---

[1] His idea is the glorification of the Iranian race, as compared not only with the Semites but also with the Greeks. From this point of view, he rewrites the history of Esther and Xerxes with the most delicate appreciation of the conditions and circumstances (vol. ii. pp. 159-74). He also boldly attacks the history of the Persian wars with Greece from the Iranian side, and presents the facts for the first time, so far as I know, in this light.

a political, dogma, it did not tempt him to misrepresent the opinions or the conduct of men and of parties. The honest facts of the great war illustrated his theory with all the meanness and the jealousy of the actors, and still more with the accidents that so often turn the balance in human affairs. He seems bound by no political theory, prejudiced by no special form of government, and his historical vision was far too wide and clear to permit of hero-worship in the modern sense. For these reasons Herodotus, with all his imperfections, his childishnesses, and his superstitions, has left us a more interesting, a more important, and, I think, a more instructive work than his rival, Thukydides.

This latter was an Athenian, in all the narrowness of the word—a quality which it seems strange to assert of the best educated people in the world. But the expression can be amply justified. No men ever had narrower sympathies than the Athenian despot-democrats. They despised all nations except their own. They despised all divisions of that nation except themselves. They even despised all those among themselves who were not strictly politicians. They looked with contempt upon all foreign history and civilization; on all simpler or more primitive Greeks; on all their own women, servants, and old men, because sickness or war had excluded them from the fever of public life. This, was the attitude of Thukydides. His plan is very shrunken and small when compared to that of Herodotus. It excludes the collisions and the contrasts of races, the ornaments of anecdote and digressive description, above all, the analysis of any rational motives or springs of action, save those of cold calculation and political expediency. Two passions only suffice in his estimate of human character: ambition and revenge. With them, indeed, his cold narrative is often dyed deeply enough. But all the more trivial and uncertain, and therefore more deeply interesting causes of great effects in history—the action of caprice in the despot, of love and partiality in the statesman, above all, the influence of women transgressing the time of leisure or the day of pleasure—these he not only neglects, but deliberately excludes from serious life. Amestris and Gorgo, Demokedes and Xerxes, as personalities, are to him nonexistent in sober history. His genius applied itself to show that all the events of a great war could be explained apart from these unworthy trifles.

His work is a great history, because it was written with passion to support a theory, and his positive theory was a vindication of the policy of the great Perikles, as being such as would have saved both Athens and Greece, had it been carried out consistently. But this was not enough. He must not only explain and develope the policy of Perikles; he must exclude those to him unworthy and incredible influences, which all the Athenian public persisted in attributing to the great statesman. **Cold and** distant as Perikles was—avoiding society, and keeping aloof from the perpetual talking of his countrymen, never smiling, rarely lamenting—the theory of Thukydides, that his whole life was one of **pure and earnest politics** was natural enough, and had doubtless many adherents. **But the** weight of contemporary evidence does not support it. The historians and philosophers of his own and the succeeding generation, the comic poets, and their highly competent scholiasts, who lived near enough **to catch the echo of** the time—in fact all our authorities, **save** Thukydides, believed that behind the mask of **cold earnestness was a warm and** passionate nature, **revelling in** pleasure, and **led by** the ministers to that **pleasure.**[1] The Peloponnesian war, for example, had its deep causes in the jealousy of race and the collision of large interests, according to **both** these authors **and** Thukydides, yet they asserted the flame to have been kindled, **not by** the **Korkyraean dispute, but** by a much smaller and meaner one, nearer home, and affecting the interests not of nations, but of one individual, Aspasia. They persisted in asserting that **the** great man was led against his better reason by **the charms** of this able and **fascinating** woman. **They regarded** her as **a power in** the State. When

---

[1] Βασιλεῦ Σατύρων, τί ποτ' οὐκ ἐθέλεις δόρυ βαστάζειν, κ. τ. λ. says the comic poet Hermippus of him.

Perikles defended her, he was moved, as he was moved but once again in his life. When she allied herself to a low fellow after his death, she at once made him one of the leaders in the State.[1]

It has always appeared to me that Thukydides is covertly combating this belief about Perikles all through his history. His positive theory was, as I have said, that the cold, clear policy of his ideal statesman would have been the real salvation of his country. Its negative side was this: that human affairs, depending on computations of commercial interest and of political expediency, are not swayed by the interference of any such capricious agents as gods or women. The religious scepticism of his

---

[1] Dr. Sauppe, in his article (Göttingen Transactions, vol. xiii.) on Plutarch's Sources for the Life of Perikles, from which I have taken these details, disbelieves the last story on very German grounds. Lysikles is known to have been a political leader one year after the death of Perikles; Dr. Sauppe therefore argues, first, that Aspasia must have been in too much grief to have thought of a new *liaison*; and, secondly, that were it so, there was no time left for her education to produce its effects. On the former point I speak hesitatingly, not being thoroughly informed as to the amount of grief usual in such characters upon such occasions. But, if the German professor has made it his special study, in order to arrive at the truth in the case of Aspasia, he ought to give us his evidence, which appears flatly to contradict popular notions. As to his second point, the suddenness of Lysikles' rise appears to me the strongest argument for, and not against, the story.

day made it easy for him to get rid of the theory of Providential interposition; the question of female influence was much more serious. His work was indeed too great and dignified to admit of direct controversy, and his open allusions to these influences are very few indeed. He speaks once pointedly concerning the elasticity of interpretation necessary to the credit of oracles. He speaks once contemptuously, in the person of Perikles, of the interference of women in public affairs.[1] But I think we can see an indirect refutation of the latter underlying his argument in many places. Not merely is his absolute silence concerning Aspasia remarkable and intentional, but his reflections on the Trojan War seem to insinuate how previous writers, especially including Herodotus, had as it were trifled with the serious conflicts of nations, and ac-

---

[1] II. 54 and 45. Though I consider Thukydides quite capable of interpolating with this sentiment the real speech of Perikles, whose connexion with Aspasia gave room for an obvious retort, there are, nevertheless, historical grounds for his having really uttered it, which are worth mentioning, as they have hitherto escaped the historians of the period. When Perikles had, on a previous occasion, delivered a funeral oration, the women, who seem at Athens to have had no other opportunity of hearing an orator, were so transported with admiration, that they overwhelmed him with garlands and with acclamations, a proceeding exceedingly disagreeable to his distant and dignified composure. It is the repetition of this unpleasant enthusiasm that he apparently guards against by his cold and contemptuous advice.

counted for them by an absurdly inadequate cause. To talk of Helen as the origin of the Trojan War was exactly as absurd as to refer the outbreak of the Peloponnesian War to Aspasia and her girls. And as the latter war could be accounted for by purely political considerations, so the mythical conflict around Troy had no other origin.[1] As men would ever remain the same, and be able to refer to his analysis of the Peloponnesian War as a permanent lesson in politics, so the olden time only differed from his own in possessing less money and fewer ships, not according to the visionary fancies of poets and old women. With this supreme contempt of trifles, with this deep enthusiasm for the policy and intellect of Perikles, he wrote his great defective history. The most remarkable portion of it is that which is the least historical. For the speeches which he composed, and put into the mouths of his various characters on suitable occasions, were no mere ornaments, but dramatic representations of the motives underlying his facts. They contain most of his conclusions and convictions. They

---

[1] He does not positively deny that Helen may have served as an excuse, cf. 1, c. 9. Ἀγαμέμνων τέ μοι δοκεῖ τῶν τότε δυνάμει προὔχων καὶ οὐ τοσοῦτον τοῖς Τυνδάρεω ὅρκοις κατειλημμένους τοὺς Ἑλένης μνηστῆρας ἄγων τὸν στόλον ἀγεῖραι. He has stated just before what the cause of all the earlier wars had been, ἐφιέμενοι γὰρ τῶν κερδῶν.

are, in fact, in combination with his personally expressed reflections, the exposition of his historical, or rather political theories.[1]

The two great Greek historians are peculiarly suitable examples, when we are discussing the proper method of writing critical history. For the defects of the one are supplied by the merits of the other. So far as vividness and simplicity of narration, faithful reproduction of details, artlessness and honesty of purpose are concerned, Herodotus is far superior to his rival. He is also superior to him in the loftiness of his conception, which includes, I may say, the destinies of all the known world, and reduces them to a great harmony under one principle. But so far as we lay stress on dignity and severity of style, elimination of superstition and gossip, and the development of a distinct and precise political theory, no author, ancient or modern, has ever surpassed Thukydides. Yet as regards what was to him ancient history, he is hardly a more critical writer than Herodotus. To those who desire with modern lights to study the remote beginnings of Greek history, he is even far less useful, for while the simpler Herodotus reproduces more or less faithfully the original legends handed down to him, Thukydides casts all

---

[1] The Melian dialogue, for example (v. c. 85-112) has been proved, to my mind, unhistorical by Mr. Grote, and can, therefore, have no other object in his work than to illustrate a theory.

their information into the crucible of his political theory, and produces (as has been well observed) a result which is neither legend nor history.[1] His results appear indeed probable, being constructed upon vulgar and ordinary human motives; but as a million other results are equally probable on similar motives, in the absence of positive evidence such history may be only more misleading than good childish wonders.

I have also chosen the great Greek historians as illustrative examples in discussing critical history, because the accident of our classical education has made them more familiarly and accurately known to us than perhaps any other, and because their briefness and their acknowledged excellence render them in other respects equally suitable for such a purpose. They will serve us likewise, though not so well, when we proceed to the next question before us, that of *teaching* critical history. This latter is indeed a far more important subject to the generality of mankind. To write a critical history for the advancement of learning is conceded only to a few men of exceptional genius; whereas the teaching of history, and the compiling of works intended to lead ordinary minds into the subject, require a large number of labourers, and must ever be in consider-

---

Grote's History, I., p. 545 (large edition)

able demand. And be it remembered, that the office of teaching history, humble as it may often seem, is nevertheless one of the conditions whereby genius may either be checked and turned aside, or stimulated and encouraged. Surely, many of our ablest minds are not originally cast for one particular purpose, which they must attain in spite of all circumstances, but are equally adapted to several lines of research; and so an interesting and suggestive introduction to any one of these studies contrasts it with its rivals, and determines young minds to follow it far oftener than we imagine. Here, too, there is place for accident in human affairs. I am convinced, for example, that as we lose a great many mathematicians by tormenting our boys with idle and senseless repetitions of Euclid, until they become convinced, from their necessary hatred of the only science they are taught, that they have no taste for any science at all,—as we so lose mathematicians, we also lose many historians by the equally stupid and clumsy teaching of our handbooks. If our children learn ancient history as a sort of almanac—made up of names and dates and tables—it is no wonder they dislike it. On the other hand, I have never yet known a boy of any literary taste, who has not formed an early attachment for history, if encouraged to read the large and philosophical works which are usually reserved for the University course. The conclusion naturally forced upon us is this: if the necessary size and length of these *chefs d'œuvres* make it inexpedient to have nothing else for the use of younger students, what compromise can we effect so as to reduce our histories in length, and yet make them pleasant, useful, and suggestive books?

The problem of teaching history is therefore neither easy nor unimportant; and it is only when we come to weigh the difficulties that beset us, and the errors we must avoid, that its real intricacies emerge into view. If the almanac style of handbook is obviously dull and repulsive to the young, we must take care that we do not fall into the opposite extreme, and substitute an historical novel for history. Of course such books as *Anne of Geierstein*, and *The Last of the Barons*, and Creasy's *Old Love and the New*, do teach a great deal of history, and I should prefer to have children taught through them than through what may be called the modern *logographers*;[1] yet still where the chief interest is centred upon the fictitious situations and motives of the hero, the mere framework and background of historical facts do not come with sufficient importance before the mind. And so the emotions which are imaginary are remembered, and the facts which are real are forgotten, or at least inaccurately learned.

---

[1] I mean of course logographers, in the earlier or historical sense, such as the composers of the bald annals before Herodotus.

This is one danger; and here is another, which is not confined to the handbooks for the young. It is the love of vague generalities and wide theories about historical epochs, without a proper and careful digest of facts. The whole fashion of the day tends in this direction. Essays, and broad views, and comprehensive sketches, suit the hurry and the idleness and the love of generalisation of those who wish not to know a subject, but merely to talk or write brilliantly about it. Broad views are doubtless the finest features in our great historians. But if they are presented without a full statement of their evidence, and if they are used as a substitute for facts, they contradict the very use for which they are intended. It is only when they explain and connect the strict and unvarnished facts, that they aid our memory, and increase our knowledge.

I often apprehend that the present tendency of Oxford culture is to encourage the writing of these sketchy theoretical essays, brilliant in style and conception, but impatient of real labour; and, since we regard Oxford, in literary matters, as best indicating the tone of the rising intellects of the day, it seems all the more necessary to insist that mere historical theorising is not history, and that this science, like every other, requires to be studied in minute detail, and with honest and tedious labour.

But as far as our handbooks are concerned this danger is still a prospective one, and has not yet arisen, though I believe it certainly will arise. For we are still under the bondage of an old fallacy, which is the belief that young minds are unable to grasp or understand generalities, and that philosophical reflections are to them unpalatable and uninteresting. I predict that with the increasing precocity of our children this fallacy will soon be exposed. But quite apart from any precocity, in truth nothing is so seductive to young minds as a broad general theory. There is usually no difficulty in *understanding* historical theories. In the great philosophical work of Mr. Grote there is not a page which is not perfectly intelligible to a boy of fourteen. There is also no reading boy of fourteen who would not be delighted at being allowed to study Mr. Grote's account of the Persian wars, or the Sicilian expedition, with all its detail and circumstance, instead of the barren skeleton of the compendiums. I can well remember my own feelings on the subject, and many experiments upon others have convinced me that they were not exceptional. Chronological or statistical discussions only are, to my thinking, unpalatable to the young and unsuited for their study.

Such then are the difficulties between which we must steer, if we wish to produce the proper effect upon the rising generation, and enlist their co-operation in the study of ancient history, without confining themselves to elegant generalities. As I said before, the proper and attractive representation of any great subject to the young is not to be regarded as lower and easier work, as the mere exercise of a popular style, and of shallow thinking. For in the present day, when the various branches of our knowledge have become so radically subdivided, each line of study, once begun, leads the mind into a certain groove, and tones it with a certain temper, that makes it almost inaccessible to the attractions of heterogeneous subjects. It is vain to object to this specialisation of mind; probably the strict subdivision of knowledge is now a necessary condition of its soundness. But it certainly brings with it this consequence, that a mind turned into a new channel diverges more widely every day from those into which it might once have been easily directed. If we wish in our day to make an historian we must secure him early; and the right way to do so is to provide him with such elementary text-books as will attract him to the science, and not disgust him with it.

I have been speaking hitherto as if the student were to be enlisted merely for the benefit of the science, and not for his own. It is, perhaps a selfish view, and yet would that learned men were oftener imbued with it! A real votary of his favorite pursuit should not merely court it himself, but ever proselytise around him. He should ever seek to help and to correct himself by the aid of others, and to work as much by stimulating others as by exerting himself. If it be then selfish to endeavour to enlist every mind we can in following our own pursuit, without regard to its usefulness or the claims of kindred sciences, it is a very large and unselfish selfishness, of which no one need be ashamed. There could hardly be a nobler or more interesting competition, than if many able representatives of different fields of knowledge were to contend together to persuade and to monopolise the rising generation around them. It would no longer be the conflict of Virtue and Vice for the youthful hero, but rather the friendly rivalry of several virtues.

Were they all dressed honestly in their real attractions, and were all their solid merits dispassionately weighed, none would rank higher than the study of history, and of ancient history too. I shall not dwell on the hackneyed argument that the highest study of mankind is man, or, what is really true and important, that the estimating of probable evidence is a finer and more practical training than long and precise demonstration. All this is familiar to every intelligent reader.

But let us turn to a larger question than the education of individual minds, and consider in what the higher and broader education of our national mind consists. The faculties of an individual may be developed in a thousand different ways, and many of these may be equally advantageous to his own life and to that of the state in which he lives. All this variety must be conceded in individual culture. But national culture is a narrower subject, and cannot be attained in these myriad ways. The prosperity of a nation appears to depend almost completely (apart from physical conditions) on the education of the public mind in *religion* and in *politics*. And it is in these very branches of knowledge that it seems impossible for our children to receive a broad education. For they must be entrusted in early years, not to the care of enlightened rulers (as was proposed by Plato), but to that of ignorant servants and of bigoted parents, who take care to infuse their own narrowness as the highest virtue into the politics and religion of their children. I am not in favour of abolishing this bigoted first instruction. For I cannot see how we can ensure earnestness in uneducated teachers without bigotry, and of all things in educating the young earnestness is absolutely necessary. It is not, I think, possible to begin with indifferentism; and, if it were, the child trained up as an indifferentist could never understand the fire of political and religious bigotry, and therefore, never attain a correct estimate of the motives that sway the great majority of men.

Bad and narrow as it may be, there is therefore something to be said for a one-sided training of children in politics and religion. It makes these subjects of first-rate importance in their minds, and enables them to appreciate the passions that have hitherto swayed the world. But this is only the *attitude* into which the pupil is put and kept, as when he is about to learn the art of dancing or of fencing. To keep him there permanently is to do him a wrong; for though it is absolutely necessary to excite his *emotions* about religion and politics, almost every one of the opinions he has been taught, and on which he exercises these emotions, may require remodelling. Yet, if you remodel them for him forcibly, you are likely to do him still greater injury. Second-hand broad views are a most contemptible and useless creed. If I am right, that mind is best imbued— perhaps that mind is alone really imbued—with liberal and just principles on religion and politics, which has been brought up in honest bigotry, and which *thinks itself free*.

If this process be of such value in forming the national mind, what study is so likely to secure it as that of history, and more especially, of history remote from the present day? Our political animosities and religious antagonisms reach back some centuries in reality; they are imported by our historians into still older periods; and I know not any avenue by which bias and bigotry attempt more frequently to enter unsuspicious minds, than by what is called mediæval and modern history. Nevertheless, even in modern history, we can consult authentic documents, as well as the advocates of either side, and so materials for a sound judgment in politics can be obtained by any honest student. But I maintain that an intelligent appreciation of ancient history is free from most of these risks. It is, of course, quite possible to write the histories of Greece and Rome with a strong bias. The great apology for Democracy by Mr. Grote, the great panegyric on Cæsarism by Dr. Mommsen, the angry polemics against Napoleonism by M. Beulé, afford us signal specimens among the three literary languages of Europe. We have however in this case not only the resource of comparing rival theorists, we can consult the great ancient artists who have told the annals of their nation with prejudices, perhaps, but with prejudices so different from ours, in an attitude so perfectly independent, that we can easily read them with critical composure, however hot and intolerant our views of present affairs may be.

Some people will think that in consequence of this independent attitude ancient history stands too far apart from modern to afford us any political lessons at all. Nothing can be farther from the truth. It has been often observed, and by the highest authorities,[1] that the social condition and the civilisation of Greece and Rome are far nearer to our own than is most of the intervening period. If early

---

[1] Cf. e. g. Arnold, in his edition of Thukydides, vol. III., pref. p. xviii., a passage which contains some very sound reflections.

in time, this civilisation, as we know it, was not only fully developed, but old and at last effete; and I hesitate not to affirm, that the feelings and the principles displayed in Thukydides and in Polybius are far more modern, in the philosophic sense of the word, than those of the Crusaders or of the Schoolmen. While, therefore, the great questions of our own time, such as Democracy, Federalism, or the Balance of Power,[1] are all to be met in the history of these ancient, but not antique, nations, we can consider them with minds freed to a great extent, if not altogether, from the colouring of modern party spirit. I am therefore justified in saying that there is no study by which a man can better think himself free of those narrow or bigoted notions, which we cannot and would not prevent his learning from earnest parents in his early youth.

These observations apply, it is true, to the development of what may be called modern antiquity,

---

[1] Some authors have been led, from the modern form of the expression, to imagine that is a new principle in politics. Wherever the name may have originated, the thing is almost as old as history. The oscillating attitude of the smaller Syrian kingdoms between Assyria and Egypt afford a very ancient example. The conduct of Sparta towards Athens, after Ægospotami, and of Athens towards Sparta, during the Theban supremacy, may be cited from Greek history. The policy of the Lagidae with respect to Syria and Macedon has been ably appreciated by Th. Mommsen, "History of Rome," book iii., chap. viii.

and not to the more remote and obscure epochs of human culture, about which these essays are chiefly concerned. The scanty fragments of the older civilisations may fairly enough be considered to have merely an antiquarian, and not a really historical, interest. For we have as yet insufficient materials before us to construct an adequate account of the times, and to paint a true picture of the politics, of the society, and above all, of the leading minds, in ancient Egypt or Assyria. In reply, I need not plead that such a task may yet become possible, but cannot be accomplished without preliminary researches, such as those I have endeavoured to describe. It will be shown in a subsequent essay that our materials are rapidly increasing, and that a sketch of the literature, for example, of ancient Egypt, beginning with the fifteenth century B.C., is even now more than a mere dry skeleton.

But this answer is not necessary. Researches into the origin of given results have ever been of the deepest interest to inquiring minds, and are, moreover, found useful when least expected. Is it not the greatest mark of our depth and progress in physiology and in pathology, that, not content with empirical observations on health and disease, men are striving to discover the hidden structure of tissue, and the origin of life; and that, under the title Histology, this purely speculative science is assuming a recognised place among the various branches of learning ? Is there not a profound interest in these obscure questions of the origin and the elements of life, which is justly, even now, absorbing popular attention more than the plainer practical sciences ? If this be so, and the origin of individual life is so precious a secret, why should not the historian be allowed the same curiosity to analyse and resolve into its elements a result not less complex, not less gradually constructed, not less mysterious in its first formation, in the first infusion of that mystery called life into its elements, and in its subsequent growth and development ? The protoplasm of physical life, however minute in its parts, has already come within the increased power of our observation. Who can tell whether the protoplasm of social life, however distant, may not yield to like zeal and to like patience ?

ESSAY II.

The Value of Legends in Critical History.

"Es ist sehr klar, dass in der Mythologie zweierlei vorkommt, *Angabe des geschehenen, und gedachtes.*"

K. O. Müller.

ΕΥΕ. ἔσθ' ὅποι κατὰ τῶν πετρῶν
ἡμᾶς ἔτ' ἄξεις; οὐ γὰρ ἔστ' ἐνταῦθά τις
ὁδός. ΠΕΙ. οὐδὲ μὰ Δί' ἐνταῦθα γ' ἀτραπὸς οὐδαμοῦ.

Aristophanes.

THERE are sciences that have sprung, or apparently sprung, from the brain of a single genius. We can fix, as it were, the day of their birth, and can watch them in their swaddling clothes, when we compare the laboured tentative exposition of their founder, with the clear and more precise statements of his successors. But there are sciences of obscurer origin, that shoot from the soil insensibly and increase by slow degrees. Their development may indeed be marked off into epochs by the labours of illustrious men, or by the strong spirit of certain ages of the world, that force the human mind into new paths, and will scarce permit a straggler. Yet withal we cannot ascribe the glory of their parentage to one man or to one age.

Mere Probability no true Criterion. 31

It is to this class of sciences that critical history belongs. Prefigured in bald relief by the cold catalogues of Egyptian genealogist and Greek logographer; hewn out in colossal proportions by the genius, and adorned as it were with gold and ivory by the rich fancy of Herodotus; reduced in conception, but purified in the marble of Thukydides, critical history disappeared with the gloomy splendour of Tacitus, scarce to reappear in fifteen centuries with the light of the Reformation. Since that time its scope is enlarged, and its interest enhanced, yet even now, when it has occupied the attention of great minds for centuries, its first principles are hardly fixed, and its basis is as yet uncertain.

Contemporary history has indeed, since the work of Thukydides, been agreed to consist in the collecting and collating the reports and documents of eye-witnesses. But contemporary history is the smallest and in some respects the easiest part of the science.[1] It is by confining himself almost exclusively to this narrow branch that the lesser genius of Thukydides has ever been able to eclipse, for a moment, the simpler and less precise but far vaster and more comprehensive spirit of Herodotus. For

---

[1] Of course all history must be written, not during the occurrence of the events, but after they have run their course and attained to some fixed conclusion. Contemporary history, therefore, means the history of events which have happened during the life and within the personal recollection of the historian.

when Thukydides comes to estimate the records of the past, as preserved in legend and in tradition, we find him judging, as I have before explained, on *principles* exactly the same as the predecessor at whom he cavils, though his cool and sceptical temper led him to apply these principles somewhat differently. Both authors agree in setting up *probability* as the criterion for accepting or rejecting the evidence of tradition, and, as every one knows, probability varies not only with the age in which we live, but with our individual tempers and education.

Thukydides agrees with our notions in rejecting all supernatural agency as improbable, and in this particular attracts the modern historian more than Herodotus, who readily admits it. But unfortunately he also rejected such other alleged causes as seemed to him too trivial or unworthy to produce great results. He would therefore have omitted in an oriental history those family disputes and transient female influences, which Herodotus justly regards as having often wrought great and fatal results. And in his Athenian history he did omit, intentionally, all mention of the influence of Aspasia, which appears from many contemporary allusions to have been of considerable importance.[1] In this

---

[1] Nothing shows more clearly the wonderful importance of style and of *literary* genius than the way in which such authors as Thukydides and Tacitus blind modern commentators in questions of evidence. Tacitus has been clearly proved, from his

respect Herodotus approaches our modern historians nearer than Thukydides. He generally tells all the versions of a story, even those that he personally discredits, and thus, while stating his own belief, leaves the reader means of judging differently for himself. This attitude was only recovered within the last century. Earlier historians after the revival of learning, not only criticised and sifted the legends of antiquity imperfectly, but endeavoured to impose their results upon the reader authoritatively, without leaving him the right of choice. Such a method of composing history upon theory is now justly condemned, and even the most remarkable historian of our day, Theodor Mommsen, excites dissatisfaction, and at times even suspicion, by the scantiness of the authorities which he cites in support of his novel and striking theories.

But while a complete statement of evidence has been considered more and more essential ever since the days of Niebuhr, the use of probability as a test of historical truth has withstood the assaults of sceptics up to the present day. It seems, in fact, impossible for a man of that keen imagination necessary in great historians to destroy *all* the legendary antecedents to positive history. As an effect without a cause is in-

---

own statements, thoroughly untrustworthy, and Thukydides, though more consistent, may yet be convicted of strong partiality. Cf. pp. 5 and 13, *notes*.

conceivable, so one who has spent years of his life among the records, and so to speak in the society of an ancient people, cannot but frame some picture from the prehistoric legends that lie before him. He will in vain employ all his caution, he will in vain summon to his aid all the sceptical tendencies of his age; nothing will save him but the total absence of imagination, and therefore of the historic faculty, or the tyranny of some positive theory which compels him to violate his nature.

We might at first suppose that a strong sceptical tendency in a great mind would in itself be sufficient to check the imagination. Nothing is farther from the truth. It would be much easier to support the thesis that any mind whose imagination can be thoroughly checked will never take its place among the great leaders of the age. At all events, ruthless scepticism and a vivid imagination are constantly combined in great historians. I shall not quote the very remarkable case of Ernest Renan, whose well-known writings on the New Testament combine these qualities to an extent perhaps unparalleled in historical literature; for M. Renan cannot be classed among great historians. But consider Niebuhr and Mr. Grote. Thorough-going as their scepticism appeared to their contemporaries, we already find them both attacked for easy faith, and for endeavouring to reconstruct from mere probability the legendary histories of Greece and Rome. In the case of

Mr. Grote, this is the more remarkable, as he has himself shown with great learning how former sceptics had ever failed to maintain their attitude consistently. Both with him and with them it was impossible to consider the great body of legends as purely fabulous, or as a picture of social life only. So many of them harmonise completely with ascertained facts, and are so consistent with known conditions, that in spite of theory they have practically maintained their historic value.

I know but one even approximate example[1] of perfectly consistent negative scepticism, not maintained to support a new theory, but from the calm determination to accept nothing short of convincing testimony, such as is demanded in a judicial inquiry. This example will be found in the works of the late Sir George C. Lewis. But it was, I think, this imperturbable temper that marred the greatness of his mind. Profoundly learned in the records of Greek and Roman antiquity, he seems to have studied

---

[1] I say *approximate* advisedly, for though I at first thought his writings a strict example, I find that even to him consistent scepticism was impossible. Thus, for example, in his Letters, p. 346, he evidently holds the old conservative view concerning Homer, and believes that we have the poems in the same shape in which Herodotus and Thukydides read them. I have no doubt that any one who took the trouble of toiling through his professed works on ancient history minutely, would find other instances of the same inconsistency.

them so to speak from without, and never to have really lived within their sphere. His critical mind approached them candidly indeed, and with interest, but with neither enthusiasm nor excitement. He was far too perfect a Commissioner ever to be a great historian. He studied the life of the Greeks and Romans exactly as he studied the causes of discontent in Malta and in Ireland. His works upon their alleged acts and arts are blue books and not history. No emotion ever animates the placid flow of his style, no play of fancy ever colours the transparent clearness of his thoughts.

But judicial is not historical inquiry, and the man who not only rejected, but ridiculed the splendid researches of his day in Egyptian and Assyrian philology,[1] showed that his scepticism, fair and logical as it seemed, disabled him from appreciating those delicate chains of evidence, that raise an uncertain conjecture through the many phases of possibility and probability to a sure discovery. In the inability, or perhaps the dislike, to estimate the value of cumulative evidence lay his fatal defect as an historical inquirer.

But although Mr. Grote may differ from him in practice, in theory he must be classed with Lewis, and it becomes a question of the greatest importance

---

[1] A reply to his arguments will be found in the next essay.

to estimate their negative theory of scepticism as to legends.

They held that the natural and the supernatural were so chemically fused in them that no *a priori* analysis—that nothing but the positive test of credible evidence, could possibly separate fact from fiction. Mr. Grote farther laid stress upon the point that probability was no test of truth, for that there might exist plausible as well as extravagant fiction. His conclusion was simply this: that there might or might not be historical basis for a legend, such as those told in the Homeric poems; in fact, that in these legends, as a whole, there probably was some such basis, but that independent evidence alone could establish it: on the other hand, that any one of these stories, hitherto supposed to be semi-historical, might be a pure invention, created to meet the cravings of religious emotion or patriotic feeling, and possessing no basis in facts whatever.

In accordance with this theory, he recounted the pre-historic legends as evidences of Greek national feelings and manners in early times, but refused to accept them as materials for his history, with a very few exceptions. The Return of the Herakleidae, for example, associated with the Invasion of the Peloponnesus by Dorian tribes, is admitted by the great sceptic to be on the verge of history, and to be true in the main. He rejects, of course, many of the details, he even reconstructs the main features of the campaign, which he believes to have been gradual and tedious, and not decided by a few great battles. But he in this case admits the evidence of a legendary history, professing to be the last remarkable series of events in the memory of the men who lived at the dawn of contemporary records.[1]

Both by his general theory and by this very remarkable example, which is said by his critics to be inconsistent with it, Mr. Grote, if he threw doubt and discredit on any hasty acceptance of legends, did not in any way discourage historical students from seeking independent evidence, or from endeavouring in every possible way to extract from them well-attested facts. When, for example, it was discovered that great and ancient ruins covered the sites of Argos, of Mykenae, and of Troy, and when men inferred from this that the existence of these ancient cities in the very places described by the legends showed a basis of fact for the Trojan war—when all this was discovered Mr. Grote would only remark that in such case independent evidence had been found, and that probably many other details might yet make their way by the same process into sober history. The same would doubtless be the attitude of Bishop Thirlwall, and of the great Germans, Th. Mommsen and E. Curtius, who have

---

[1] This view is partially conceded by Mr. Cox, ii., p. 182.

done so much to reconstruct the earlier histories of Greece and **Rome**.[1]

There is indeed in Mr. Grote's theory **one** positive element to discredit the legends. He believes that **they may be pure** inventions created to satisfy the religious or emotional wants of primitive men by clever poets. He even gives an example of such invention in **the case of a scandal** disseminated about **Lord Byron** by Goethe without **any** historical foundation.[2] Seeing that the story was suggested by one of his own poems, in which he was supposed (though falsely) to have depicted himself, the case is hardly a fair one. There are reasons to believe that Lord Byron may have intended deliberately **to mislead** the public, which he thoroughly despised. And moreover, however mistaken men **may have** been as to the locality of the adventure, part of it certainly occurred, probably in several different places. If Mr. Grote had cited the supposed crusade of Charlemagne, it would have been a better example; but even here it has lately been shown that a basis of fact was

---

[1] These latter cannot indeed be classed in exactly the same category with their English fellow-labourers, for they spend no small labour and ingenuity in drawing inferences from casual allusions in the myths, inferences which can hardly be considered demonstrated, but which are certainly probable enough to take their place in ancient history. Prof. E. Curtius is, indeed, in my opinion, far too easy of faith.

[2] Cf. *Westminster Rev.*, 1843, vol. i., p. 316, *sq.*

greatly exaggerated, and that political missions or relations between the Emperor and Haroun-al-Raschid were magnified into a personal visit.[1] The legends about William Tell are now said to be pure inventions; but the existence of this personage has been proved by M. Häusser, in addition to the acknowledged Germanic[2] features of the story. Yet even were this proved a real specimen of pure invention, which is not the case, this example will hardly establish its existence among a simple and primitive

---

[1] Cf. *Revue Arch.*, N. S., vol. iii. pp. 36-50. The whole question has been treated exhaustively in the great work of Léon Gautier, entitled *Les Épopées Françaises:* cf. vol. II., pp. 260-71, especially secs. II. and III., on the historical basis and modifications of this celebrated legend. Eginhard, in his *Vita Karoli*, expressly says the Emperor entered into relations with Syria and Jerusalem, to assist poor Christians. The *Chronicon Benedicti*, by a monk of Mount Soracte, circ. 950, is the earliest specimen of the legend, which is simply produced by the monk transcribing loosely and dishonestly the 18th chapter of Eginhard's *Vita Karoli*, and ascribing to the Emperor himself what the historian had told of his ambassadors. The two narratives are given in parallel columns by M. Gautier, II., p. 265, *note*, and are profoundly instructive on the growth of myths by distortion. It is historically certain from Eginhard that in 799-800, A. D., the patriarch of Jerusalem sent to Charlemagne sacred relics, and also the keys of the Holy Sepulchre. The Emperor sent an embassy in return.

[2] Strange to say, beyond this branch of the Aryan family, the story has been chiefly found in perfectly foreign races, such as the Finns, Turks, and Samoyeds, cf. Cox, II., p. 101. This fact will be shown of great importance hereafter.

race of men, when deliberate deceit is, according to Mr. Grote himself, out of the question.

Exaggeration and distortion are not only possible, but certain; pure invention is the very reverse, for we know that the human mind has a very scanty faculty indeed of new creation, and has recourse to all possible combinations and re-arrangements of old materials in default of this faculty. It is not even likely that pure inventions of poets would be appreciated by their hearers when really produced. Nor is it by such means that the early poet would enlist the sympathies of his hearers, but by gathering together the faint and scattered traces of some early tale told to them as children by garrulous mentor or aged crone, and which they longed to hear again and know, as a man longs to know some quaint melody, which, when first heard, is strange indeed, and yet familiar—in some sense new, but stirring up old emotions long hidden in the soul.

But I need hardly urge other arguments against the theory of invented legends, when it is the fundamental principle of the newer school of sceptics that no such thing is possible. If Mr. Grote questions the legends because they are probably later than the period which they profess to describe, a more advanced school attain the same conclusion by asserting them to be centuries older than that period; and while they accept his conclusion, they do it by refuting his argument.

Accordingly, the labours of Mr. Grote and Bishop Thirlwall are already old-fashioned. They attempted nothing but a negative criticism. They merely suspended their judgment on the legends. Now there has arisen a new school, that of the Comparative Mythologers, who not only deny that the legends have been proved historical, but assert that they can be proved mythical. The last expression of this school in England is the elaborate work of Mr. Cox,[1] who seeks to establish the astounding position, that all the myths and legends of all the Aryan races can be resolved into a primitive stock of figurative phrases and conceptions about the sun, the dawn, the clouds, and the night, and that there is no ancient epic which does not revolve round these physical conceptions. He professes, indeed, not to question that there are possibly historical facts shadowed in some of the legends. It would be impossible for any man of sense to do so, seeing that innumerable legendary stories have sprung up around great names, preserved to history by independent evidence, such as Cyrus, Alexander, and Charlemagne. But if I understand the spirit of his book, and interpret rightly the main intention amid a crowd of details, his object is not only to throw historical discredit upon the legends, as not proven, but to throw discredit on the very attempt

---

[1] *Mythology of the Aryan Nations*, London, 1870.

to prove them, or to seek any basis of fact in these early traditions. The main outlines of all of them are to be explained mythologically, and any residue of history they ever contained is too small to be considered of importance. If in all their leading features, the Iliad, the Odyssey, the Thebaid, and the Herakleis of Peisander, are nothing but obvious variations of the same solar myth, how idle to seek under them any serious historical significance! Mr. Cox professes to have so interpreted the whole body of legends preserved to us not only in the Greek and German epics, but in the Celtic, Teutonic, Indian, and Iranian folk lore.[1]

This theory is of more serious import than the negative criticism of Grote and Lewis, for two reasons. It actually professes to interpret the legendary traditions of the ancients; it discourages every attempt to seek an historical explanation of any of them. The theory is positive, and also exclusive; for although the comparative mythologers admit that they will at once bow to contemporary witnesses or other evidence admissible in a *judicial* inquiry, yet they candidly tell you that such will

---

[1] The Sclavonic legends are most unaccountably omitted. By his theory Mr. Cox actually (*Mythology*, &c., i. 91, *note*) professes *to have* explained *everything in the legends!* His assertion is indeed true. The theory does explain everything, and should, as we shall see, not have been confined to Aryan legends, but have embraced those of all the world.

never be found, and that it is idle to proceed to any other explanation than that which they have given.

As the discussion turns upon evidence, two questions must be definitively answered. First, are we to be confined in writing ancient history to such evidence as would be received in a court of justice or strictly judicial inquiry alone? Secondly, have the comparative mythologers, who exact this from their adversaries, proved their own conclusions with the same sort of evidence?

It must be acknowledged that the science of comparative mythology, as originated by MM. Kuhn and Max Müller, has some scientific basis. But in the face of farther developments, hazarded by them and their followers, it is highly necessary to state what that basis is. A number of myths existed, they say, especially among the Greeks, conflicting with the higher moral sense of that people, attributing to their deities immorality, and sometimes absurdity. It was suspected that these stories were not understood by the poets that repeated them, but were relics of some earlier condition of things. An investigation of the Vedic mythology showed (α) that the names of some old Indian deities corresponded *letter for letter*[1] with those of the Greeks; (β) that their *etymological intention* was the same,[2] (γ) that the myths in which the

---

[1] That is to say, according to fixed laws, by which certain letters replace one another in sister languages.

[2] "It is useless almost," says Mr. M. Müller (*Lectures* II.,

Vedic deities appeared were *closely analogous* to the adventures of the Greek deities, and yet were plainly susceptible, even in the minds of the Indian poets, of a physical explanation. The mythologers assert that in that primitive age these gods and heroes could be identified with such objects as the sun or the dawn, without in consequence losing their consciousness and personality. Any object possessing motion or change[1] appeared to them endowed with life, and often even with personality. Under these circumstances it was inferred that the particular myths of the Greeks, which showed this close correspondence with the picturesque personification of the sun and dawn, were ancient relics of a time when the various branches of the Aryan family had not been separated, that these stories had originally been poetical translations of the same physical facts, and could find in them, and in them alone, their justification.[2]

---

p. 471, *note*), "to compare mythological names without first discovering their etymological intention."

[1] Not *every* object, as Mr. Cox absurdly says. I do not believe that any savage ever supposed the stones he met on his way to have life. The fact that the names of these motionless and therefore lifeless objects, are masculine in many languages shows, I think, that the appearance of neuters was not coeval with the abstraction of life from inanimate objects.

[2] The mythologers have, as we shall see, been charged justly (*Edinburgh Rev.*, Oct., 1870) with exaggerating the similarity between the stories, which is very slight indeed to a calm critic unbiassed by theory.

It was farther inferred that such explanations, borrowed from comparative mythology, were not only applicable to myths about the gods, but also to the adventures of heroes told in legendary history. That this might be so, was considered evident from the fact that in the Greek and other legendary histories the relation of gods and heroes was so intimate, the transition from one to the other was so gradual and uninterrupted, as to afford no means to the historian of discriminating them with any safety.

And there is yet another principle, adopted in the legends of all nations, which appears to make this inference more certain. Owing to the poverty of human invention, which is unable to devise independent adventures for each hero, or to the weakness of memory, which forgets his peculiar features, or still more to the existence of floating traditions, wandering in search of a local habitation and a name—owing to one or all of these causes we meet in almost all nations with *recurring legends*. Under this expression two apparently distinct facts are implied. First, the application of the same story by different nations to their respective national heroes. Secondly, the repetition of the same story by the same nation about successive heroes or events. Of both these facts there is ample and conclusive evidence.

Everybody knows how the same story is told of Cyrus and of Romulus being nursed by a wolf or bitch. Paris indeed received the same attention from a bear.[1] But it is really surprising to find complicated legends, like the story of Polyphemus and Odysseus in the *Odyssey* or that of Rhampsinitus in the second book of Herodotus, repeated with hardly any change, except the names of the actors, in the **Blinded** Devil of Teutonic, and the Shifty Lad of Gaelic, folk lore. Most people who hear this partial statement for the first time will suppose with **Mr. Cox** that these stories can hardly have resulted from coincidence or from borrowing, but rather from a special appropriation by different branches of the Aryan family from a common stock of legends. The second case of recurring legends is one which prevails even in our own day. It may be exemplified in the Greek mythology by such cases as Orpheus, Theseus, and Herakles all descending to hell, the constant appearance of the Dioskuri in battles,[2] and so forth. In modern times it still sur-

---

[1] Cf. Cox, vol. I., p. 116, *sq.*, and II., p. 365. There are similar points in the legends of Wolfdietrich and Sigurd.

[2] The history of these legends is curious. The earliest case in Italy was probably that of a battle on the Sagra between the Krotoniates and Lokrians, the many marvels at which made it pass into a proverb. Then comes the story of the battle of Regillus. Their last appearance was as late as the day that Perseus was conquered at Pydna, B. C. 168. Cicero gives a very interesting account of it, as follows—(*de Nat. Deor.*, ii. 2) —" Ut et apud Regillum bello Latinorum, quum A. Postumius dictator cum Oct. Mam. Tusculano prœlio dimicaret, in nostra

vives in the habit of attaching good stories, jokes, and smart sayings, to the most notable wit of the day. When he dies, and is forgotten, the same anecdotes are repeated of some other man, like the beacon lights heralding the news of the fall of Troy, where one transmits its blaze to the other, so that the last, in the words of Aeschylus, was—

οὐκ ἄπαππον 'Ιδαίου πυρὸς.

All these facts collected by the comparative mythologers make it possible that a great many of the myths and legends of antiquity are not historical, but merely repetitions of some very ancient beliefs, the common property of the Aryans—perhaps of all primitive races; and of these beliefs some are clearly to be explained by the physical phenomena of nature. But do they prove that all legends are such? Do they prove that every great national epic of the Aryan family has merely a mythological import? Do they make all inquiry into the historical basis of

---

acie Castor et Pollux ex equis pugnare visi sunt, et recentiore memoria iidem Tyndaridae Persen victum nuntiaverunt. P. enim Vatinius, avus huius adolescentis, quum e praefectura Reatina Romam venienti noctu duo iuvenes cum equis albis dixissent, regem Persen illo die captum, senatuique nuntiavisset: *primo quasi temere de republica locutus, in carcerem coniectus est;* post, a Paullo litteris allatis, quum idem dies constitisset, et agro a senatu et vacatione donatus est." He mentions the battle on the Sagra, but tells another story about it, which does not introduce the Dioskuri.

these epics idle? For this is the position to which the comparative mythologers have advanced.

Let us re-state the evidence on which the discoveries of the comparative mythologers commanded our acceptance. There are some cases where the Greek names of gods or heroes correspond letter for letter (according to well-known laws) with Sanskrit names. *Ushas* and Ἡώς, *Saranyu* and Ἐρινύς, *Harits* and Χάριτες, are apparently the same words. This is the first condition. But we do not find that the characters of the individuals denoted by all these names correspond closely. It cannot with any justice be asserted that the legends of the nine *Harits*, or horses of Indra, are the least like the Three Graces of Greek mythology. In this case then the third canon is not observed.

But let us take a more prominent example. Professor M. Müller and Mr. Cox assert that Saramâ and Ἑλενή are identical. The certainty of this statement may well be denied. No doubt the *s* may correspond to the *spiritus asper* of the Greeks, and the *r* to the Greek *l*, but why should the *m* appear as *n*, except in exsonance. Sanskrit *terminations* in *m* are constantly replaced by Greek terminations in *n*, because the Greek language does not tolerate final *m*, but in *insonance* (Inlaut) the case is not so clear. The comparison of *Sarameyas* and Ἑρμείας is against it, for here the Sanskrit *m* is preserved. In this then the first canon is not satisfied. The second is not even applied. As to the third, Saramâ is not stolen, but *recovers* for Indra the cattle stolen by the Panis. The legends are therefore totally irreconcileable. But this is not all. As Indra's cattle are stolen by certain evil powers of night, called *Paṇis*, it was inferred that the latter corresponded to Paris in the Iliad, and that this part of the legend was therefore mythological and not historical. The conclusion again fails, because the first condition has not been strictly fulfilled. There is no evidence that the Sanskrit *n* can be represented by the Greek *ρ*, and the Paṇis are more generally (I think) plural, whereas Paris is singular. Yet still the other resemblances are strong, and the theory may be admitted as possible. Nevertheless, "*in a judicial inquiry*," an obstinate juror might be found very troublesome, if these difficulties were urged. Many more might also be suggested. Paris is no dark robber, but a fair and beautiful youth, the special favourite of the gods, and described by the Homeric bard with a luxury of imagery that would rather suggest the rising sun than a power of darkness. We shall see presently how this difficulty is answered.

But the mythologers do not rest there. If Helen be the dawn and Paris the powers of night, Achilleus must be the sun, which defeats the darkness, and brings back the Dawn. His place in the story (our second condition) suits this view well enough, but what of his name? It is connected, according to M. Max Müller, with *Ahalyá*, said by Kumârila to be the *goddess of night*. He thinks *it may have meant the Dawn*.[1] But this is so far from certain, that it could by no means be proved in a judicial inquiry. It is in fact an assertion that black is white.[2] It is not necessary that Achilleus should appear at all in Sanskrit, except he be a solar hero of the original Aryans, which is the point yet to be established. That his relations to Helen indicate something of the kind is possible, but this does not the least disprove his historical character; for it is well known and acknowledged among the mythologers to be a common practice to attach such legends to historical characters. In fact an uncritical age is sure

---

[1] "*It is most likely* that she was meant for the dawn," are his words, *Lectures*, II., p. 502. Mr. Blackie (*Edinburgh Transactions*, vol. xxvi., part I., p. 57) calls attention to the weakness of this proof, without quoting details.

[2] The uncertainty of such conjectures will be best brought home to the reader by stating the probabilities in this case arithmetically. I do not suppose that the chances in favour of Kumârila's assertion are worth more than $\frac{1}{2}$. M. Max. Müller's conjecture cannot possibly claim a higher probability than $\frac{1}{4}$. That a word used for the Dawn should be transferred to the Sun is, without farther evidence, so unlikely that if we allow it a value of $\frac{1}{5}$ we are very liberal indeed. The probability, therefore, that Achilleus is derived from Ahalyâ (apart from linguistic difficulties) is $\frac{1}{2} \times \frac{1}{4} \times \frac{1}{5} = \frac{1}{25}$! Have conclusions resting on such premises the smallest scientific value?

to do so, if we judge from the examples of Cyrus, Alexander, and Charlemagne. The fact that Paris has a second name, Alexandros, makes an historical basis for the Trojan still less improbable; for, supposing the legends of the dawn and sun had been imported into an historical legend, it would be natural to fit a new name to the hero who was obliged to play the part of the wicked power. If so, Alexandros would be his real, and Paris his mythical name. I am not setting this up as a theory, but rather as an answer to the presumptuous dogmatism of the mythologers. They say that they have shown Achilleus, Helen, and Paris to be mere mythical figures. Such is not the case. Not one of the names can be satisfactorily explained by Sanskrit analogies. They need not have told us that there may be mythical elements of great age and of physical import introduced into the Trojan legend. About the residue, which they have not explained, they have no right to make any assertion. In my opinion, the legends are far more likely to have clustered around some historical basis than to have been spun out of two or three barren enough[1] physical conceptions. I may be wrong, but so may they.

---

[1] The mythologers will quarrel with such an assertion. They have employed all the figures of poetry to paint these conceptions in the brightest colours. This was necessary to their theory, but is, as will be shown, foreign to a simple and primitive condition of the human race.

They stand no longer on the basis of certainty, but of bare probability.

Yet Mr. Cox, not content with this very questionable victory, hastens to mask the strongholds that have not surrendered, and to advance to farther conquests. It is his theory that every national epic is nothing but an adaptation of solar myths. He is, therefore, bound to explain the Odyssey from the same point of view. The contrasts between the heroes of the two poems are striking enough. One is young and the other old, one is impetuous and the other wary, one is short-lived and the other of mature age. Let us add that no single adventure is common to Achilleus and Odysseus. In one point alone they agree.[1] *The names of neither can be explained from Sanskrit analogies.* For if the more modern form *Ulixes* seems to suggest the Sanskrit word for εὐρυκρείων, that epithet is not applied to solar heroes, but rather to Agamemnon, their opponent.

But all these things are very small hindrance. As the expedition eastward symbolises the rescue of the Dawn from the powers of Night, so the voyage of Odysseus is nothing but the representation of the course of the sun through the sky towards the west. If so, the climate of Greece, or rather of the origi-

---

[1] The reader who desires to see some wonderful analogies developed between Odysseus, and Phoibos, and Herakles, between the ship Argo and the Trojan horse, &c., may consult Cox, II., p. 174, *sq.*

nal Aryans, must have been a very cloudy and unpleasant one indeed. **Every** possible hint at a similarity with any other god or hero is collected by Mr. Cox. If he is wise, so was Prometheus and Medeia, and Asklepios and Melampous; if he was crafty, **so was** Hermes. "**If he uses** poisoned arrows it **is not** because the Achaian chieftains **were** in the habit of using them, but because the weapons of Herakles were steeped in venom, and the **robe of** Mêdeia scorched the body of Glauke; if he submits to be the lover of Kirke and Kalypso it is because Achilleus solaced himself with Diomede for the loss of Brisêis," &c.[1]

What follows **is still** more striking. If Odysseus contends **with his** enemies for the possession of a lady, so did Achilleus. In the one case she is a wife, **and** in the other not; in the one the hero is armed with divine armour and at the head of his troops, **in the** other almost alone and in rags. But what does this signify? **Had not** Achilleus a friend who was killed, and has not Odysseus a son who was

---

[1] I., 266. It is worth while to point out the very loose reasoning in this passage. Of course the point in favour of the mythologers, as concerns the poisoned arrows, **must** be this, that their use was not an ordinary practice among **Greeks**, and that they hence indicate a solar hero. Does Mr. Cox mean to assert a similar peculiarity in the second *rapprochement*, which he cites? The intelligent reader will be more disposed to consider it *sublunary* than *solar*.

wounded?[1] Was not Hektor dragged round the walls of Troy, and Melanthius mutilated in a courtyard?

Surely this is a travesty of mythological explanation. Neither are the details at all similar, nor is any attempt made to show any identity in name between most of these so-called parallel heroes. Of Polyphemus we are told that he represented a thunder-cloud with the sun peering through like a single eye—a curious confusion. His delight at drinking the wine of Odysseus is the delight of Indra (the Indian thunder god) at receiving the *soma*, or nectar of the gods. These are selected from many similar examples.

But I should do the learned author great injustice by omitting to state and discuss the *principle* on which he ventures such startling assertions. It is a principle which may be called the *Flexibility of myths*. "In the Vedic system," says Professor M. Müller, "there are as yet no genealogies, no settled marriages, between gods and goddesses. The father is sometimes the son, the brother the husband, and she who is in one hymn the mother is in another the wife. As the conceptions of the poet vary, so does the nature of the gods."[2] " The same

---

[1] So Odysseus himself was only wounded by a boar, but Adonis killed; "nor *can we doubt*," says Mr. Cox (II., p. 172), "that this boar is the beast whose tusk wrought the death of Adonis"!

[2] *Chips*, II., p. 75.

object," adds Mr. Cox, " would at different times, and under different conditions, awaken the most opposite and inconsistent conceptions. But these conceptions and the words which expressed them would exist side by side without producing the slightest consciousness of their incongruity ; nor is it easy to determine the exact order in which they might arise. The sun would awaken both mournful and inspiriting ideas, ideas of victory and defeat, of toil and premature death."[1] It will be seen, as usual, that the pupil far outruns his master. M. Max Müller's statement amounts to no more than this, that the relationships of the gods were not fixed—a thing very likely to be the case in an age so primitive that no relationships were fixed. This confusion is a very common occurrence among the present primitive races on our globe;[2] and there are not wanting traces in the Latin and Greek languages, which point to a similar state of things before the early Aryans separated.

I am prepared to admit not only this sort of variation, which must surely have taken place; even really inconsistent ideas might be evoked by the same object, as Mr. Cox says, under different cir-

---

[1] Cox, I., p. 41, and p. 258, *note*.
[2] See the interesting collection of facts in Sir J. Lubbock's *Origin of Civilisation*, pp. 60, *sqq*.

cumstances; but in the name of all honest inquiry we must object to this being called in to explain every difficulty. Such a principle is, from its very nature, loose and elastic. If the greatest caution be not used in its application it will mislead and not elucidate. By itself it is of course useless. It may help to clear away difficulties that remain when a real analogy is established; such is its only use. When we are told that the single eye of Polyphemus is to be explained by the sun looking through a cloud, seeing that if Polyphemus is to be mythically explained at all, he must be a power of night, hiding Odysseus, the solar hero, in his cave, we cannot concede such a confusion on a mere random assertion.

---

[1] If Polyphemus' eye be the sun, then Odysseus, the solar hero, extinguishes himself, a very primitive instance of suicide. But Polyphemus affords matters for other curious reflections (Cf. Cox, I., p. 389.) Were we disposed to follow up the brilliant *reductio ad absurdum* in the fifth number of *Kottabos*, where M. Max Müller is identified with the sun god, and his whole life and acts reconciled with that hypothesis, there might be ample reason for seeing in Polyphemus a rude prototype of the great professor. Πολύφημος = πανομφαῖος = Professor of languages. He lives in an island of the west, to which he is not indigenous, but is reputed to have been sprung, like many foreign importations, from the sea. (Cf. Germ. *meerkatze*, lit. foreign cat, *meerschwein*, &c.) His brilliant eye is darkened by a number of brutal obscurantists, justly styled *nobodies*, who persist in considering him a free thinker. Yet they take all they can of the good things he has provided in his cave, and then escape from his power under the cover

If the identity of the name Paris with the Panis of the Veda were certain, if the etymology of both of them were certain, and reducible to a common idea, then, since the principal position of Paris in the Iliad corresponds to the powers of night, we might give some weight to an explanation of the famous passages describing him as fair and glorious, from the flexibility of myths. But as the matter now stands, neither of the first two points is made out, and, consequently, the inconsistency of the Homeric description with that of the Veda is an argument against identifying them. If comparative mythologers allow themselves to be carried away by such inferences their works will soon resemble those of the last century, which they delight to ridicule, and from one of which M. Max Müller[1] quotes the following: "Caput quartum, VIII. Vulcanus idem ac Moses. IX. Typhon idem ac Moses. Caput quintum, II. Zoroastres idem ac Moses; Caput octavum, III. Apollo idem ac Moses. IV. Pan idem ac Moses. V. Priapus idem ac Moses," &c., &c.[2] To identify, for example, all the cases of suicide by hanging, in the Greek legends, with the action of the Iranian *Azhi Dahaka*, the throttling snake, is less amusing, but not less absurd.[3]

---

of sheepskins, an idea still symbolized by the practice of wearing a sheepskin hood, when escaping from university bondage.

[1] *Lectures*, II., p. 402.   [2] Huet, *Demonstratio Evangelica*.

[3] Cox, II., p. 188. The idea of *throttling* is due to Mr. Cox, not to the Persians.

"Of course," says an able writer,[1] "with such tests at hand, the process of verification is easy enough. It would be difficult to find, or even imagine, a case where it would not apply. Every hero, for example, is born and dies, and as the sun rises and sets, here is a striking coincidence to begin with. Again, every warrior fights for himself or others with a common weapon, or a peculiar one, and experiences either victory or defeat, and in either of these different alternatives he is equally a solar hero. With regard to his relationships, he is either a lover and bridegroom, or rejected and disconsolate, married or single, father or son, has offspring or has not, is monarch or subject, oppressor or oppressed; and on either alternative he is equally a solar hero." The passage concludes, "When stripped of special details and literary embellishments, the method of solar verification is thus of extreme and even obtrusive simplicity. It consists in making a brief abstract of a hero's character and career, fathering the descriptive outline on the primitive race with the designation of solar, and then applying the outline to the hero's actual history, and identifying his name with the solar assumption. And the curious mixture of suppositions, facts, and circular reasonings is by a singular misnomer called science."

---

[1] *Edin. Rev.*, Oct., 1870.

Such are the consequences at which we may arrive on any theory if we allow ourselves to be carried away by mere possibilities. There is a fallacy, called by Archbishop Whately the *thaumatrope* fallacy, in which the illusion is produced by rapidly presenting to our minds a series of separate ideas, and ringing the changes on them till we are confused and believe them all identical or connected. A logical reader is strongly reminded of this fallacy when he finds the sun, the dawn, the storm-clouds, and the gloaming, kept going like a number of balls in a juggler's hand. Any hero can play any part. If he is spoken well of he must be the sun, if not, he is the night. Whether he murders or marries or deserts a maiden or a widow, she is the Dawn. What is still more unscientific, if he have two or three letters of his name identical with any other mythical name, identity of character is asserted. This is a habit which our comparative mythologers ought not to acquire, seeing that even the most advanced comparative mythologers of Germany cannot forget the difficulties before them. Even Professor Max Müller cannot develope his theory without much hesitation. Far from being satisfied with any random similarity, he professedly requires complete identity of letters, a knowledge of the etymology, and even an identity of accent, before he is satisfied. Thus, he hesitates about *Septem-*

triones.[1]   He hesitates about Paris, as we have seen.
He hesitates (though little) about Hermes, because
the form *Heremeias* does not occur. He hesitates
concerning *Aditi* having the meaning of the Infinite.[2]

All these **are the doubts of** a scientific linguist;
and yet all of them are assumed to be definitely
determined by Mr. Cox.[3]

Nevertheless, he is **very** severe towards **what he**
calls the Euemerists, for drawing conclusions from
probabilities or possibilities. Surely his own inferences should be subject to the same criticism. **He
has set up for his** opponents the test **of a judicial**
inquiry; the candid reader will judge whether his
work, in most points, can submit to the same ordeal.
As to linguistic tests, he confesses[4] that he is dis-
posed not to be very exacting, and that he believes
in exceptions to the laws of language. But **the**

---

[1] *Lectures*, II., p. 365. Though, in matters of the kind, it is impossible to speak very positively, *it seems not improbable* that the name *triones* may be an old name for star in general.

[2] Cf. *ibid.*, II., 500, *note*. "*This is doubtful*, but I know no better etymology." The reader will find similar caution used in *Chips*, II., p. 133. I may add, however, that the greatest of Greek etymologists, G. Curtius, rejects many of the derivations which even M. Max Müller considers sound. So far are we still removed from the *judicial inquiry* stage.

[3] For *Septemtriones*, cf. Cox's *Aryan Mythology*, I. p. 47, for *Aditi*, I., p. 333.

[4] I., p. 327, *note*. What is meant by this statement of Mr. Cox I am at a loss to conceive. He might as well talk of exceptions to the laws of nature.

identity asserted by the mythologers between Vedic and Greek mythology is based on nothing but arguments from names and from phrases, alleged to be the same in both. The Edinburgh Reviewer shows (p. 338) more pointedly than I have done, how the few *phrases* which can be quoted from the Vedas are ludicrously inadequate to bear the gigantic responsibility thrust upon them, and that they require a very magnifying medium to afford even a starting point for the theory. As to the argument from *names*, he does not enter upon it very explicitly, but contents himself with censuring the undue worship of etymology in the present day; in this point, indeed, agreeing with Mr. Cox in estimating linguistic reasons lightly. As I do not, I have rather essayed to show that the mythologers cannot prove the linguistic argument to be decisive. It is, moreover, highly inconsistent of the comparative mythologers to cast the smallest doubt on deductions from the laws of language, for the very existence and the first origin of their theory is due to linguistic laws, and to them alone. It is verily the usual ingratitude of upstarts to scorn the support which first raised them from their low state.[1]

The conclusions, therefore, of the mythologers

---

[1] I am sorry to see that Prof. Blackie (*Edinburgh Transac.* xxvi. pt. I., p. 47) thinks "the best etymologies are only accessories to a scientific mythological explanation, especially as he

from language are only probable at best. But the position of probable conclusions in history is far too important to be considered polemically only; we shall therefore postpone this inquiry till we have discussed the two remaining arguments which our opponents propose. They may briefly be called the *geographical* and the *psychological*.

The former will not detain us long. We are told that as all the mythical wars in Greece contain expeditions from east to west, or west to east only, this is the strongest corroboration of the solar origin of these myths.[1] But surely, *supposing that we admit this as a fact*, for argument's sake, it would be considered a strong point by the Euemerists also. All great wars among Greeks must have taken place in these directions. All great expeditions must have followed these routes. At the dawn of positive history we find Asia Minor, Greece, and Lower Italy the homes of the Hellenes. In whatever order they were occupied it seems very im-

---

almost directly refutes this assertion himself in the same article, § 27 (2) where he shows that different words are more easily identified than different mythological persons.

[1] Cox, I., p. 204. "Whether the old Vedic hymns contain the germ of the Iliad and Odyssey, or whether they do not, it seems impossible to shut our eyes to the fact that the whole mythical history of Hellas exhibits an alternation of movements from the west to the east and from the east back to the west again, as regular as the swaying of a pendulum."

probable that it was any other route than that from east to west; if the colonies warred with the mother states, if they returned to their homes peaceably, it must have been from west to east. The whole tide of Hellenic life, with rare exceptions, ever ebbed and flowed in these very directions.[1] But as there are exceptions in positive history, so there were exceptions also in legendary history, and *it is not a fact* that these movements are as regular as those of a pendulum. What about the war of the Seven against Thebes? It was an expedition nearly due north for most of the contending chiefs. What about the return of the Herakleidae? It was due south. Mr. Cox is tortured by his theory into asserting that it is from west to east:[2] truly a most extraordinary statement! The geographical argument, therefore, is based on a misstatement of facts, and even if we

---

[1] It has often been remarked that this direction is common to almost all primitive migrations, and that a mountain chain running from north to south has never been able to check the progress of nations in the same way that east and west chains have done. Whatever reasons we may assign, whether it be that the climates vary so widely on opposite slopes in the latter case, or whether primitive men felt safer in following the course of the sun, at all events the present divisions of Europe and Asia, compared with the ethnical unity of America, will illustrate the principle. In the old world most of the chains run E. and W., in the new N. and S. Such exceptional chains as the Ural, Caucasus, Apennines, and Pindus, have never barred migrations.

[2] Cox, I., p. 206.

concede this statement to the mythologers, it tells fully as much in favour of their opponents as of themselves.

We pass to the psychological argument, which bases the whole system of interpretation by the Sun and Dawn alone on an analysis of the mental condition of savages, or of primitive races; and I would draw special attention to this side of the theory, which has hitherto been very slightly examined by careful critics. Comparative mythologers draw very poetical and very detailed pictures of these historical infants, and give us to understand that they have studied their habits closely. "His mental condition[1] determined the character of his language, and that condition exhibits in him, as in children now, the working of a feeling which endows all outward things with a life not unlike his own. Of the several objects which met his eye he had no positive knowledge, whether of their origin, their nature, or their properties. But he had life, and therefore all things else must have life also. He was under no necessity of personifying them, for he had for himself no distinctions between consciousness and personality. He knew nothing of the conditions of his own life or of any other, and therefore all things on the earth or

---

[1] That is, of the primitive Aryan. The quotation is from Cox's *Aryan Mythology*, I., pp. 42, *sq.*

in the heavens were invested with the same vague idea of existence. The sun, the moon, the stars, the ground on which he trod, the clouds, storms, and lightnings were all living beings; could he help thinking that, like himself, they were conscious beings also? His very words would, by an inevitable necessity, express this conviction. His language would admit no single expression from which the attribute of life was excluded, while it would vary the forms of that life with unerring instinct. Every object would be a living reality, and every word a speaking picture. For him there would be no bare recurrence of days and seasons, but each morning the dawn would drive her bright flocks to the blue pastures of heaven before the birth of the lord of day from the toiling womb of night. Round the living progress of the new-born sun there would be grouped a lavish imagery, expressive of the most intense sympathy with what we term the operation of material forces, and not less expressive of the utter absence of even the faintest knowledge. Life would be an alternation of joy and sorrow, of terror and relief; for every evening the dawn would return leading her bright flocks, and the short-lived sun would die. Years might pass, or ages, before his rising again would establish even the weakest analogy; but in the meanwhile man would mourn for his death, as for the loss of one who might never return. For every aspect of the material world he would have ready some life-giving expression ; and those aspects would be scarcely less varied than his words. The same object would at different times, or under different conditions, awaken the most opposite or inconsistent conceptions. But these conceptions and the words which expressed them would exist side by side without producing the slightest consciousness of their incongruity; nor is it easy to determine the exact order in which they might arise. The sun would awaken both mournful and inspiriting ideas, ideas of victory and defeat, of toil and premature death. He would be the Titan, strangling the serpents of the night before he drove his chariot up the sky; and he would also be the being who, worn down by unwilling labour undergone for men, sinks wearied into the arms of the mother who bare him in the morning. Other images would not be wanting; the dawn and the dew and the violet clouds would be not less real and living than the sun. In his rising from the east he would quit the fair dawn, whom he should see no more till his labour drew towards its close. And not less would he love and be loved by the dew and by the morning herself, while to both his life would be fatal as his fiery car rose higher in the sky. So would man speak of all other things also; of the thunder and the earthquake and the storm, not less than of summer and winter."

From what source is this picture drawn? Certainly not from an investigation of the tribes that still live in their primitive condition in remote quarters of the globe. These tribes, whether they roam in the prairies of North America or inhabit the forests of India, whether crushed in their development by the cold of Siberia or the heat of Africa, have many points in common, so many that patient inquirers are beginning to form some general idea of what all tribes or races must have been in their earliest condition.[1] We may safely assert that there are no cases at all parallel to the fancy picture of the mythologers. There are plenty of savages that worship the sun and moon, that personify moving objects, because they cannot conceive motion without life,[2] and that have formed myths about physical phenomena. But we look in vain for all this wonderful riot of imagination about the daily operations of nature, this terrible anguish about an ordinary sunset, this outburst of joy in the summer dawn, when their nightly grief had scarce lulled them to sleep.

---

[1] If it be objected that these tribes belong to lower races, without answering the assumption of an original difference of race, it may fairly be retorted that there is no evidence of any higher intelligence in the original Aryans than in the present New Zealanders.

[2] So Schoolcraft says of the Red Indian *Totem* (vol. II., p. 19), "It is always some animated object, and seldom or never derived from the inanimate class of nature." The widely-spread worship of sacred stones appears to be symbolical, and not from attributing to them life.

"Years might pass," says Mr. Cox, "*or ages, before* the sun's rising again *would establish even the weakest analogy*, but in the meanwhile men would mourn for his loss, as for the loss of one who might never return." I cannot but think that the smallest philosophy, or the smallest study of human nature, must refute such an absurd supposition. Surely the most certain point in all psychology is the rapid formation of firm beliefs founded even on insufficient evidence. The association of ideas, the principle of expectation that the future will resemble the past, furnish us with convictions almost before we can express them. The school of Hartley, James Mill, J. S. Mill, and Bain go so far as to maintain that associations formed in our earliest infancy afford us even those irresistible convictions commonly called *a priori* Laws of Thought. Such a theory could never be maintained for a moment by thoughtful men, were it not agreed that every human mind is so constituted as to infer laws spontaneously and rapidly from any repetition of phenomena. The first inductions will be made from the most imperfect data; even the most stupid children will infer a law from two or three examples. A being in whom years of sunrises and sunsets would not establish a very strong conviction (instead of the "weakest analogy") must be a complete idiot, and perfectly incapable of providing himself with the necessaries of life, far less with a poetical mythology.

And if we go back far enough to deprive the primitive Aryans of *ages* of experience about the sun's daily course we shall come to a time when they, like the savage races of the present day, showed no curiosity at all on the subject, and were perfectly listless, as savages are wont to be, about all natural phenomena that did not disturb their life, or interfere with their comforts.

> " Nec plangore diem magno solemque per agros
> quaerebant pavidi palantes noctis in umbris,
> sed taciti respectabant somnoque sepulti,
> dum rosea face sol inferret lumina caelo :
> *a parvis quod enim consuerant cernere semper*
> *alterno tenebras et lucem tempore gigni,*
> *non erat ut fieri posset mirarier umquam*
> nec diffidere, ne terras aeterna teneret
> nox in perpetuum detracto lumine solis.
> sed magis illud erat curae, quod saecla ferarum
> infestum miseris faciebant saepe quietem."[1]

The condition then of the human race postulated by the solar theory of myths appears to be inconsistent with itself, and impossible. For it is, as to association of ideas, or inferring from experience, a state beneath that of an infant or an intelligent domestic animal ; as to imagination and sympathy, a state as advanced as the most poetical minds of

---

[1] Lucretius, *de Rer. Nat.*, v. 971-81. He appears to have met comparative mythologers in his day who tried to impose their imaginations about primitive men upon him.

our own age; as to language and expression, a state so perfect that it must either have been produced by direct revelation, or developed by the progress of myriads of centuries.[1]

We must not forget to add that these keenly sensitive and remarkable men, though their migrations must have produced many strange and striking adventures, are asserted by the mythologers to have observed and recorded nothing but the one fixed phenomenon, that should certainly have failed at a very early period to impress them by its eternal repetition. They were unable to remember any great war or battle; they did not preserve intact the portrait of any national hero; they forgot to chronicle any crisis in their tribal life. And yet they exceeded us all in the keenness and quickness of their sympathies! Is this assumption reasonable, and are we to admit, for the sake of the mythologers, that the memories so indelibly retentive of a few physical phenomena, and so rich in clothing them with the dress of fancy, were incurious of all human affairs, and of those real tragedies in their life, *which afforded them all the metaphors wherewith they adorned the struggle of the sun.*

The able critic of the theory in the Edinburgh Review, already cited, takes up another aspect of the question, and shows equally that the nature

---

[1] I am glad to see myself supported, at least in substance, by Sir J. Lubbock, *Origin of Civilisation*, p. 221, *sqq.*

of the memory required by the theory is absurd, from a psychological point of view. For while all the various names and even phrases in which solar phenomena were expressed must be accurately remembered, it is equally necessary to the theory that their meaning must be forgotten. "This," as the reviewer justly remarks, "postulates in the Greeks of the mythopoeic age the existence of a verbal memory at once supernaturally strong and supernaturally weak, and that too in relation to the same things" (p. 344.) Such a condition is indeed very consistent with the state of imagination and of folly which I had shown to be equally demanded by the theory, but it will create great additional difficulty when regarded from a plain common sense point of view.

Surely such a race of men are rather postulated by an ingenious theory than suggested by facts and sound analogies. If bitter grief and exulting joy, if fear and wonder are a necessary basis for a physical explanation of myths, I cannot but think the change, not of day and night, but of the seasons, would afford a far better ground-work.[1] We know as a matter of history that the destruction of the verdure and the flowers of spring by the summer's heat, and the death of autumn in the winter, have

---

This was the attitude of Wilhelm Müller in his *Deutsche Mythologie*

not only suggested many ceremonies to ancient nations, but that even now, in this mature age of the human race, they affect our prosaic and positive minds with a sadness which we cannot reason away.[1] For even though we foresee the result with certainty, the revolution of the year is too slow to console us with the excitement of expectation. Yet I am not sure whether even so we could fairly explain the amount of wonder and terror assumed by the comparative mythologers. If we consider the mental attitude of young children towards natural phenomena, we shall find them perfectly accustomed to the change of day and night before they have words to express themselves; and the change of the seasons, if it does influence the general state of the spirits, is too gradual to produce sudden and violent emotions.

But there yet remain those striking and occasional phenomena, such as storms and earthquakes, which occur frequently enough in some climates, but always irregularly. These, as they still do, must always have produced the deepest emotions in primitive men, not only from their impressive nature, as phenomena, but owing to the actual disasters that followed in their wake. I think therefore that on *psychological* grounds, the theory supported by MM. Kuhn, Roth, and others (called by Professor M.

---

[1] "To the number of these plaintive ditties belong the song *Linus*, mentioned by Homer, the melancholy character of which is shown by its fuller names, Αἴλινος and Οἰτόλινος. It was fre-

Müller the "Meteorological Theory"[1]) is decidedly to be preferred to the solar theory, supported by the English works on the subject. Of course linguistic grounds are of far more importance, and will outbalance many improbabilities, but the linguistic authorities have not yet agreed in their verdict. In the meanwhile, let us not permit imaginary sketches

---

quently sung in Greece, according to Homer, at the grape-picking. Linus was originally the subject of the song, the person whose fate was bewailed in it; and there were many districts in Greece (for example, Thebes, Chalcis, and Argos) in which tombs of Linus were shown. This Linus evidently belongs to a class of deities or demigods, of which many instances occur in the religions of Greece and Asia Minor; boys of extraordinary beauty, and in the flower of youth, who are supposed to have been drowned, or devoured by raging dogs, or destroyed by wild beasts, and whose death is lamented in the harvest or other periods of hot season. The real object of lamentation was the tender beauty of spring destroyed by the summer heat, and other phenomena of the same kind, which the imagination of these early times invested with a personal form, and represented as gods or beings of a divine nature. According to the very remarkable and explicit tradition of the Argives, Linus was a youth, who, having sprung from a divine origin, grew up with the shepherds among the lambs, and was torn in pieces by wild dogs; whence arose the 'festival of the lambs,' at which many dogs were slain. Doubtless this festival was celebrated during the greatest heat, at the time of the constellation Sirius, the emblem of which, among the Greeks, was, from the earliest times, a raging dog." K. O. Müller, *Hist. of Greek Lit.*, p. 23. He quotes many other cases in the sequel.

[1] Cf. *Lectures*, II., p. 518, *sqq.*

of primitive men in impossible conditions to be thrust upon us as arguments on either side.

A larger and more important question remains to be discussed—a question too weighty to be handled polemically : it is the position of probable conclusions in the study of ancient history. I am using the words *probable* and *certain* in their popular sense, for I know that no conclusions as to matters of fact can be strictly demonstrated, and that therefore in the mathematical sense any evidence that can be obtained in history is only probable. But from a wider point of view, there are facts admitted to be certain, and opposed as such to others not supported by sufficient evidence. All historical inquirers are agreed that the independent evidence of several contemporary witnesses removes all reasonable doubt, and that even when such evidence can be obtained indirectly from the generation immediately succeeding the actual witnesses, we are still within the domain of positive history. But beyond this point the modern English school abolish all history, for likening their method of inquiry to a judicial investigation, they repudiate any evidence that would not be of use before a jury.[1]

I cannot but think that were this position logically maintained, even contemporary history would become impossible. No sketch of a great cha-

---

[1] This is the position of Sir George C. Lewis, *Credibility*, &c. vol. I., p. 16, *sq*.

racter, or of a great national development can be completed without much conjecture, without many inferences on very delicate evidence indeed, which could never be stated to a jury, and the weighing of which depends upon that subtile diagnosis, which is the essential difference of a great and skilled observer. It should never be forgotten that the great value of special training in any field of knowledge is to enable the inquirer to appreciate evidence inappreciable by mere common sense. If history be a special science, it is as irrelevant of the sceptics to test its conclusions by an appeal to a jury, as it would be to test by the same criterion the inferences of a skilled physician from obscure and fugitive symptoms. Nor is it any disrespect to a British jury to assert their incompetence of deciding questions which the lawyer and the judge (as such) are equally incompetent to decide.

All such conclusions are indeed but probable, some of them but possible; yet are they therefore to be refused a place in our histories? Fortunately, the readers addressed are not a British jury, compelled to give a verdict forthwith, and bound in every case to disbelieve what they can doubt, but a body of trained men able to weigh evidence with nicety, at liberty to suspend their verdict, and to whom suggestions and hints are valuable, as leading them to new and confirmatory researches.[1]

---

[1] I believe all great historians act on these principles. For

There are no doubt two kinds of probability; one is called *a priori*, which merely consists in not conflicting with any known facts. This, which should rather be called possibility, is seldom of any value in history, because a great number of cases are equally possible, and equally in harmony with the *a priori* conditions of the case. But as soon as any actual evidence can be attained, we have a different sort of probability, which falls short of certainty, because our evidence is not quite trustworthy, or because it does not tell us enough to draw a conclusion. This latter sort of probability must, in my judgment, play a prominent part in the ancient history of any nation, provided it is regarded merely as such, and continually subjected to farther verification. The researches of comparative mythologers are at present for the most part of this nature. They are not by any means (as I have shown, and as it is fully admitted by the most scientific among them) certain discoveries, but rest upon such probable evidence as may be corroborated by additional discoveries. It is possible that a more complete knowledge of the Veda may discover to us the derivation of the word Panis, and that

---

example, Th. Mommsen, when discussing in his *Hist. of Rome* the probable complicity of Julius Caesar with Catiline's conspiracy, says, "That in particular Crassus and Caesar had a hand in the game may be regarded—*not in a juristic, but in an historical point of view*—as an ascertained fact." Vol. IV., part I., p. 181, (Eng. Ed. of 1866.)

Greek analogies may show Πάρις to correspond to it. In the meanwhile, it would be absurd to deny the comparative mythologers the right of stating and ventilating their conjectures on the subject, provided they do not overstate or overestimate the certainty of these conjectures. For the very same reason historians must assert their own right of stating inferences from tradition as probabilities.

This privilege, which the mythologers exercise very freely indeed, without always confessing it, they deny to the historians upon two grounds: first, that the legends preserved in the " *Epos* of the Aryans," being probable only in the first sense, are not capable of being verified by any positive evidence; secondly, that the mythological theory of the origin of legends explains everything. The first assertion seems a very bold one indeed to make, so much so that the more cautious theorists confine themselves to saying that the legends have not yet been verified, adding however, ironically, that they will be delighted to submit to any positive evidence when produced. They point, like Mr. Grote, to the chemical fusion, if I may so call it, of supernatural with ordinary events, which renders it impossible, in their opinion, to detect the several factors.[1] Conceding great difficulty, it would be very hard to prove the

---

[1] Cf. Cox, vol. I., chap. ix., and Grote's *Hist.*, part I., chap. xvi.

impossibility. All the sceptics, whether mythologers or otherwise, admit that there are historical elements in the Greek legends. Surely, until every possible evidence on the subject has been exhausted, historians are bound to endeavour in every way to winnow the wheat from the chaff. Who knows what archaeological evidence may yet turn up? For example, the discovery of very ancient and extensive ruins on the sites of Mykenae and Troy—two cities of no importance in historical times—shows that the Homeric poems dealt with real cities, and not with a mere Greek localisation of mythical countries. These poems would have lost all their effect if they had invented a war between two great existing states which had never been at feud with each other. Whether, therefore, there was really a Trojan war in prehistoric times or not, the firm geographical basis of the Iliad can only be satisfactorily accounted for by a conflict between the states of Greece and the northwest coast of Asia Minor.

Now this very conclusion is ridiculed by Mr. Cox as so barren and unimportant, that it may be cast aside as useless. Let us therefore approach it historically, and see what probable conclusions can be derived from it. As an isolated fact it tells very little indeed, but in relation to other legends its high importance will soon appear. Every one is aware that the consistent tradition of the Asiatic Greeks asserted them to have come, not from the east, as the Aryans did originally, but as a return-wave, if I may so say, from Greece. No nation forgot their foreign origin so rapidly as the Greeks, but it was their custom when they did so to consider themselves αὐτόχθονες, and not to invent a false foreign origin. So lively a faith in the advent of their ancestors from Greece makes it *probable* that the so-called Ionic migration was not a solar myth, but a fact. Now this probable conclusion receives strong corroboration from the so-called barren fact that the Iliad presupposes a conflict caused by the Greeks of Hellas invading Asia Minor, and sets forth, rightly or wrongly, a previous outrage on the part of the Asiatics as a sufficient justification for the invasion. When we add the peculiar and striking consideration that a series of lays celebrating the victories of Greek heroes over the princes of Asia Minor was apparently composed, and certainly popular *in the cities of Asia Minor* at the dawn of their positive history, the explanation irresistibly suggests itself, that these lays must have been intended to excite the courage and the ardour of invaders by representing their ancestors as having obtained deathless glory in the same conflict. To adorn this ancient duel, myths and folk lore would be put under contribution, gods and heroes would be set upon the stage, and great victories would be described, which posterity would endeavour to rival. But existing conditions would forbid the poets to add a permanent occupation to **the victory,** for the very same territory was now being conquered, inch by inch, by the descendants of **the former victors.** After the historical conquest, it **was natural that these** splendid epic lays should **be** cherished, as were afterwards the **lyrics** of Tyrtaeus, **by the victorious** settlers whom they had inspired.[1]

There is a case **very similar in later** Grecian history. The restoration of the Messenians by Epaminondas led **to a similar** outburst **of epics** concerning the **old Messenian** wars—epics which would certainly **have been** regarded **as devoid of** all foundation **by the sceptical** critics, had **not** fragments of the contemporary Tyrtaeus survived. Still the romantic details about Aristomenes seem to belong chiefly **to** these later epics, and I have little doubt that many stories about him **have their parallels** among other Aryan nations. If it **were really** the case that no historical William Tell could be discovered, and that he must have been discovered, had he existed,[2] still the legends about **his contest with**

---

[1] This view is substantially that of Professor E. Curtius.

[2] This is the position taken by M. Albert Rillier in his remarkable book on the *Origin of the Swiss Confederation*. He has however contemporary documents for his basis, so that his inquiry is by no means so hazardous as those concerning earlier myths. The defect of his work is I think the absence of any rational account *how* the story originated. M. A. Maury, in an interesting review of the work published in the *Journal des Sa-*

Gessler point to a period when such sentiments were highly gratifying to the Swiss, and show that when the story was composed there was a feud between the Swiss and the Emperor. The part of Gessler is very remarkable, if the whole of it was invented as one of plausible fiction. But however the fifteenth century chroniclers may have invented a story they knew to be false, I am supported by Mr. Grote that in early ages deception—deliberate deception—is out of the question. It is therefore likely enough that there may be some basis for the Trojan war beyond the excited feelings of the Greek invaders in the Ionic migration.

But hitherto the accruing evidence has been rather against it, for the comparative mythologers have shown, with some amount of *probability*, that a good deal of the romantic matter may be mythical, and that therefore Achilles and Helen have their figures so decorated with fiction as to render them perfectly undistinguishable. Believing, however, that the Iliad is "rooted in geography," to use an expression of Mr. Simcox,[1] it seems *probable* that the homes of these unhistorical heroes, at all events, indicate the homes of the leading invaders, and this

---

vants for July, 1870, promises to supply this gap in a future article. The war between France and Germany has unfortunately stopped all succeeding numbers.

[1] *Academy* for August, 1870.

inference agrees with the tradition which brings them from various parts of Greece. As Mr. Cox tells us "that no historical knowledge can be gained from the legends of Hellenic colonization in Asia Minor," I am sorry to annoy him by adding another *probable* inference. The tradition that the young blood of Hellas crossed over to Asia Minor accords remarkably with the rapid and brilliant development of that country, as compared with Attica and the Peloponnesus. So the Italian and Sicilian colonies rapidly outstripped the mother country in absolutely historical times; and should we be told that a richer soil and climate produced these results, the answer is obvious, that the Greeks can hardly then have first occupied the coast of Asia Minor, but if they came from the east can hardly have avoided colonizing it as early as their European peninsula.

It appears then that the naked fact of a war having taken place between Mykenae and Ilion is of the greatest moment in adding an independent probable argument to prove a conclusion hitherto resting on other probabilities alone—the conclusion that the legends asserting the Ionic migration are historical. And any one who knows how to estimate the accumulating force of several independent probabilities tending to the same conclusion, will see good reason to reject the supercilious advice of the mythologers, that such probabilities, and such isolated facts, are of no importance. It is indeed a matter of great patience to hear men rejecting facts as unimportant, and extolling fancies as of the most profound interest; nor can we conceive it possible to know, whether any, even the most trivial, fact of such antiquity, may not some day assume the very greatest importance in history. For surely we can never know where and how additional evidence may be found. Mr. Cox has devoted his tenth chapter to show that all the tribal names of the Greeks are based on mythical etymologies. He rings his usual changes on such similarities as ἰοστέφανος, Ἴαμος, Ἰώ, Ἴωνες, and such as Ἀχιλλεύς, Ἀχαιοί, to which he might as well have added ἄχος, ἄχυρον, and every other word that begins with ἀχ. Let me again remind the reader that unless the derivations of these proper names are carefully determined, accidental coincidences with one another, and with Sanskrit parallels, are perfectly untrustworthy.

It is strange indeed that the very men who have been most successful and meritorious in exposing the blunders of the so-called "Volks-etymologien" should themselves fail to guard against the very same description of error. But even Professor M. Müller seems to agree in considering that the tribal names occurring in the Greek epics are historically worthless, and can give us no reliable information as to the geographical distribution of the Greeks before the dawn of contemporary history. If this scepticism means anything, it means this, that the

Homeric lays[1] afford no evidence that the Achaeans lived in Greece, or the Lykians in Asia; for that these and all the other names of tribes had a mythical significance for ages, before they were localised and adopted by special divisions of the Greeks; and that for all we know, the geographical localization of these names may be perfectly at variance with their legendary distribution. If applied to the legendary distribution of names in the Homeric lays, this statement is utterly false. There was so close an agreement between the designations of the various tribes in Homer, and their historical position afterwards, that none of them ever found the smallest difficulty in identifying themselves with their legendary forefathers.

So accurate is, in fact, the agreement, that a thorough-going sceptic might suggest it as a proof of the late composition of the Iliad. The principal

---

[1] It will be seen that I do not assert the unity of either Iliad or Odyssey. In fact the arguments of Professor Kirchhoff (*die Composition der Odyssee*, Berlin, 1869) have persuaded me that the Odyssey is patched together like the Iliad, though somewhat more cleverly. But I am at a loss to see how the composite character of the poems disproves the historical basis of the several lays, and yet this is evidently the opinion of Mr. Cox, when he urges it against the conservative unitarians. As the unity of the poems does not prove their historical value, so their composite character does not destroy it; on the contrary, short separate lays are more likely to be really ancient than a sustained and complicated epic.

tribes, he might say, must have wandered often and changed abodes often in prehistoric times; if the Iliad shows a distribution identical with that of historic times it is because the poem or poems were not composed till all these arrangements were settled, and its geographical arrangements are merely copied from historical facts. But such an admission would be perfectly suicidal to a comparative mythologer, whose whole theory is based upon the *great antiquity* of the general outline, and in particular of the geographical features, of the legendary Epos. And indeed even the greatest sceptics are agreed that the individual lays, on which our Iliad and Odyssey are founded, must be referred back to a period long before the dawn of history.

It would be equally impracticable to argue that the geographical titles of the tribes had been copied from the legends, and made to fit the arrangements there described. We can hardly conceive people calling themselves by ancient titles for such a reason, when it would be much easier to adapt a legend to account for their original name were its derivation forgotten; and in any case a curious piece of evidence has lately come to light, showing that the appellations Achaeans, Lykians, Tyrrhenians, and some others, were appropriated by special tribes at a period certainly earlier than the composition of even the scattered lays that make up the Iliad and Odyssey. The Vicomte de Rougé[1] has lately copied from a temple at Karnak, and translated, an inscription set up by king Merenephtah, perhaps the very king in whose reign the children of Israel departed from Egypt, and whose date is clearly to be placed in the end of the thirteenth century B. C. Among the names of various naval tribes, who appear to have been at that time in search of settlements (for the inscription tells us they brought with them wives and children) those above-mentioned occur. The correctness of M. de Rougé's deciphering has been carefully tested by German Egyptologers, and is now generally accepted. If not certain, it is at least so probable as to demand a place in our ancient history, and certainly far more probable than many of the identifications attempted, on scantier evidence, by the mythologers. These tribes then probably possessed their historical names before they settled on the coasts of Hellas, and they have a really historical import, whether they be derived originally from solar legends or not. Interesting as is this discovery in itself, it is of the last importance in showing that all possible evidence concerning prehistoric Greece is not yet exhausted. The frequent mention of Egyptian expeditions into the Aegean, coupled with the notice to which I have alluded, leads us to expect new light from farther Egyptian

---

[1] See his very remarkable articles in the *Revue Archéologique*, N. S., vol. xvi., pp. 35 and 81.

excavations. Whether M. de Rougé will be able to show any historical basis for the legend of Danaus, I know not, but it may possibly turn out more than purely solar, as the mythologers assert, and should not be rejected without complete proof against it.

I return, and but for a moment, to the other hardy assertion of Mr. Cox that his theory *explains everything*. It has been proved to excess that the statement itself is utterly exaggerated, and that the theory, whatever its prospects may be, as yet explains very little. There is, however, a far more damning fact yet in store for it. Even when it does explain a story perfectly, such explanation by no means excludes an historical basis.

One celebrated instance will settle the question. The story of Sigurd, the hero of the *Edda*, with all the accessory characters, and all the adventures—a favorite example of a solar myth with the new school—is so closely imitated, to all appearance, in the *Nibelungen Lied*, the great German epic composed centuries after it, that here, if anywhere, comparative mythology appears to have won a great victory. The names are the same, and the adventures are very like. It would then follow necessarily that the later poem at all events (if not both) was mythical and not historical. But strange to say, there is an historical basis for this later poem—an historical basis so certain that not even the mythologers can gainsay it. Closely as the names appear to correspond to those of the Edda, they correspond just as closely to historical personages who lived after the Edda was known and referred to in literature. Sigurd represents Siegbert, king of Austrasia, 561–75 A. D. Gunther represents Gundicarius, king of Burgundy, in 435 A. D. So Brynhild, Irenfried, Dietrich, and Atli, are the reflections of Brunehault, Hermannfried [Irminfrid?], Theodoric, and Attila.[1]

Here then, when comparative mythology might possibly have explained everything; here, when in default of other evidence we should all have been quite content to accept its explanation, it is shown to be a false and delusive guide. Its explanations, when applied to legends of men, if they can be distinguished from legends of the gods, do not exclude all historical origin, and are therefore almost worthless. Scientific linguists know this difficulty, and have cautioned their followers, but in vain.[2]

That the nature of comparative mythology makes

---

[1] See a full description of the plot of the *Edda*, and of its age, and that of the *Nibelungen Lied*, in Max Müller, *Chips*, vol. II., pp. 113-5, from whom I borrow these details, and who is answerable for the forms of the names. He quotes them to show that there are mythical elements in the story older than the Austrasian kings. I quote them to show that there are historical elements in the story younger than some parts at least of the Edda, and not borrowed from it.

[2] Cf. M. Max Müller's judicious remarks on the subject of Cyrus and St. Patrick in his review of Mr. Cox's *Tales*, in *Chips*, II., pp. 169-72.

new evidence more accessible than the nature of legend, must be readily admitted. That the mythologers have done excellent service in showing analogies between the names of gods and heroes in different branches of the Aryan family, is also true. That the habit of transferring adventures from one prominent character to another was common in olden times, as it is now, they have proved clearly enough. But the wholesale conclusions they are now asserting cannot be received, least of all from men that affect such strictness as to evidence.

One more argument remains to be urged. This too is a general objection, and affects the whole method of the later comparative mythologers. *Real coincidence, even in complicated legends, is by itself no proof of their common origin*, for it is constantly found in the beliefs of nations totally distinct in race, and consequently in mythology. If therefore the process of inferring unity of origin from *mere coincidence of names* in divers legends has been proved perfectly untrustworthy, it is not difficult to show that similar inferences from *mere coincidence of stories* are equally precarious. So strictly true is it that the new science has no claims to respect whatever, if the three canons above stated (p. 45) are not all strictly obeyed. As was before remarked, at first hearing such strange coincidences will readily convince men of a common origin, but modern researches have shown irrefragably, not only that the most diverse nations in the world devise exactly the same customs and entertain precisely the same ideas on many conventional matters, but also that they have devised similar legends. Thus, the mythology of the Aryans resembles in many points that of the Semites, though these races have been separate in language and religion for ages before the Aryans left their first home, even granting that they ever were united. So also the Aryan myths find their parallels among the so-called Turanian nations, and even in America. The legends of Tell and of Polyphemus, for example, to which we have already adverted, characteristic as they may appear, occur among Turks, Finns, and Siberians.[1] If therefore mere coincidence of myths prove anything, it proves a great deal too much, and shows not only the single origin of our race, but that Adam and Eve constructed for all nations all the legends to which they ever could attain!

On Mr. Cox's own showing, the myths of Egypt and of Syria, particularly of Osiris and Adonis, are just as parallel to the northern European legends as the Greek legends are.[2] He adds the cases of Semiramis, of Minos, and of Samson. So some Indians of South America believe in the origin of men from stones, like the myth of Deukalion, and the similarity of Dagon with Proteus, and some stories of the

---

[1] On Polyphemus, cf. the Essay of Wilhelm Grimm, *die Sage von Polyphemus*. On Tell, Mr. Dasent's Introduction to his *Norse Tales*.

[2] Cox, I., p. 400, *note*.

American Indians afford similar matter of comparison. I quote from the *Saturday Review*[1] the following illustration:—

"Another still more extraordinary example of wide diffusion is to be found in a nursery story told by Mr. Chambers, called 'The Milk-white Doo.'[2] The incidents are as follows:—A labouring man brought home a hare to his wife, and desired her to cook it for dinner, but while it was on the fire she tasted and tasted at it till she had tasted it all away. Not knowing what to do for her good man's dinner, she killed her little son, and boiled him. When the boy had been eaten, his little sister gathered his bones, and buried them below a stone before the door. While lying there, according to the story—

> They grew and they grew
> To a milk white doo,
> That took to its wings
> And away it flew.

In the course of its flight it came to two women washing clothes, upon which it sat down on a stone and sang—

> ' Pew, pew,
> My minnie me slew,
> My daddy me chew,

---

[1] July 30th, 1870.
[2] *Popular Rhymes of Scotland.* (Edinburgh. 1870.)

My sister gathered my banes,
And put them between twa milk-white stanes;
And I grew and I grew to a milk-white doo,
And I took to my wings and away I flew.'

The women were so charmed with the song that they offered it all their clothes if it would sing it again. And the bargain having been concluded, the bird then flew till it came to a man counting a great heap of money, all of which the dove obtained upon the same terms as the clothes. Lastly, it came to two millers grinding, and by them was presented with a mill-stone. It then flew away back till it lighted on its father's house-top, and when by-and-by its sister came out, it threw down the clothes to her; when the father came out, it threw down all the money to him, and lastly, when the mother came out, it threw down the mill-stone upon her and killed her.

"Such is the queer absurd story which used formerly, if not now, to be familiar in every Scottish nursery. Mr. Chambers mentions that it is also prevalent in Germany under the name of the *Machandel Boom*, or the holly-tree, and that the song of the bird spirit in Lower Saxon is almost the same word for word as in the Scottish version. Its diffusion, however, is a vast deal wider than this; for it prevails not merely in Scotland and Germany, but in England, in Hungary, in Languedoc, in Modern Greece, among the Bechuanas in South Africa, and, strangest of all, some of its traits are even to be found in a popular tale recently published from an Egyptian papyrus contemporary with the abode of the Israelites in Egypt. There cannot be much doubt that the story is a parable intended to teach that retribution is in some mysterious way attendant upon evil deeds, and it may possibly in addition to this have some mythological meaning which it is perhaps vain now to hope to recover."

Of course nothing but confusion can result, if we do not call in some farther proof of common origin, such as strict identity of names, and of the derivation of these names. And even then we must be cautious not to deny absolutely an historical basis, till such basis is positively disproved by contemporary records. With these limitations, the science of comparative mythology must be hailed as having done some service in expounding the primitive ideas of our forefathers, and the extravagance of its pretensions, a feature common to almost all new sciences, should not blind us to its solid merits. A few years more will probably put us in possession of many interesting additions to the great collections of parallel customs and beliefs made by Waitz and other anthropologists.

Surely the comparative mythologers have not sufficiently weighed the importance of this most mysterious uniformity in the human race. It will make a close attention to similarity of names, in both sound and etymology, of absolute necessity in convincing us of the single origin of parallel legends. But even beyond this, its recognition will open to us a new page in the forgotten life of prehistoric ages, and will show us that, as every other part of our nature obeys its laws, so even the riotous faculty of the imagination is checked by some secret rein, and guided unconsciously upon beaten paths.

ESSAY III.

The Egyptian Hieroglyphics.

Et manebant structis molibus litterae Ægyptiae priorem opulentiam complexae.
TACITUS.

IN the last discourse it was our intention to show that there may be evidence for ancient history found in legends, and that the sceptical and mythological schools which have endeavoured to destroy the value of such evidence have only succeeded to a small extent, and have been unable to make good their destructive position. The importance of legends however by themselves must be conceded to be small, if they are not supported by documentary evidence, or by such remains of human culture as can lead us to corroborative conclusions. The object of the present Essay is to discuss the oldest and most remarkable of the documents left us by early races, and to examine their importance in constructing a rational and real ancient history.

But when we approach these documents we find

the attitude of our sceptical opponents and our own difficulties completely altered. The oral statements of the legends are in general easily understood, but their value as evidence—the truth of what they have delivered—is under question. In the case of written documents, there can be no doubt of their great value as evidence, if contemporary, but their meaning has been the subject of long and violent controversy. For the fullest and apparently the most important of them—those found on the magnificent ruins left us by the Egyptians, the Assyrians, and the Persians—were not only written in characters, of which the meaning had been lost, but the very languages of these nations were of uncertain family and of unknown structure. All men were agreed that if they could be read, they would tell us much of the secrets of a forgotten world. But how were they to be deciphered?

If a known language is concealed under strange characters, provided these characters be used consistently, it is no difficult task to ascertain their respective values, and to discover the meaning. If an unknown language is presented to us in known characters, we can at least pronounce its sounds, and so form an opinion as to the affinity it shows in roots and in structure to other known languages; if there be such analogies we can through them approach its meaning. But when *both language and characters are unknown*, how are we to proceed?[1] And even supposing that ingenious men construct for us a translation, what guarantee have we that it represents the original sense?

These were the perplexities encountered when men attempted to read the inscriptions of Egypt and of Assyria. And yet it was plain that little could be accomplished in our knowledge of antiquity without this achievement. It was plain both from the historical evidence left us by the Hebrews, and from the observation of the most intelligent Greeks, that the oldest recorded human culture had been established in the valleys of the Nile and the Euphrates.

The Egyptian inscriptions were not only far more accessible, but they were in themselves more striking than those of Persia and Assyria. The most vulgar tourist could not but wonder at their bright colours, their pictorial forms, and the extraordinary art and finish of their execution. Yet almost no evi-

---

[1] This difficulty appeared to Sir G. C. Lewis so insurmountable, that in his *Astronomy of the Ancients*, a sort of blue-book containing all the Greek and Roman evidence on the subject which he could collect, he declares the deciphering of the Egyptian language under such circumstances to be *impossible*. Whether it is so or not, the old Egyptian language had long since been shown not to be under such circumstances, and Lewis struggles in vain to disprove the close and certain analogy it bears to the modern Coptic.

dence was forthcoming on their meaning. The literature of Alexandria, which would doubtless have contained all the requisite indications for solving the difficulty, has perished all but a few fragments, chiefly transcribed for us in the works of ignorant and careless compilers. The earlier Greeks and the Romans who could have informed us on the subject were such bad linguists, and so little interested in other peoples' speech, that they were content with the versions told them by the priests in Egypt, and say little or nothing of the Egyptian language, save what any intelligent observer might have remarked, viz.—that there were two or three different kinds of writing, used for different purposes, and that two of them were confined to sacred purposes.[1] It was after

---

[1] This is now known to have been a mistake. M. Chabas, commenting on the Papyrus Rollin (in Lepsius' *Zeitschrift für Aegyptische Sprache*, &c., for July, 1869, p. 85) observes:— "Beaucoup de gens y apprendront, ce que ne devrait de nos jours être ignoré par personne, à savoir que l'écriture hiéroglyphique se prêtait à tous les emplois des écritures ordinaires, et n'était nullement réservée pour l'usage hiératique : qu'elle ne constituait en aucune manière une écriture sacerdotale, inséparablement associée à la science sacrée, mais qu' elle servait aux petits commis des exploitations rurales, aux surveillants d'ouvriers, aux marchands et aux artizans, pour la tenue de leurs notes de comptabilités, aussi bien qu'aux hiérogrammates pour la rédaction des hymnes religieux et des panégyriques des rois." Nevertheless, at a late epoch, there can be no doubt that hieroglyphics, being cumbrous and antique, were specially used for sacred and monu-

their example that the three observed kinds of characters were called: (1) *Hieroglyphic*, consisting of full pictures carved on stone, and coloured brightly according to certain conventional rules, or sketched in outline; (2) *Hieratic*, a cursive character not at first sight pictorial, but derived directly from the former, intended for writing longer documents on papyrus, and consequently abridged and facilitated graphically. (3) There was a still more abridged form in which it is impossible to discover any vestige of pictures without comparing it closely with the older forms. This was called *Demotic*, or Enchorial, and was used for popular purposes.

---

mental purposes. This was the condition of things known to the Greeks; and indeed even in old times there are traces of similar language. The epitaph of the artist Iriousen, on a *stele* in the Louvre declares: "I know also the secret of the divine language," that is, of the hieroglyphics. Cf. Chabas in the *Revue Archéologique*, old series, xiv., p. 68, *note;* also his *Mélanges Égyptologiques*, i., p. 116.

[1] Some later inquirers think that it was not derived from the hieroglyphic through the hieratic, but independently, and perhaps from a different dialect. M. Chabas (loc. cit.) opposes, by implication, this opinion. Demotic was certainly as old as Herodotus, who mentions it not as a novelty, but along with the other kinds. The Coptic dialects of Memphis and of Thebes differ considerably, and this accords with an allusion in one of the ancient hieratic papyri, which speaks of the inhabitants of the Delta and of Elephantiné as unintelligible to each other. Cf. Chabas, *Voyage d'un Égyptien*, Berlin, 1860, p. 12.

Such were the various species of Egyptian writing, but as the Hieroglyphic was soon recognised to be the fullest and clearest description, from which the others were derived by mere curtailing of its elaborateness and accuracy, the attention of the learned was concentrated upon it, and as from a clear understanding of it, the reading of Hieratic follows easily, and that of Demotic is only a question of time and care, we may here chiefly confine ourselves to it alone.[1]

It is worthy of observation, however, that the study of Demotic, though De Sacy through it led the way for Champollion, by showing its phonetic character clearly from the transcriptions of names on the Rosetta stone, was not brought to a scientific condition until the labours of the German Brugsch, who has published a grammar and dictionary of the language, and has translated by far the most interesting demotic relic we as yet possess—the so-called *Roman de Setna*.[2]

---

[1] It so happens that we now reverse the method used in the days of Clemens Alexandrinus (A. D. 211), when demotic, being nearest to the spoken Coptic, was first taught, then hieratic, and then hieroglyphics. Mr. Goodwin (*The Story of Saneha*, in *Fraser's Magazine* for February, 1865, p. 185) calls this a "perverse method," but surely he forgets that the close proximity of the Demotic idiom to the Coptic made it then, when Coptic was a living language, far the easiest for a beginner in Egypt.

[2] See his article in the *Rev. Arch.*, N. S., vol. xvi., p. 161. He found the papyrus in the coffin of a Coptic monk in November, 1865.

The Leyden Papyrus, known as Pap. Anastasy 65, which has been published in the great collection of Leemans, gave an enormous impulse to this study, as a large number of magic formulæ, and of words, are *transcribed* into Greek, thus affording good materials for a Demotic alphabet.[1] M. G. Maspero has also written a very interesting essay entitled *Études Démotiques*.[2] He gives translations of some curious magic formulae from the Leyden papyrus, and also of a moral treatise preserved in the Louvre, which corresponds in its sentiments to those expressed in the more ancient funereal monuments. But as yet far less progress has been made in this branch than in the two older graphic systems.[3]

---

[1] The reader will find a full description of it in C. J. Reuvens *Lettres à M. Letronne* (Leyden, 1830), and a shorter one prefixed to Leeman's plates. A long list of works on demotic are given by Mr. Birch, *Introduction to the Study of Hieroglyphics* (in Wilkinson's *Egyptians*), p. 282. There are also several demotic texts with Greek translations published in Lepsius' *Denkmäler*, vol. xii., pl. 73-5. The best sketch of the literary history of demotic researches is that of M. Brugsch, *Grammaire Démotique*, pp. 6-8.

[2] In the *Recueil de Travaux relatifs à la philologie Égyptienne*, &c. (Paris, 1870.)

[3] "Il faut le dire," says M. Maspero (*Recueil*, p. 18), " ce que jusqu'à présent a rebuté les savants et les a empêché de continuer les recherches si heureusement commencées par M. Brugsch, c'est l'aridité même des écrits soumis à leur examen. L'interprétation des inscriptions hiéroglyphiques ou des papyrus hiératiques est toujours récompensée par la découverte d'un fait

Turning **then to the full hieroglyphic** writing, which consists of coloured pictures, it was almost unanimously asserted by the ancients, and **it** seemed evident to modern observers that these pictures must **be a** representation **of** ideas, and not **of sounds. Before** considering this distinction it will be desirable to review briefly **the first** developments of *writing* among men. The Egyptian method is in fact so very different from ours, that it must **be** compared **with those of early nations and not with the** aged experience of a later **world.** We must in fact endeavour **to do with greater accuracy what the**

curieux ou d'une oeuvre nouvelle ; l'histoire de l'Égypte, de **ses** moeurs, de ses **habitants** est sortie toute entière de ces déchiffrements féconds. **A côté des Annales** de Thotmès III, des panégyriques d'Una ou de **N'ûm-h'otep, des** oeuvres de Ptah'-h'otep, d'Enna et de Pentaûr, **que** nous offrent **les** textes démotiques ? Des prières **funéraires, des** formules magiques hérissées de noms **baroques, des contrats de** vente ou d'achat, et, pour compenser **tant de sécheresse** et de pauvreté, **une seule** oeuvre véritablement littéraire, le **roman de** Setna. Après **avoir reconnu** cette triste vèrité, **bien** des personnes ont pensé que le résultat final ne **valait pas** la peine qu'il fallait se donner pour l'obtenir, et **se sont rejetées vers des** études plus intéressantes **et plus** productives **en** apparence.

"Pourtant, l'étude des textes **démotiques n'est** pas moins **nécessaire** à l'avancement de la science **que celle** des autres textes. S'ils n'ont par eux-mêmes qu'une valeur médiocre, la langue dans **laquelle ils** ont été rédigés mérite un examen approfondi Intermédiaire **entre le copte et** l'Égyptien classique, elle nous met **sous** les **yeux tous les** changements que le cours des siècles avait apportés **dans la** langue **antique des** Pharaons. Elle **n'a plus ni la** fermeté **parfois obscure de l'idiôme** primitif, ni l'élé-

comparative mythologers have attempted on another question, and seek to place ourselves in the attitude of the first discoverers of graphic notation.

Writing in the widest sense may here be defined **the communication** of man with man by means of *visible permanent signs*. It differs from spoken language in being visible, from **transient** gestures in being permanent,[1] from the **representations** of art in being a system of signs, which are not intended to be studied in themselves, but rather as the marks of something different and beyond them. The most primitive **permanent** forms of communication by

---

gance redondante qui marque les écrits du nouvel empire, ni même la concision un peu froide des époques saïtes ; elle est terne et décolorée, sèche et verbeuse à la fois. Les tournures traînent et languissent ; les termes inutiles s'accumulent, les régimes du verbe sont répétés de deux ou trois manières différentes à grand renfort de pronoms et de particules ; on dirait d'un vieillard qui bégaie longuement des mots à défaut d'idées. Seul, le roman conserve les traces du style antique, et, sous sa forme récente, laisse percer quelquefois la forme primitive.

"Ce sont ces changemens, ces altérations, ces dépérissements progressifs, cette décomposition lente mais certaine, qu'il faudrait noter et préciser, afin non seulement de montrer aux Égyptologues comment l'Égyptien est mort, mais de faire voir aux philologues de tout espèce les diverses phases d'affaiblissement et de vieillesse par lesquelles peut passer une langue avant de mourir."

[1] I am assured by a friend that the North American Indians have reduced gestures to a very complete system of communication, and use them when they meet under doubtful circumstances, without approaching one another. He showed me many of the signs which he knew and had used.

sight are the pictures of the **North American Indians** and of the Mexicans, which represent **the facts to be** communicated as **a whole,** without conveying them in any definite language, or separating **the parts of the sentence.** The celebrated petition, for example, **of** the Indian chiefs **to** the States' President in 1849, given by Schoolcraft,[1] **and commented** on by Steinthal, Sir J. Lubbock, and **others, is of this** character.[2] Seven chiefs, represented by the **beasts from** which they took their **names, and with their** eyes and **hearts respectively joined by lines passing from the** first chief to each **of** the rest, to show the **unanimity of their object, are** depicted actually going **to see the** President. **Four lakes** are in the back-ground **to indicate the territory, which was** the subject of the mission.

This letter is depicted, **not in any** language whatever, **but purely in** ideas, **and such** documents, **which want** interpretation more **than** the hand-

---

[1] In his magnificent *History, &c. of the Indian Tribes in the United States* (published by **the American Government),** part i., plate **60.** There are a number of other specimens in the **work.**

[2] Cf. Steinthal, *Entwicklung der Schrift*, p. **64,** and Sir J. Lubbock, *Origin of Civilisation*, p. **45.** It is not to be commended in this latter work, that such **palpably worthless** drawings of **savage** life as Lafitau's should be **mixed up with** accurate sketches, **and spoken of as equal in** value. A very formidable but not complete list of books **on** American antiquities and languages is given in Léon **de Rosny's** *Archives Paléographiques*, No. ii., pp. 100, *sq.* Pickering's **Essay** and Knapp's Lectures, two **very important works, are not mentioned.**

writing upon Belshazzar's wall, prove how utterly impossible any literature would be with **such** a graphic system.

Similarly, Alexander Von Humboldt gives, in his *Vues des Cordillères*,[1] a graphic picture of a lawsuit tween a **Mexican** and a Spaniard for a farm, before three Spanish judges.[2] Though these pictures were

---

[1] Page 50, and the exposition in pp. 55-6 of the folio edition.

[2] Zoëga (*de usu obeliscorum*, pp. 525-52) has an excellent discussion on the North American and the Mexican systems. He shows that the Mexicans had actually used many symbolical pictures for separate words, and had made no inconsiderable progress towards writing. Their representing of proper names by pictures of animals was, as Humboldt observes (*Vues des Cordillères*, p. 64), a step to phonetic writing, as it was the sound of the beast's name and not the beast itself which was indicated. Yet Zoëga does not call it picture-writing, but picturing, and justly so. "In universum autem ut ex monumentis hactenus recensitis definiam hujus picturae scripturaeve naturam, illud maxime facit ad eam dignoscendam, quod non singulis figuris singulas ideas successive exprimit, ut in hieroglyphicis suis faciunt Ægyptii, sed figures ea ratione ordinat et componit, ut complexu suo locisque et actionibus ad invicem relatis totam rem exprimendam insimul significent, *quemadmodum* **apud nos fit in tabulis pictis**. Ab eo vero quo hodie nos utimur pingendi genere duabus **praesertim** rebus differt : primo, quod in **ea nulla habeatur** seu pulchritudinis seu accuratae imitationis ratio, **quanquam barbara** quadam elegantia et operosa minutarum quarundam rerum delineatio : neque in **figuris componendis** claritati studeat aut facilitati, sed multum relinquat conjecturae : secundo, quod plurimas res tropice exprimat aut aenigmatice, quod rarius fit apud gentes cogitata sua alphabeticarum litterarum ministerio declarare assuetas." (*Op. cit.* p. 532).

drawn up by the Mexicans at every trial, and though they appear to have composed lengthy annals and rituals in them, they differ only in the degree of execution from the former instances, and make no attempt to analyse the sentences, or to distinguish between the several notions implied in the action depicted.

I believe there are traces even in Egyptian of this purely pictorial stage, as might be expected in a system which, like that of nature, preserves along with all its developments the older and ruder forms. The *vignettes* in the Funeral Rituals and the great pictures on temple walls, illustrated by texts such as that published by M. Naville,[1] may have been the original text, expounded by writing proper as men advanced, and ultimately preserved as an illustration where it had originally been the only exponent.

It was not till the separation and correlation of notions was distinctly portrayed that we can consider the development of writing proper to have commenced, and we shall therefore now postulate this condition, which indeed in itself implies no inconsiderable progress of the human mind.[2]

---

[1] *Textes relatifs au mythe d'Horus*, from the temple of Edfu. (Paris, 1870.)

[2] The earliest forms of Chinese writing which we possess show no transition from the pictorial stage, and may possibly have been derived, not from pictures, but from *Quippus*, as Steinthal suggests, according to the Chinese tradition quoted by Klaproth

Suppose we desire to think about any object, such as a horse, we may either keep an image, an idea of a horse, before our minds, or we can use the word *horse*, to answer the same purpose, whether as a sound or as a written symbol, not like a horse, but by common consent suggesting this object. We can employ this alternative even in silent thinking, for men often keep their own ideas before them by a silent soliloquy in words. Similarly, if a man wishes to call up the idea of a horse in another's mind he may do it either by showing a picture, or by writing or speaking the word *horse*.[1] The former kind of

---

(*Aperçu sur les diverses Écritures de l'ancien monde*), and by Abel-Rémusat (*Gram. Chin.*, p. 5). [The **Chinese say that** they originally used for communication knotted strings, or *Quippus*, and that the founder of the empire, **Fou-hi**, derived from them about **3000 B.C.** a system of writing in broken lines, called *K'ho-teoù* (by Klaproth, p. 3, *koua*) of which a specimen is said to exist in the inscription of Yü, of which I have not seen a copy. There seems no doubt however that the present Chinese graphic system is derived from rude pictures, which are given in the authors above cited. Tradition says that the minister of the emperor **Houang-ti**, about 2500 B.C., substituted an ideographic system for the older method, and from this the present Chinese characters have descended with sundry modifications. Strange to say, **A. von Humboldt** (*Vues des Cordillères*, p. 70) shows that the **same revolution** took place among the **Mexicans**, among whom **ancient** *Quippus* were found by Boturini. The Toltec invasion, in the seventh century A. D. appears to have been the cause of the change.

[1] Whatever theory we may adopt as to the way in which the mind thinks of general ideas, there can be no doubt that we

communication is called ideographic, the latter phonetic.

Now, all the evidence we can gather points **to the fact that universally,** among the nations of the world, **phonetic and alphabetic** writing are neither the **earliest nor the most** easily invented. Seeing that primitive man used few abstract **or general** ideas when he wished to record a fact **concerning** some common object, he did **not at first, even after he had** separated **his thought into its component parts,** think **of putting down separate signs which would** suggest the *names*, but signs which would suggest the things themselves. And so **he drew a** picture of each thing **or act which** suggested **it to the** reader. This is properly **called** *picture writing*, **as** distinguished from *graphic pictures*, **because it** endeavours **to** convey **by pictures the separate thoughts or** ideas **of the writer, and because the** ideas **of the writer are written** down, **and not** the sound **which he uses. This sort of** character is called ideographic.[1]

---

often think individual **objects directly and not through the in**tervention of any verbal symbol. **I am of opinion that** to imaginative minds even general **ideas, and certainly many** abstract **ideas (such as** *honour* and *virtue*) are represented more frequently **by an** *emotion* **than by a word.** The sense of merit, for example, stands **in many minds for a** representation of virtue.

[1] Here **are some Egyptian** ideographs that explain themselves:

But as this system can only represent isolated objects, and of these **only such** as **are** material and visible, it can hardly even in this second stage **be called** a graphic system. Such a system must be able to represent such nouns as goodness and time, **justice** and **eternity.** It must also represent sentences, and such components of sentences as adjectives, prepositions, and verbs. The Egyptians, as is now well known, must have advanced **to** this farther development in very ancient times, for in their earliest monuments there is, in addition to the **graphic** pictures and the picture writing, a complete phonetic system. But they never abandoned their earlier solution, which consisted of using certain common objects symbolically to represent abstract ideas and relations. A lute[1] was used to picture the idea of good, an enraged ape[2] that of anger, transitive verbs were **noted** by a pair of thin legs walking, and so **forth.**

But there must presently arise **cases where no** suitable symbol **could be** found, and then the Egyptians **resorted to an expedient which** at first sight appears **highly unreasonable, but which** nevertheless contains the germ **of a** great **discovery.** When no symbol could be found **to answer,** they did not scruple **to** use the picture of **a thing** totally different in sense, if its *name* had the same sound, just as if we desired **to** represent the idea of right, and drew a picture of a **wright** or a rite to represent it.[1] Thus it seems probable that the lute was called *nefru*, and good **was also** *nefru*, and **they** therefore represent **the idea of good by a lute.**[2]

This is a new principle, for it consists in representing *sounds*, yet this was at first done so indirectly **that it** must have caused confusion rather than improvement in the graphic art. This very confusion, however, stimulated thoughtful men to remedy it, and indeed any **such symbolical** system must **be replete with other** difficulties. For had **even a sufficient** number of distinct symbols been attainable, the multitude of such signs to represent all our ideas separately becomes **so enormous that no** ordinary mind, **perhaps no mind, could ever recollect** them.[3]

---

[1] In a primitive language like the Egyptian, **which was not** derived from earlier literary **dialects,** these **words** would probably be all spelt as they are pronounced, **so** that the difference of *spelling* **is not a** point of weight in the present comparison.

[2] It must have been owing to this ancient practice that **the Egyptians kept up** the habit of occasionally **adding two determinations to a group of** letters, one of an object, however different, that had **the same sound ;** the **second of the object really** designated **in the passage.** Cf. Birch, *Introduction to the Study of Hieroglyphics,* in Wilkinson's *Egyptians,* &c., p. 226.

[3] Even the Chinese, **who have developed** ideography with greater **success and** circumstance **than** any other nation, and who speak a **language with fewer** inflexions and with less grammar (in the **proper sense) than any** other literary idiom in the **world, were obliged to** make **phonetic** additions **to their ideographs.**

And waiving this difficulty, **the representation of grammatical flexions seems almost** impossible. It is probable enough that men were perplexed and checked by these difficulties for centuries. The first **growth and** beginnings of civilisation were, **I am** convinced, slow and gradual beyond our **conception, and its** history older by thousands **of** years than the **limits** assigned by **theologians and by** sceptics.[1] But at last some unknown genius, who **ought verily** to be classed higher **than Sir Isaac Newton in the** history of civilisation, **bethought himself, that al**though **the ideas in** the minds of men were almost innumerable, **the sounds by which** the tongue con-

---

These additions form, according to Abel-Rémusat's Chinese grammar, about **one-half the** writing, and seem, from this remarkable case, to be essential **to** the written representation **of any language.** The proportion of phonetic groups **to pure** ideographs in Egyptian writing is at least two to one. Champollion says (*Précis du système hiéroglyphique*, **second** edition, p. 313), that **on the** Rosetta stone, where **fourteen** imperfect lines of Egyptian **correspond to 486 Greek words in** eighteen lines, there **are in** all **166 different signs, some of them** repeated so that the total **sum of signs used is 1419.** There **are** only seven pure ideographs, **or pictures,** representing ναός, εἰκών, ξόανον, τέκνον, ἀσπίς (asp), and στηλή.

[1] **I am gratified to find myself corroborated** in this opinion, long after it was written, by the **recent** utterance of one of our highest authorities, **Dr.** Lepsius, in his remarkable Essay "*on the assumption of a so-called stone age in Egypt*" in his *Zeitschrift für Aegyptische* **Sprache,** &c. 1870, pp. 91-3. I shall revert to this passage hereafter.

veyed them were but a few, ordered and **transposed** with great variety. **He** was probably led into this track **by the very confusion** which I **have** already **noted in** the Egyptian writing—that of suggesting **an idea by the picture** of a different idea which accidentally **had** the same sound for its name. So this great discoverer was led to think that if, instead of painting ideas, men would confine themselves to suggesting the sounds used in communicating them, a far **smaller number of oft-repeated** signs would suffice.[1]

We can **fancy** his **contemporaries** thinking lightly of the discovery. It abandoned the distinct pictorial system, which appeared eminently suggestive of the sense, **and perhaps best suited to** the instruction **of the young and the** ignorant. It was **subject to the grave** ambiguity of signifying two **different objects which happened** to have the **same**

---

[1] I find that Champollion (*Précis*, chap. x., § 72) speaks of this unknown discoverer (who may possibly have been the originator **of the phonetic system of Asia, as well as of Egypt, owing** to his great **antiquity and the early prominence of his** country), in very similar terms: "La solution d'un tel problème," says he, " offrait une grande difficulté, et celui qui la trouva le premier, changea, sans le savoir, la face du monde ; il décida à la fois de l'état **social de son pays, de celui des** peuples voisins, et de la destinée de toutes les générations futures." The Egyptians called him **the god Thoth.**

name, by the same signs, thus destroying the clear distinction established by the pictorial representation.¹

He cast aside too the dream which must, I fancy, have been present to the minds of the earliest thought-painters—that of constructing a pictorial representation to suit many languages simultaneously, just as the Chinese system suits all the surrounding nations. By confining himself to sounds he aban-

---

¹ This inconvenience occurs particularly often in Egyptian, where only the consonantal skeleton of the words, as a rule, was written phonetically, so that differences of vowels were left unrepresented. For example, *clyde, cloud, clad, clod*, might in this language have all been written CLD. Still worse, *star, estuary, Istria*, might all appear as STR. The analogy of Chinese is most instructive. As Steinthal observes (*Entwicklung der Schrift*, p. 96), in a language where the roots are monosyllabic, and must necessarily have many meanings attached to the same sound, purely phonetic writing would be very unintelligible, and even inferior to a partially ideographic system. The syllable *tscheu* in Chinese means: to enclose, a whirlpool, to sway, a lake, an island, a kind of plant, of tree, of wine, a fabulous horse, a she-ass, the name of a dynasty, silk, deep, to help, to quarrel, to walk, to answer. Were all these not represented by different ideographs which have the same sound, Chinese would be far more difficult to read than it now is, perhaps impossible. Champollion (*Gram. Égypt.*, § 85) saw that this was one of the chief causes of the use of *determinative ideographs*, by which the varying vowels were at least indirectly indicated. Cf. also his *Précis*, p. 366.

doned this splendid, but unpractical idea, and confined himself to the graphic reproduction of his mother-tongue alone.

But among the many difficulties he must have encountered, we should specially remember that of analysing words into single letters. Tell an ignorant churl, who has never learned to read, or has seen writing, that the word *hound* consists of five letters and the word *cat* of three, and he will not understand you, for the word seems at first to be a single indivisible sound. Had all words indeed consisted of one syllable, as in Chinese, the discovery might never have been made; but in words of two or three there was even to the ignorant ear an apparent break, and accordingly there is great evidence that the earliest attempts at representing sounds did not divide words farther than into their component *syllables*. Such a word as *baboon* would, in these systems, be represented by two signs only. This condition of things was exemplified by the Assyrian cuneiform character, and the old Persian still bears traces of it.[1] It may also be asserted, within limits, of the Hebrew and Aramaic, where the vowel-points are but a later addition, and not required by the old speakers of the language, who seem easily to have supplied the ne-

---

[1] These points will be discussed in a subsequent essay.

cessary sound. The earliest sort of phonetic writing was then *syllabic*, not alphabetic; it did not write individual letters, but combinations of vowels and consonants, generally, indeed, a consonant and its succeeding vowel.

It was the next great step in the history of writing when men learned to separate the consonants from the vowels in a syllable, and to note all the former by separate signs.[1] And it is very curious to observe how they adopted the same device in various alphabets to convey the sound of single letters to their readers. The Phoenician, which we have inherited, did not differ in this from the Egyptian. Both represented the letter A, for example, by a thing of which the name began with A. And although, in the case of Chinese and Assyrian syllabic writing, the original pictures have been so completely conventionalised for tachygraphic purposes, that in very few cases is the object originally represented by the sign now discernible, there are the strongest reasons to believe that the same device was there

---

[1] Very few of the old alphabets invented in the East allow separate signs for all the vowels. In the Indian and West Iranian graphic systems, for example, the short *a* is not written. So far as I know, the Zend, the Armenian, and the Greek alphabets are peculiar in noting all the vowels, and the two former are not old.

also adopted.[1] Thus, the Phoenician *aleph* (alpha)
means an ox, and the oldest form of the letter represents rudely an ox-head. *Bet* (Beth) means a
house or tent, and such was the oldest form. This
principle holds good throughout the whole Phoenician alphabet, and must have been employed by

---

[1] Champollion (*Précis*, p. 356) suggests that a perfectly *arbitrary* notation might arise by a man who was acquainted with
the writing of a foreign nation inventing a set of symbols for his
own. I think that both the graphic systems used by the old
Persians were most probably so formed, to judge from the *fuller
notation of the vowels*, a feature which does not occur, so far as
I know, in primitive graphic systems. Their cuneiform system
would then be adopted from the older writing of the Sakae or
Scythians or Susians, whichever they were, and their Zend alphabet, in which we have the Avesta, at a far later period, from the
Semites. (Cf. Spiegel, *Altbaktrische Grammatik*, p. 14.) But quite
apart from conjectures, the guesses of Champollion have as
usual turned out to be discoveries. Four authentic cases are
on record, two of which are among modern savages, where, owing
to their contact with writing nations, gifted men have invented
a system of syllabic or alphabetic signs. It is well known that
the Coreans invented an alphabet for their own language, in addition to the Chinese signs in use among them. They fix the
invention in the fourth century A.D. We also know from Moses of
Chorene that the Armenian alphabet was thus framed late in the
fourth century by his master, a saint called Misrob, who spent
years in attempting to find a character suitable to the Armenian tongue, and at last was vouchsafed a vision of it in a dream
in answer to prayer. Cf. Moses of Chorene, *Hist. Armen.*, lib. iii.,
caps. 46, 53, also Schröder, *Thesaurus linguae Armenicae* (Amster-

the writers in very ancient times, for the name of no nautical object occurs in their alphabet, a very strong proof that they did not reach the sea, or at least live in ships till after its invention. But though the Phoenician, and its source, the Egyptian alphabet, agreed on this point, they differed on two other all-

dam, 1711) pp. 30, *sq.*, and M. Pichard's *Moïse de Khorène*, p. 63. The other cases are both quite modern, in fact in the present century. A Cherokee Indian, named Sequoya, devised a syllabic set of characters, 82 in number, and has himself described his gradual conquest of the difficulty, and the prejudices of his tribe. I have seen this curious account in a note to Talvj's Translation of Pickering's *Essay on the North American Languages*. The original authority is Knapp, *Lectures on American Literature* (Boston, 1829). Schoolcraft, though he gives the characters (part ii., p. 229, *sq.*) is silent on this precious psychological history. We may notice lastly the Vai-Negroes, near Sierra Leone, for whom a man called Doalu invented a syllabic system of 200 signs, between the years 1830-40. He professed to have been taught in a dream by a white man—sufficient evidence in itself that the contact with writing races suggested it. See the profoundly interesting account in Steinthal's *Mande-Neger-Sprachen*, pp. 257, *sq.*, who also translates some of their treatises in an appendix. The original authority on the subject is S. W. Koelle, *Grammar of the Vei Language* (London, 1854). These people turned with enthusiasm to literature and to educating their children, but were consequently set upon and destroyed by their neighbours, who considered, perhaps justly, that they were getting into their hands a magic power. This sad example shows how often in ancient times the first sparks of incipient culture may have been trodden out by the jealousy of surrounding barbarism.

important details, which are, in fact, the two concluding stages in the history of the invention of writing. First, the Phoenician, and all succeeding systems, banish ideographic signs altogether (except in numerals) as breeding confusion, and they restrict themselves to representing sounds only. They are, in fact, *purely phonetic.* This was a condition at which the Egyptian language never arrived until the new Coptic alphabet was adapted for it chiefly from the Greek.[1] Down to the latest period of proper Egyptian history its graphic system always combined pictures of ideas and symbols of sounds in perplexing confusion. Such was the case even in the demotic writing, though it has lost all trace of the original picture, and *looks* as purely phonetic as our own writing.[2]

---

[1] It is not probable that this was done till after the Christian era, for though the form of the letters in our oldest Coptic MS. is very ancient, no trace of the Coptic alphabet has as yet been found in the pre-Christian Egyptian documents.

[2] Il est extrêmement curieux de savoir, et je me suis proposé à moi-même cette question interessante plus d'une fois, pour quelle raison les Égyptiens, en créant une nouvelle écriture appliquée au dialecte moderne de leur langue, ne retinrent pas exclusivement les signes alphabétiques. Ils décèlent par ce procédé un certain penchant pour l'antique, ce qui peut-être fut ordonné par une loi speciale du pays. (Brugsch, *Gram. Dém.* p. 15.) I think M. Brugsch has hardly given sufficient weight to the obtrusive advantages of ideographs, suggested above, p. 113, and to

Finally, even when this difficulty is removed, there remains yet another, the last in the history of writing. It is to use the same sign consistently for the same sound; a precaution which would seem the most obvious of all, but which the ancient Egyptians systematically neglected, and, as if they desired to entail upon us difficulties, they had a vicious habit of using different signs for the same letter, as, for example, an arm,[1] an eagle,[2] and a reed,[3] for A; a serpent,[4] and a hemisphere,[5] for T. The great Champollion has indeed shown that this habit was no mere caprice, and he has even discovered the principle upon which they acted.[6] He first showed from

---

the *character of language* which re-acts upon its graphic system. Without the determinative ideographs we should have failed in deciphering old Egyptian, just as we have hitherto failed in interpreting the Etruscan inscriptions, though we can read them.

[6] His explanation will however not account for sundry *bizarreries* in the hieratic papyri, where it is certain that the scribes often introduced superfluous syllables, for reasons which we cannot now fathom. In one case M. Chabas has traced a desire to flatter the reigning sovereign by assimilating a word to his titles through these additions, without puzzling the readers. But though the fact has been detected and the difficulty overcome, the cause of it may never transpire. See M. Chabas' article, *Mélanges* i., p. 99, *sqq.*, and also *Leps. Zeitsch.* for 1869, p. 55. In the inscriptions of the Ptolemaic epoch, these peculiarities increased so as to become a veritable *graphic disease.*

a minute investigation of the Coptic names of the objects used indifferently for the same letter, that these names all began with that letter. He next proved that the different signs were not used arbitrarily, but that *the object most in harmony with the sense of the writing* was specially selected. Thus, in transcribing the word Emperor (αὐτοκράτωρ) into Egyptian, they always used the *eagle* sign for the first letter, as it was the proper symbol of the Roman power. It resulted farther from this principle, that as special signs were appropriated to special words, abbreviations were far more easily understood, as not merely the sound, but the sense of the word was indicated by the peculiar sign employed.[1]

These things were indeed of advantage, perhaps even necessary, yet they certainly brought with them

---

[1] It was also, as I before observed, of the greatest service in a language where a great many meanings were attached to the same syllable, so that confusion would have resulted from the poverty of a mere phonetic symbol, which only noted the sound and gave no indication of the sense in addition. Champollion showed, with his usual learning (*Précis*, p. 372), that Horapollo specially mentions the principle of implying the sense by varying the sign, and to those who may be sceptical he adduces, with his usual felicity of illustration, the parallel case of the Chinese, who at the present time have recourse to the very same device, especially in satiric writings, when they desire their sentiments to appear stronger than the bare expression of them.

enormous difficulties. And to us these difficulties are greatly increased by our having before us the inscriptions of different epochs, during which different signs appear to have become in turn fashionable. Nevertheless, they have not succeeded in baffling the acuteness of the present century. The problem is indeed so difficult that we may well wonder it was ever solved. An unknown language, written in more than 1000 signs, some of them ideographic, some of them phonetic, with the same signs used now in the one, now in the other sense, with different signs meaning the same thing, and the same sign different things—surely it is no wonder that for generations such a problem resisted all the efforts of the learned. It is no wonder that even now many old-fashioned people, who occupied themselves with it long ago, and in vain, still throw doubts upon the reality of the discovery, and the interpretation of the mystery.

But, now that we have explained the nature of the Egyptian writing synthetically, assuming all the difficulties as discovered, and putting together briefly the history of this celebrated writing from its first origin—having done this as best we could, we must reverse the process and explain how all this gradual development was ascertained, and how we know that all these asserted difficulties are not random guesses to conceal our ignorance. We must therefore apply analysis, beginning from the lower or modern end, and show, step by step, how these things were proved, and all these perplexities discovered and unravelled.

Let us now place ourselves in the position of the learned men who in the last century turned their attention to Egyptian writing. They found before them numerous inscriptions on stone, since increased by the discovery of papyri, in three distinct characters, as the Greeks had observed. The farther observation of the Greeks, that one of them consisted of picture-writing, seemed amply confirmed by the appearance of its signs, which consisted of very clever drawings of common objects,[1] as well as also by the great number of the signs, which far exceeded that of the sounds produced by any human tongue. The Greek authors are indeed very consistent and positive on this point. With the exception of a single passage in Clemens Alexandrinus, so obscure that it lends itself to many interpretations,[2] all our Greek allusions agree in speaking of the hieroglyphic system as ideographic. They even gave the meaning of a few signs which are common in the inscriptions, and as to the interpretation of which they had been well informed. But as

---

[1] Like the specimens above given for the reader.
[2] Cf. the commentaries of Letronne in Champollion, *Précis*, p. 378, *sq.*, and of Bunsen, *Egypt's Place in Universal History*, vol. i., p. 344-53. Still better is the article by M. Lauth in the *Proceedings* (*Sitz. ber.*) of the Munich Academy, for 1868, vol. ii., pp. 328-58. He corrects some inaccuracies of Bunsen's.

to the hieratic and demotic characters, they appeared more cursive, better suited to the transcription of long documents, and more like phonetic than ideographic writing. It was, accordingly, the first prevalent theory, that the same language was written in pictures by means of the fuller character, and in letters by the two latter. It is now unnecessary to specify more particularly the points of dispute in this stage of the inquiry.

Meanwhile the French expedition to Egypt supervened. The great Napoleon had obviously larger and deeper views than that of mere military occupation, for he was accompanied by a staff of competent *savants*, whose magnificent *Déscription d'Égypte* gave to Europe the first accurate indication of the monuments and inscriptions of the country. In this, as in all his other enterprises, the first Napoleon showed a grasp of mind far superior to that of ordinary despots. So it happened that in 1799, a French engineer officer, M. Broussard, throwing up earthworks at Rosetta (the modern Reschid) discovered a large black slab, somewhat mutilated, with an inscription in hieroglyphics, in demotic, and in Greek. The French *savants* who accompanied the expedition fully appreciated the value of this discovery. They copied the inscription, and packed up the stone to be sent to France; but the victory of the English, a few days after, threw it into the hands of Sir William Hamilton, the only

Englishman in Egypt who had the smallest knowledge of the subject, and so it was deposited in the British Museum. By this accident a text was discovered, of which the Greek version stated that it was an ascription of divine honors to one of the Ptolemies, or Greek kings of Egypt. The conclusion of the Greek version also told us that the same inscription was transcribed in the three characters, and that the hieroglyphic and demotic versions were mere transcriptions of the Greek text.

But although the sense of an hieroglyphic inscription was thus certainly ascertained, how was the value of each character and its sound to be determined? For without reading the sounds, and analysing the words, a mere general notion of the sense of the inscription was of little service. It was therefore of the last importance, that in the Greek version the name of Ptolemy was preserved, and that about the corresponding place in the hieroglyphic inscription, there was an oval ring, inclosing a group of characters.[1] It was accordingly conjectured that this ring was the sign of the proper name, espe-

---

[1] Here is the memorable group. I omit for simplicity's sake the additional characters for the epithet " beloved of Ptah :"

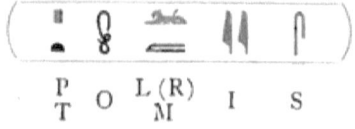

cially as long series of sitting figures on the temple of Karnak had these rings placed over them, apparently indicating their names or titles.[1]

It were tedious to detain the reader with all the false conjectures[2] made in deciphering this celebrated inscription, based on the assumption, or perhaps the false indication, of the Greeks, that the hieroglyphic signs were purely ideographic. We may better start from the great discovery (at first a mere conjecture) made independently, and about the same time, by Thomas Young and Champollion,[3] that the character was a mixed one, containing partly pictures of objects, partly signs of sounds.

Champollion tells us that he was led to the discovery by the labours of De Sacy, the great

---

[1] This had been guessed long before by Zoëga, who indeed also guessed the phonetic nature of the character. Cf. his treatise *de usu obeliscorum*, p. 556, for the testimonies of the ancients on this latter point. It has since been ascertained that the oval ring was a sign of royalty, and that names of private individuals were written without it, though generally followed by the picture of a man to determine their meaning.

[2] An amusing account of them is given in Mr. Birch's learned *Introduction to the Study of Hieroglyphics*, appended to Sir J. G. Wilkinson's *Egyptians under the Pharaohs*, pp. 194-5.

[3] M. Champollion Figéac has proved that the discovery was announced by his illustrious brother in a paper read at Grenoble, in 1810. This clearly establishes his priority. Cf. *Rev. Arch.* N. S. vol. xiv., p. 592.

Orientalist, and **Ackerblad**. Both these **authors had** shown that **the Greek** proper names on **the Rosetta** stone were **transcribed** *phonetically* in **the demotic version.**[1]

As far as I can make out from the **controversy, which was** long and bitter, **as to the** respective **claims** of different **discoverers,** Young's **most important** contribution was *to assert the ideographic nature of many demotic symbols.*[2]

It was **also observed that the more cursive and** alphabetic-looking **hieratic and demotic characters** were abbreviations of the fuller pictures, and **it was** conjectured accordingly **that** although there were **in them no proper pictures,** they might nevertheless **contain signs for ideas. These** signs might, as in **Chinese, appear to be mere** phonetic symbols, and

---

[1] Cf. *Précis*, p. 15, "Notion précieuse qui **est devenue en** quelque sorte **le** germe veritable de toutes les découvertes faites depuis sur **les** écritures Égyptiennes." **Mr.** Birch describes (*Introd.*, &c., p. 193) how these results were obtained. The words Alexander and Alexandria in the 4th and **17th lines** of the Greek version, corresponded to two similar **groups in the 2nd and 10th** lines of the demotic. **A group occurring** in almost **every** line was guessed to mean *and*. **A group repeated 29 times** in the **demotic version** corresponded **to** *king* in the Greek, where this **word** occurred about the same number of times.

[2] M. Brugsch, now the highest authority on the point, says (*Gram. Dém.*, p. 12), **that** demotic contains at least as many ideographic **signs as hieratic writing, a** fact which surprises us greatly when **we first compare the general** appearance of the two systems.

yet serve as a sort of abbreviated picture, suggesting the object directly, and not through its name. But all these conjectures were at first only applied to the characters inside the ring. The first difficulty was to determine their order, which might be, as in Hebrew, from right to left, or as in our system, from left to right.[1]

Another discovery settled this point for Champollion. A little obelisk, found in the island of Philae, was brought home by Mr. Bankes of Dorsetshire, and was found to be inscribed with a dedication, in hieroglyphics and in Greek, to a Ptolemy and his sister Cleopatra.[2] There was a ring in the hieroglyphic inscription identical with the famous ring in the Rosetta stone—the ring for Ptolemy.

---

[1] Subsequent researches have shown that hieroglyphics, which were always very subservient to artistic considerations, and accommodated themselves to the space and other conditions prescribed by architecture, were written both from right to left, and *vice versâ*, as well as occasionally in vertical columns. Hieratic and demotic writing are always from right to left.

[2] This inscription, with the Greek translation at its base, had been copied by M. Calliaud, in 1816, and commented on by Letronne and Champollion in the French scientific journals in 1822. Here is the writing of Cleopatra:

The last sign is the feminine termination in *t*, in this case not pronounced.

Another royal ring was there for his sister Cleopatra. By a fortunate coincidence this name has several letters in common with Ptolemy.[1] By means of this key, and by assuming from the analogy of other systems that the objects depicted signified the initial letter of their Coptic names, both groups were spelt out, and Champollion was in possession of eleven *phonetic* signs of the old Egyptian language. It now became plain, that in this case the signs were not syllabic, but really alphabetic. Applying these principles to monuments which appeared to be of the Roman epoch, and attempting to decipher the royal rings upon them, Champollion found an almost complete list of the Roman emperors, each with his title "Emperor" (αὐτοκράτωρ) added ;[2] and this title

---

[1] These names are otherwise interesting, as proving the interchange of *r* and *l* in Egyptian, as well as also the existence of homophone letters for *l* and *r*.

[2] The last emperor whose name occurs in hieroglyphics is Decius (A. D. 249-51). It is not a little remarkable, that this emperor, in whose time the cruellest persecution of the Christian faith commenced, marks the very date when Christian writing and Christian literature completely crushed and superseded the old wisdom of Egypt. Cf. Lepsius' article in his *Zeitschrift* for 1870, p. 30. M. F. Lenormant (*Rev. Archéol.*, N. S., vol. xxi., p. 106) believes he has found a still later name, that of the usurper Achilles, who was conquered and put to death in Egypt by Diocletian, A. D. 296. The emperor followed up his victory by a reconstruction of the government of the country, and if Suidas be right (sub. voc. χημεία), by a persecution of the old faith,

when once deciphered was a clue to all similar inscriptions.

The very completeness of the list, and the perfect clearness with which he proved the phonetic writing of the names, made some of his opponents suggest that the hieroglyphic signs were only put to this use in order to transcribe the names of the foreign lords of Egypt. But by farther researches Champollion showed that not only the naturalised Ptolemies, but well-known old Egyptian kings—in particular, Psammetichus, Shishak, and Ramses, had their names written in phonetic characters also. This demonstrated the antiquity of phonetic writing in Egypt—a thing which should never have been doubted after the statement of Herodotus, that *demotic* was used in his day; for demotic was agreed to be chiefly phonetic.

These discoveries made it certain that the hieroglyphic inscriptions could only be read by ascertaining the *sounds* of the old Egyptian language. If the whole writing were pictorial or symbolical, the sense might be discovered without knowing a single sound. If a lute means *good*, and an ostrich feather *justice*, the writers might convey to us their meaning without expressing it in words, just as the North

---

and the burning of the old magical books. M. Lenormant is disposed to ascribe to him an edict forbidding the use of hieroglyphics, so that this would be the period of their disuse.

American graphic pictures do. But as soon **as it** became certain that the Egyptians used an alphabet also, an additional discovery became necessary; we must discover the sounds of the Egyptian language.

To meet this difficulty many learned men, even **in** the last century, bethought them of the modern Egyptian, or Coptic language, which was expressly stated by early Christian fathers **to be almost the** same as the demotic or vulgar Egyptian, though written in a different alphabet, chiefly borrowed from the Greek.[1]

This point was conclusively settled in the affir**mative by the** labours of Quatremère, in the beginning of the **present** century. But unfortunately the Coptic language had become almost extinct in Egypt during the last century, to make place for Arabic.[2]

---

[1] **Though** borrowed chiefly from Greek, the Coptic alphabet was shown by Champollion to have taken six signs for its un-Greek sounds from the old hieratic characters (*Précis*, pp. 113, 130). This observation **has been** curiously verified by the discovery of certain Egyptian prognostications **written *in* Greek** cha*racters* on the back of the papyrus containing the λόγος ἐπιτάφιος of Hypereides. **The very six signs mentioned by** Champollion are added to the Greek letters. (Cf. *Lepsius*' *Zeitschrift* for 1868, p. 19.) They are the following:

ϵ = ⲡ   ⲇ = ⲧ   ⲋ = ⲍ or ⲥ   ⳤ = f   ⳟ = ⲍ and ⳝ = ⲃ.

[2] M. F. Lenormant gives us the welcome information that

There is nothing so vexatious as the constantly recurring fact that the most precious relics of antiquity, having lasted through centuries of neglect and oblivion, are destroyed when they are on the point of coming within the grasp of modern research. The greatest historical document ever discovered in Egypt, now known as the Turin papyrus, which contained an apparently complete and authentic list of all the Egyptian kings, and the duration of their reigns, was allowed to go to pieces in Europe in the year 1820, through sheer carelessness, and is now indeed preserved like precious gold, but in one hundred and sixty-two disarranged and incomplete fragments.

A sitting statue of Baal, in one of the ruined temples of Lebanon, an antiquity without parallel in its profound interest, was completely destroyed three years before the French Government sent out M. Renan, in 1860, to investigate and collect the Phoenician relics in the country.[1]

Coptic did not completely die out, as has been unanimously asserted, in the eighteenth century. On the contrary, M. Brugsch, now consul at Cairo, found it still spoken by several families of Jacobite Christian Copts in old Cairo. He gives us some hopes that he will publish commercial letters written at the present day in Coptic. M. Lenormant conversed with these people in November, 1869. See his article *Rev. Archéol.*, N. S., vol. xxi., p. 108.

[1] See his Report, *Rev. Archéol.*, for 1861, p. 330. A great

But why need we prolong our indictment against that jealous fate which conspires with ignorance to hide from us the evidences of ancient culture ? The case of the Coptic language was not so hopeless as it might have been. For in the last century there was a school of Coptic priests at Rome who could still speak the language of their sacred books, and from the information they possessed, together with the publication of the Coptic version of the Scriptures, modern scholars have obtained a very good knowledge, not only of the grammar, but of the vocabulary of the language. It is probable that more materials will yet be found in Egypt. A Coptic papyrus, which I have never yet seen described, was found in the coffin of a monk, along with the curious *Roman de Setna*, by M. Brugsch a very few years ago. But already through the various versions of almost all the Scriptures, the numerous homilies of Coptic saints, and rituals, very large lexicographical progress has been made. A few de-

---

part of these losses are due, in the East, to the iconoclastic fury of the Mahommedans, as well as to their extreme jealousy of any relics older than the rise of their religion. They do not, however, monopolise Vandalism. The Irish Protestants have defaced many beautiful antiquities, because they commanded the reverence of their Roman Catholic neighbours. " As face answereth to face in water, so doth the heart of man to man."

tails as to this curious language will be necessary to the right understanding of our subject.[1]

In a Coptic grammar, written in Arabic, by Athanas, bishop of Kous, in the eleventh century, A. D., which has been translated by Quatremère, the following passage occurs: "The Coptic language is divided into three dialects, that of Misr, which is the same as Saidic, [or highland—viz., that of Thebes,

---

[1] The deserts of Egypt were in the fourth century a favourite resort of hermits, and the Egyptian monks played a prominent part in the early controversies of the Church, so that we need not be surprised at their literary activity. The reader who wishes to make a closer acquaintance with the language may consult the grammars of Schwartze and Tattam, and above all, the vast exposition of the dialects by Schwartze, in his enormous work *Das alte Aegypten*, where one thousand densely-printed quarto pages are devoted to the subject. (Part i., vol. ii., pp. 1034-2040.) In addition to *Zoëga's Catalogus codicorum copticorum in Museo Borgiano*, which contains a great many texts, and is not difficult to procure, M. G. Schwartze has published a very excellent critical edition of the Psalms, which is probably the best text-book for studying the language. I select from it Psalm i., vv. 1 and 2, to show the alphabet, in which any scholar will recognize the Greek words borrowed from the Septuagint.

Ⲟⲩ ⲙⲁⲕⲁⲣⲓⲟⲥ ⲡⲉ ⲡⲓⲣⲱⲙⲓ ⲉⲧⲉ ⲙⲡⲉϥϣⲉ ϧⲉⲛ ⲡⲥⲟϭⲛⲓ ⲛ̄ⲧⲉ ⲛⲓ ⲁⲥⲉⲃⲏⲥ .ⲥ. Ⲟⲩⲇⲉ ⲙⲡⲉϥⲟϩⲓ ⲉ ⲣⲁⲧϥ ϩⲓ ⲫⲙⲱⲓⲧ ⲛ̄ⲧⲉ ⲛⲓ ⲣⲉϥⲉⲣⲛⲟⲃⲓ .ⲥ. Ⲟⲩⲇⲉ ⲙⲡⲉϥϩⲉⲙⲥⲓ ϩⲓ ⲧⲕⲁⲑⲉⲇⲣⲁ ⲛ̄ⲧⲉ ⲛⲓ ⲗⲟⲓⲙⲟⲥ .ⲥ. Ⲁⲗⲗⲁ ⲉⲣⲉ ⲡⲉϥⲟⲩⲱϣ ϣⲱⲡⲓ ϧⲉⲛ ⲫⲛⲟⲙⲟⲥ ⲙ̄ ⲡϭⲥ .ⲥ.

in Upper Egypt] the Bahiric, called from the province of Bahirah [probably maritime, and known as Memphitic], and the Bashmuric, used in the country of Bashmour. At **the** present day only the Bahiric **and Saidic are in use.** These different dialects are derived **from the same language."** This passage of undoubted authority, **in a work** which contributed greatly to **the sound knowledge of Coptic,** has occasioned a protracted **controversy as to the** nature of the dialects. We have many manuscripts in two widely different dialects, **and as these** classes of manuscripts have been **consistently discovered** in the Memphitic and Thebaic regions respectively, there can be no doubt that they are identical **with** two of the dialects mentioned by Athanas. **But** the very existence of Bashmuric has been questioned by some, while others have actually collected and published alleged remnants of the dialect, which **was extinct as a spoken language in the eleventh century.**[1]

---

[1] Münter supports the negative side, while Engelbreth has published the so-called Bashmuric fragments, which certainly differ in many important respects from both the other varieties, but which do not very well agree with themselves. Schwartze has been able to show (*Aegypten*, ii., p. 1128) that three distinct varieties are discoverable in the Bashmuric fragments of Jeremiah, of Isaiah and St. John's Gospel, and of the Epistles of St. Paul respectively, and he has, to my mind, proved the existence and distinctness of this division of the language, which

The very locality of this dialect is a matter of grave doubt, for while most authors believe it to have been the coarser speech of the wild inhabitants of the Delta marshes, Champollion, probably the highest of authorities, thinks it was the dialect of middle Egypt.

Assuming however, without farther digression, the existence of Bashmuric to be established by Schwartze's labours, it appears that this version of the Scriptures was derived from the Saidic or Theban, which it most resembles, and that both differ considerably from our oldest Greek manuscripts (especially the *Codex Alexandrinus*), a fact which proves their great antiquity. The independence and literary character of the Bashmuric version has also been inferred from its considerable and independent variations as compared with its Saidic original.[1] Both dialects were phonetically decayed, and

---

can hardly differ from the third dialect of Athanas. The great authority of Brugsch is on the same side, who farther observes (*Gram. Dém.*, p. 94) that the Bashmuric almost always preserves the oldest forms, especially the demotic *a*, which the other dialects have weakened to *e* and *o*.

[1] Champollion shows with his usual acuteness (*Précis*, p. 367) that when the various dialects differed in sounds *the same hieroglyphics had represented the various sounds in the older language indifferently*. This is the case with the mutes and aspirates of Greek names transcribed by the same hieroglyphic, and interchanged in Theban and Memphitic. It is also the case with the

therefore *linguistically* later than the Memphitic, from which almost all the words transcribed by Herodotus and other ancient authors seem to have been taken. Nevertheless, of the extant manuscripts, those in the later dialects are far the earliest in date, for none of the Memphitic appear to reach back farther than the tenth century, A. D., whereas the Saidic are as early as the sixth century, at all events. This is proved both by the form of their writing, which resembles our oldest Greek manuscripts, and also by the fact that many of them are accompanied by Greek translations, whereas, after the Arab conquest, the Greek is replaced by Arabic. The form of the letters points indeed to an older date, possibly the second century B. C., but as yet there is no trace of the Coptic alphabet in the pre-Christian papyri discovered in Egypt. If, as Leemans asserts, the oldest Coptic MS. we have (the *Epistles of St. Antony*) dates from the latter part of the third century, and our latest demotic document, copied by De Saulcy, dates from the joint rule of M. Aurelius and Commodus towards the end of the second century, the transition of *character* probably took place between these limits. Transition of *language* there was none at that time, for a late demotic papyrus

---

sounds *r* and *l*, which represent one another in Theban and Bashmuric. To a linguist this is a very strong proof that old Egyptian was the mother of these dialects.

in the Leyden collection was found by M. Brugsch to contain parts of the Book of the Dead in *pure Coptic*.[1]

We have on the other hand the remarkable document above alluded to (p. 131), where an Egyptian text was written in Greek characters, with the necessary demotic additions for peculiar sounds, and this document Mr. Goodwin discovers from astronomical data contained in it to be of the year A.D. 154. He shows clearly[2] that the language is older and different from the earliest Coptic MS. which we possess in any of the dialects. There appears to be a far better papyrus of the same kind, bought from the Anastasi collection by the French Government in 1857, which, however, has disappeared or become inaccessible.

I have ventured on these brief and dry details, in order to show how the language has been scientifically studied, and can be properly employed in the present investigation.

Champollion having made himself master of

---

[1] Cf. Leemans, ii., p. 82, and also Brugsch's description of it, *Zeitsch. der Morgenländ. Gesell.* vol. vi., p. 250.

[2] *Leps. Zeitsch.* 1868, pp. 22 and 23. I may add that the fact of the Demotic *Roman de Setna* being found in the coffin of a Coptic monk of the fifth or sixth century, shows that the character was understood, at least by the learned, up to that time.

Coptic, as any one must do who desires to read old Egyptian, saw that the older names for objects would be represented more or less accurately in the later language. The very archaic character of the Coptic language made this inference exceedingly **probable.** In the fifth chapter of his *Précis* he has **verified** the hypothesis by one of the finest specimens of scientific induction to be found in any literature.

His task was to demonstrate that the **phonetic** signs used in transcribing Greek and Roman proper names, and also in the names of some old Egyptian kings, were equally used in ordinary hieroglyphic writing. He desired to show farther **that** the words so read phonetically, displayed a close affinity to the Coptic names for the same objects.

His first essays were naturally made upon those numerous sepulchral monuments where the proper names had been read (by the aid of Greek transla**tions), and** where short connecting words were obviously expressive of the relationships **between the** persons named. As there **were** often pictures added of the deified deceased receiving **offerings** from his family, accurately represented as to age **and sex,** the conjecture as to what relationships **should be expressed was often** narrowly limited. Now **the Greek** author Horapollo, who wrote **a** special **treatise** on Egyptian **writing,** had **stated** that the signs below given (a goose and vulture) were used for *son* and *mother*.[1] Champollion found that this was so, and that, according to the phonetic reading of the former sign from proper names, this and the other two homophones substituted for it were pronounced SHE, in Coptic *to be born*, or *to originate*. A fourth sign used with the same sense he read MES, which appears on the Rosetta stone as a translation of γενέθλια (the nativity of Ptolemy), and this word in Coptic means *to be born* also. The identity of the Coptic and old Egyptian words for *son* was thus evident. In the second case, that of *mother*, Champollion read it MOU, or with the feminine ending, appended to all the names of goddesses, MOUT. He then compared the statement of Plutarch, who says that Isis is sometimes called by the Egyptians *mouth*, and that this means *mother*.[2] On all the monuments in Egypt, the name of Isis is followed by this sign, and in Coptic *mou* means mother.

I need not enter on other cases in detail. The title king in the inscriptions reads *suten*, and this word in Coptic means *to rule*. On the Rosetta stone the word *place* is translated by *ma*, which is also its Coptic name.

---

[1]

[2] Plut. *de Isid.* cap. 56. ἡ δι'Ἶσις ἐστιν ὅτι καὶ Μούθ, ὅτι κ. τ. λ. Σημαίνουσι δὲ τῷ μὲν πρώτῳ Μητέρα.

Champollion farther analysed grammatical forms, terminations, and inflexions, and found the same close correspondence.[1] Many curious results appeared in the course of his investigation. Among other points it may be repeated that the old Egyptian, like the Hebrew and Aramaic alphabets, omitted many vowels, of which the pronunciation appears to have been wavering, as shown by the Coptic dialects. These and such like details showed that the hypothesis was a sound one, and of the same value as if we proposed to construct the old Greek language from its analogy with the modern Romaic.

But when the indefatigable Frenchman was sent to Egypt to explore the ruins in person, he found means of proving his theory on a far ampler scale. For in the tombs at Beni Hassan he found numerous pictures of well known objects, with groups of hieroglyphics over them, which apparently represented their names. Applying what letters he knew, he

---

[1] He analyses in particular (p. 127) the plural terminations of masculine and feminine pronouns, and the terminations of verbs. Considering the infant state of comparative philology in his day, his linguistic instinct appears truly wonderful. He adds (p. 136) that he saw through the inscriptions crowds of Coptic verbal forms, which were to him a philological piece of evidence, doubtless, quite conclusive. But with the caution of a patient and honest investigator, he refrains from citing any case not absolutely certain on independent grounds.

found this conjecture correct, and that the Coptic gave him in almost every case a direct clue to the name. He then found it easy to complete his alphabet from partially read words, agreeing in sense with known names, and so the great discovery was gradually completed, sounds suggesting signs, and signs sounds, each new step verifying and correcting previous, and stimulating farther, inferences.

And indeed when he had once hit upon the right track, the discovery would have been comparatively easy, but for two difficulties to which I have already alluded. The first is a complex one, for besides all the alphabetic signs, there were both a number of pictures, direct and symbolical, and also the same sign was used now in the ideographic, now in the phonetic sense. How was he to know the proper application of them in each case? A little reflection showed him that the old Egyptians themselves must have been puzzled by the same difficulty, and must have used some means to avoid it. A written system of one thousand signs, used at random ideographically or phonetically, must ever have been perfectly useless. He therefore looked for and found indications added to the pictures, informing the reader in which sense to understand them. An open mouth,[1] for example, was added to show that the sign was intended phonetically. Often the picture of the object, which appeared under its name in the tombs, was inserted after the same group of signs in an inscription, as if to indicate the sense. By this means, by a system of *determinative* signs, which have now been enumerated very completely in Mr. Birch's dictionary, the old Egyptians met the difficulty of having the same sign meaning two different things, an idea and a sound. Among ideographic signs, those intended for simple representations of objects being admirably drawn, are easily understood, except when they depict household articles no longer in use. But when they are used symbolically, it is of course a matter of the greatest difficulty to guess what analogy guided the first inventors of the symbol. Champollion considered this point the most unsatisfactory in the deciphering, and that which would remain longest unsolved. Happily, such signs are not frequent in the inscriptions.

There are indeed some specimens of a sort of writing (*Anaglyphs*), supposed by Champollion to be wholly symbolic, which he left unexplained, and which he thought had been used by the priests as a really secret character, in contrast to the hieroglyphics. Signs for the secret names of the gods are sometimes transferred from this system to the hieroglyphic and hieratic. This view, which has been supported in later times by M. de Rougé and Professor Lauth,[1] has been denied by M. Dümichen, who says that he has been unable to find in the monuments any *systematic* secret writing, side by side with the usual hieroglyphics.[2] As, however, M. Dümichen concedes that a perfectly peculiar, and almost undecipherable system of variations, that had been known earlier, became fashionable in the days of the Ptolemies, and as he himself has published specimens of this writing, the dispute appears to me verbal, and the view of Champollion substantially correct. If not, it is but another instance of our being misled by the blunders of the Greeks, as the *Anaglyphs*, name and thing, were suggested in the famous passage of Clemens on Egyptian writing. The remarks of M. Brugsch on the subject[3] do not speak positively as to the decision of the controversy. But his examples seem to indicate that no new *principle* was used in

---

[1] *Chrestom. Égyp.* p. 144, *Munich Sitz. ber.* for 1868, ii., p 356, and *Lepsius' Zeitschrift*, 1866, p. 25, and 1868, p. 43.

[2] *Lepsius' Zeitschr.* for 1867, p. 64. Mr. Birch (*Introduction*, p. 243) not only agrees with this view, but has a theory that the twenty-second dynasty, of Babylonian origin, introduced phonetic signs for many ideographs, and so produced it. I cannot reconcile this statement with the usual belief that the so-called secret writing was more ideographic and symbolical than the other, or with that of M. Lauth (loc. cit.) that it is found on monuments of the eighteenth dynasty.

[3] *Die Sage von der Geflügelten Sonnenscheibe*, in *Göttingen Transac.* xiv., p. 180.

the anaglyphs, but merely a profusion of licenses and individual fancies introduced, which make the interpretation a matter of great patience and ingenuity, but not impossible.[1] It may therefore safely be asserted that all such exceptional inscriptions are in no respect likely to invalidate the received system of interpretation, and that they will not even themselves long resist the application of that system, with some slight modifications.

Champollion thinks that Horapollo intended to explain this kind of writing called anaglyphs, as the signs he expounds are either not found in the monuments, or, if found, seem to be in general incorrectly interpreted.[2] For of seventy physical objects, said by Horapollo to be used as signs, Champollion could only find thirty, and of these only thirteen seem correctly interpreted. Of the forty groups of symbolic signs, only two were found by Champollion, those for *writing* and for *inundation*, both very important ideas in Egypt. Modern scholars have grave suspicions whether Horapollo understood the subject.

The second obstacle was even greater, for it soon

---

[1] His essay is a very successful specimen of such interpretation. He thus contrasts the ancient and Ptolemaic inscriptions: "In jenen sind dunkle Begriffe in einfacher Schrift, in diesen einfache Begriffe in dunkler Schrift enthalten."

[2] *Précis*, p. 348, *sq.*

L

became evident that the Egyptians used different signs to signify the same sound. When the names *Berenike* and *Aleksandros* were guessed at the very outset, it was found that there were different signs for *k* and *s*. The great number of apparently phonetic signs pointed to the same conclusion. In a few cases, known names of objects varied in the writing, and so two different signs for the same sound were ascertained, and often verified from the fact that the *same demotic equivalent* was substituted for them in transcriptions.

But Champollion soon discovered a larger field whereon to pursue his comparisons. There was a long and elaborate book of Ritual which the old Egyptians placed beside mummies in the coffin, and of which several copies had been brought to the European museums. These copies, though evidently identical in sense, and in the great majority of their characters, contain frequent variations as to single signs. In hieratic copies the same sign generally represents these varieties. Without knowing the sense of the book it was clear that these must be different equivalents for the same sound, or what are called *homophones*.[1] Of course when one of them

---

[1] As M. de Rougé observes (*Chrestomathie Égyptienne*, i., p. 16), Champollion soon perceived that this complication also was chiefly due to the fancies of a later age. M. Lepsius has since established that the most ancient alphabet admitted very few

was discovered the rest became known. With the discovery of these homophones the reading of the hieroglyphics was placed on a firm footing, and it only required additional researches and farther comparisons to complete the structure of which Champollion had laid the foundations, and sketched the plan.

It would indeed be unjust to pass from this part of the subject without expressing the deep admiration that every unbiassed reader must feel on coming in contact with his splendid genius. In this, as in other studies, it is too often our habit to be led by the latest authorities only, and to neglect the great original sources, which may be surpassed in results by inferior but more recent labours. To the reader who merely desires to gather information, such a course may be the most compendious, but to him who wishes honestly to examine the evidence for a discovery, nothing will supply the place of a perusal of the original exposition, either in profound

---

homophones, and in general employed only one sign for each letter. It must never be forgotten that many apparent homophones really indicate slight variations of pronunciation, and that it requires a great deal of evidence to prove the sound of two distinct signs exactly the same. So M. de Rougé says (*op. cit.*, p. 19, *note*), " c'est ainsi que les Anglais notent avec le *th* plusieurs sons que des grammariens plus raffinés, tels que les Indiens, auraient certainement rendus par des lettres différentes."

L 2

interest or in the abiding conviction it will produce. In Champollion's *Précis*, a **work** short, easy, and exceedingly clear, we as it were **accompany** him through the successive labours, the **brilliant** inductions, the startling verifications of a career **full of** results, though, alas! too brief in years. We **see the** morning twilight, **then the** first streak of dawn, then the full brightness **of day.** The work possesses, too, that peculiar fascination exercised by minds of the highest order alone. It is not **more** remarkable for **bold** and original thinking than for profound and varied learning, for extreme calmness and caution. It is passing strange that so great a **man has not** attained more universal fame.[1]

Such was the general course of the discovery. Some remarkable verifications may here be added to those already produced **during** the discussion. No

---

[1] The *Grammaire Égyptienne,* his later work, **is decidedly a** maturer and **more** correct **exposition of the language,** but I prefer citing the **Précis, on account of its** *analytical* method, for the ordinary reader. The student of Egyptian will of course turn to the systematic synthetical treatise, since most ably supplemented by the Vicomte de Rougé's Chrestomathy and M. Brugsch's Dictionary. I quote **the following** as a fair specimen of the tone of the *Précis* (p. **301,** *sq.*) "Je connais assez à fond **les mécomptes,** les **obscurités,** les illusions, et tous les obstacles qui hérissent **et rendent si difficiles la** carrière vers laquelle j'ai specialement **dirigé** mes études ; je m'ai défait, autant qu'il a été en mon **pouvoir, de tout esprit de système,** j'ai lutté contre ce **penchant naturel qui nous porte à** voir les **éléments** de théories

doubt there was at first **a great deal of** uncertainty. So there is in every discovery. We must assume provisionally a basis for our deductions, which **if** verified **will tend to** establish, or if disproved will **refute, the original** assumption. But if this process **be** constantly repeated with success, the evidence becomes so multiplied in strength that the hypothesis **is** raised to a certainty. All this occurred in **the** present case. Starting **with a dozen sounds** ascertained **from** the **proper names in bilingual inscriptions, bringing to his aid the few words** cited by Greek authors, and those **found on the tombs and in** funeral inscriptions, no doubt Champollion **at first** conjectured **a** good deal, and his conjectures were **not always** verified. But by repeated trials and corrections, **he found** that the alphabet he had constructed produced, both in sound and in structure,

---

dans quelques aperçues, dans quelques rapprochements peu réfléchies, et dont l'imagination seule fait tous les frais. Le sort de tant d'ouvrages deja oubliés, et dans lesquels leurs auteurs ont prétendu tracer *a priori* les principes du système hiéroglyphique Égyptien, m'a servi d'un salutaire avertissement; *et le soin que j'ai pris de ne rien deviner*, mais de me tout démontrer par des faits très multipliés, évidents par eux-mêmes, observés avec attention, et comparés avec sévérité, ce soins, dis je, donnera quelque poids à mes déductions, et aux idées qui me restent à présenter, quoiqu'elles diffèrent essentiellement de l'opinion qu'on s'était en general formée de cette écriture sacrée de l'ancienne Égypte."

a tongue so like Coptic, that he could decipher its meaning. This should in itself have persuaded men of the reality of the discovery. A false reading of characters may possibly fit one inscription, or even a second like it in sense, but to imagine that any false reading will fit hundreds of perfectly distinct documents, and extract from them a consistent meaning, is to assert that a practical impossibility is actually a fact.

Though no other corroboration was wanting, it came crowding upon the discoverers. The historical facts revealed by the hieroglyphics differed indeed profoundly from the stories repeated by Herodotus about the early history of Egypt, but were elsewhere strongly confirmed. They were remarkably confirmed by the short extant quotations from the history of Manetho, an Egyptian priest, who compiled during the second century B. C.,[1] from the documents of his own people, a history of Egypt. They agreed, as we have seen, with many of the

---

[1] It has been often stated, and is, I think, generally believed, that Manetho wrote his history in Greek. But the reader will find (in Chabas' *Mélanges*, i., p. 33) the following remark: "Je regarde d'ailleurs comme un fait certain qu'aucun d'eux (that is, the Greeks who cite Manetho) n' a pu étudier le texte original, faute de connaître la langue égyptienne ; l'incorrection de la version grecque peut seule rendre compte de certaines erreurs qu'un scribe égyptien n'a pas pu commettre." M. Chabas proves his point by a most acute remark on the derivations of the word

definite explanations of Egyptian words by the
Greeks, whose general theories on the subject were
so vague as to afford no test whatever.

Yet even these proofs have at times failed to
satisfy, I shall not say sceptical minds, but minds
dogmatically attached to preconceived ideas, and
unable to grasp the new truth of the real antiquity
of civilisation. When people heard it asserted that
Moses had not arisen in Egypt till the longest and
greatest acts of her history had been played out, and
only those of lesser glory and importance were to
follow—when the king from whose bondage the Children
of Israel escaped was called a monarch of the
New Empire—when all these wonders were extracted
from the lists of kings, from astronomical calculations,
and from the plain assertions of ancient documents,
there were many who would not believe even
upon such perfect evidence; and there still remains
in the minds of the careless public a vague idea
that all the discovery is still uncertain, and the
interpretation of doubtful value. To such I would

---

hyksos ascribed to Manetho. These remarks will disprove the
statement of Mr. Birch (*Introd. to the Study of Hieroglyphs*, p. 181)
that Manetho himself even translated the work. I am surprised
that M. Lauth in his latest discourse (*die Geschichtlichen Ergebnisse
der Aegyptologie*, &c., Munich, 1869, p. 4) does not give weight
to these considerations. Dr. Ebers (*Aegypten, und die Bücher
Moses'*, &c., i., p. 217, *note*) misrepresents M. Chabas completely,
and speaks as if he attributed to Manetho himself the blundering
derivations of the name.

suggest a careful consideration, if possible, of the following fact:—

While making researches at Tanis in Egypt, in April, 1866, Professor Lepsius found another trilingual inscription in hieroglyphics, in demotic, and in Greek. It contained certain resolutions drawn up by a synod of assembled priests at Canopus, enumerating all the benefits done to the country by Ptolemy Euergetes I. (especially by the restoration of the statues carried off into Persia by Cambyses), and decreeing him and his wife divine honours. To Egyptian scholars this inscription afforded no difficulty. Read by their received principles of interpretation, it produced a sense identical with the Greek version. Who can question this verification? "The fact," says Mr. Birch, "that excepting one or two difficult passages, the contents are much easier for an Egyptologist to read off and explain than the same amount of Tacitus or Livy to a fair Latin scholar, marks at once the progress made in the deciphering of the hieroglyphics, and must afford conviction to any candid mind that such unexampled coincidence as the names, words, grammatical forms, and syntax of sentences, could only be the result of a circle of correct deductions, not the aberration [chance agreement?] of vicious hypotheses."[1]

---

[1] Cf. *Transactions of Royal Soc. of Lit.*, vol. ix., part 3, p.

To conclude: within the last three years, M. Mariette has copied from the pillars along the line of the Suez Canal inscriptions set up in four languages by Darius I., king of Persia, describing how he had undertaken the cutting of the canal, but stopped it when almost brought to a conclusion. This fact is verified by Strabo, who tells us that Darius was persuaded, but falsely, that the level of the Red Sea and of the Mediterranean varied, and that Egypt would be inundated and destroyed by opening the canal. The inscription, of which there are several mutilated copies on different stone pillars, was written in hieroglyphics and in cuneiform characters of three kinds—Persian, Assyrian, and Casdo-Scythic.[1]

349; and also Wescher in the *Revue Arch.* for 1866, p. 48. The details given by these authors are very interesting. The stone measures about 7 feet by $2\frac{1}{2}$, and contains 37 lines of Egyptian to 76 of Greek. The demotic version is on the side, and was not at first noticed. It appears (like the Rosetta inscription) to have been composed in Greek originally, and then to have been translated into Egyptian. Its date is fixed by its mentioning the contemporary *eponymous* priest of Alexander, and the *Kanephoros* of Arsinoe ii., wife of Philadelphus. These offices, being both annual, but not commencing simultaneously, have enabled scholars to fix the date of the decree as the 7th March, 238 B. C.

[1] It has been discussed from the cuneiform side by M. Jules Oppert in a memoir reprinted from the Transactions of the French Academy in 1869. The discovery of one such pillar is described by M. Mariette in the *Revue Arch.*, N. S., vol. xiv., p.

We need only concern ourselves here with one of these cuneiform transcriptions, and may choose the Persian, which is not only the best preserved, but also the most easily read of the languages in arrow-headed characters. This Persian version corresponds in sense to the hieroglyphic version, when read according to the now received system. The Egyptian copy adds indeed a good many details, intended for the special edification of the Egyptian subjects of the great king, but the facts in both are exactly the same.

Just as every independent investigator who adopted Champollion's method arrived at identical conclusions, so every new text confirmed all the previous inductions.[1]

After all these accumulated proofs, I cannot conceive any additional way of strengthening the argu-

---

433, where the monument is entitled the quadrilingual *stele of Chalouf*. This was not the first contact between the study of hieroglyphics and cuneiform writing. At an early period of Champollion's researches a bilingual inscription on a vase at Venice had afforded him an occasion of comparing his results with those of Grotefend. They both independently deciphered the name of Xerxes in the characters which they had respectively studied. I may add that I am not responsible for the term Casdo-Scythic.

[1] Cf. Mr. Goodwin in the *Rev. Arch.*, N. S. ii., p. 234. " L'excellence du système de Champollion se démontre par le fait décisif, que se système, bien employé, conduit tous les investigateurs sur la même voie et au même resultat final."

ment save that of refuting the ablest and most modern attack upon Egyptology that can be found. The critical reader who knows what the advocates of the discovery can say, may possibly wish to see, in addition, the case of the objector and its value. But we must not waste time by considering the doubts of the vulgar and the ignorant, who merely disbelieve because the results are wonderful, and because they will not take the trouble to study the process which has revealed them. Yet when we come to look for a worthy antagonist, it is not easy to find him. I am not aware that any one who has really made himself master of the subject has ventured to impugn the brilliant induction of Champollion.[1]

But in Sir George Cornewall Lewis we can happily find a man of mark, and no mean judge of legal evidence, completely ignorant indeed of comparative, and especially of oriental, philology, but in other respects highly qualified, both by general intelligence and by a very sceptical temper, to give an opinion on a subject he did not understand. It may therefore be worth while to consider *seriatim* the passage which he devotes to the subject, and to discuss the weight of each argument as it occurs.[2]

---

[1] The objections of Klaproth and Seyffarth are rather objections of detail, and concede the main principles at issue.

[2] Cf. his *Astronomy of the Ancients*, pp. 377–93, and the al-

He starts by asserting the *a priori* impossibility of deciphering any language of which the tradition has been lost, and shows very justly that Greek and Latin were never in this sense dead languages; for there has been no complete interruption in men's knowledge of them since they were spoken. But in the case of the hieroglyphics, he thinks both the language and the character were completely dead; and the difficulty was likely enough to be thought insuperable till refuted by facts. These facts should have been familiar to Lewis. Quite apart from the body of evidence adduced in this particular case, the simultaneous labours of Burnouf, Lassen, and Rawlinson in 1836 had made it perfectly evident that the language of Cyrus and Darius—a language of which both the characters and the sounds were perfectly lost—had been discovered and explained by the ingenious conjectures, and afterwards by the linguistic researches of modern scholars. By a systematic reading of the characters,

---

lusions in his *Life and Letters*, pp. 403, 409, 419, and 421. Professed Egyptologists have not condescended to reply to his arguments. In all the literature on the subject, I have found him only twice alluded to, and by M. Chabas in his *Observations sur la langue et la littérature d'Égypte Lepsius'* (*Zeitsch.* for 1866, p. 44). He says :—"De semblables critiques n'exciteront aujourd'hui qu'un sourire de pitié." Cf. also *Les papyrus hiératiques de Berlin*, p. 68.

which produced a language closely similar to that of the Zend Avesta, the cuneiform inscriptions at Persepolis and Behistun were read in such a way as to leave no shadow of doubt in the mind of any careful critic.[1]

Sir George Lewis never even mentions, far less refutes this discovery, and confines himself to regretting in one of his letters that he is totally unacquainted with oriental philology!

The next assertion which he hazards on the subject is this: that even were the characters deciphered and the inscriptions *read*, this would not in the least help to determine the meaning—a very wonderful statement, which evidently implies that the language read has no analogy whatever to any known human speech, and also (what Lewis himself distinctly rejects) that the supposed system is phonetic, and not ideographic.

He thinks he can prove it by citing the cases of the Umbrian, Oscan, Etruscan, and Lykian inscriptions. The attempts, he says, of even the most accomplished modern linguists to explain these inscriptions must be regarded by an impartial judge as utter failures.[2]

An impartial judge will rather consider Sir

---

[1] This discovery will be described in a succeeding Essay, to which the reader will refer.

[2] Cf. *Astronomy of the Ancients*, p. 387, where he reverts to this point.

George Lewis' argument to be either false or irrelevant; for if he consults any linguistic treatise of reputation on the point, as, for example, Schleicher's *Indo-European Chrestomathy*,[1] he will at once be convinced that the Oscan and Umbrian inscriptions have been clearly and scientifically explained. The case of Lykian and Etruscan is irrelevant, for the difficulty has here arisen from unknown *roots*, to which we have no clue. As the letters have all been ascertained, if we only had the assistance of determinative pictures, like the Egyptian, this difficulty would soon be removed, and no one asserts that Champollion would have succeeded in deciphering Egyptian had not both roots and grammar in addition been suggested to him by Coptic analogies.

But there were also many plain and obvious ideographs—a fact overlooked in the assertion that *reading* the inscriptions would not *explain* them, for to read ideographs is nothing, except to ascertain their meaning. In the case then of ideographic writing, the objection of Sir George Lewis is absurd, and all the more so as he himself argues that the hieroglyphics cannot have been phonetic. This is, in fact, his next formal objection to the discovery of Champollion. All the ancient evidence, he says, we have on the subject is violated if we assert the Egyptian writing to be *phonetic;* for Chaeremon,

---

[1] Published in connexion with his Comparative Grammar.

Horapollo, Ammianus Marcellinus, and others state that it was ideographic, and are *perfectly silent* as to any phonetic elements. If it were worth while, the accuracy of this statement could be disproved; for Champollion has shown that the well-known passage on this question in Clemens Alexandrinus, probably our best Greek authority, can only be explained by assuming a phonetic system in the hieroglyphics. But, waiving this point, there is no weight in the objection. The ancients were notoriously bad linguists, and a glance at the writers quoted will show that all of them (except Horapollo, who appears not to have written about ordinary hieroglyphics)[1] merely give a superficial account of the language, and naturally dwell on the feature which struck them as peculiar in comparison with their own language.[2]

From this point of view they enumerated a few

---

[1] Cf. above, p. 145.

[2] I was glad to find this opinion corroborated by M. Lauth in his excellent discussion on the account given by Clemens Alex. of the hieroglyphics. Cf. *Sitzungsber. der Münch. Akad.* for 1868, vol. i., p. 350. " Die Griechen und Römer, welche mit Aegypten und seiner Schrift in Berührung kamen, wurden von dieser Seite [the symbolical ideography] der Hieroglyphik am meisten befremdet, weil sie von ihrer Alphabet-schrift am weitesten ablag, und eben diese Grund-verschiedenheit reizte ihre Neugier. Desshalb sind die meisten Beispiele der Klassiker u. a. der änigmatisch-allegorischen Schriftart der Aegypter entnommen."

ideographs, on which modern Egyptologists *agree with them*, as we have seen above, so that their *positive* evidence has not been violated. Their *negative* evidence, or silence concerning phonetic elements, is perfectly worthless, seeing that they have hardly constructed for us a single complete sentence of Egyptian. They say absolutely nothing about prepositions, adverbs, or other particles. They give no hint concerning syntax. These are the very points where the phonetic element has been found essential in all written languages. To argue from the silence of ignorant persons to the non-existence of this element, is surely puerile in the extreme.

Lewis next combats the asserted analogy between Coptic and old Egyptian, which he considers Champollion to have assumed without proper proof. He thinks it almost certain that the language must have changed so considerably in the great interval (?) between the age of our respective documents, that no inferences can be drawn concerning the earlier language from the later. I wonder upon what evidence a man ignorant of comparative philology ventured to assert such a change. What amount of change *ought* to take place in any language within a given period is a problem which the greatest linguist on earth must refuse to determine. Our evidences show remarkable variations in different cases; but in general, while the languages of savages, who have no fixed abodes, no writing, and no literature, have been known to change very rapidly,[1] those which have been long written, which are embodied in literature, which are crystallised in sacred books and rituals, may remain almost the same for centuries. This is peculiarly the case in those stable and conservative Oriental states to which Egypt bore so close a resemblance.

I shall not cite the analogy of China, which is in all respects the example most in point, and where the written language has remained almost the same for at least 3000 years, but consider the case of Greece, which has undergone many revolutions and invasions, and whose inhabitants bear little trace of relationship with the hearers of Perikles and of Kleon. Twenty-three centuries separate the History of Thukydides from a Greek newspaper of the present day, and yet a competent linguist could easily construct the older idiom from a careful analysis, and comparison with the new. Our bilingual Egyptian inscriptions are not more than six centuries removed from the oldest Coptic manuscripts.[2] During part of

---

[1] Even in these cases there are many notable exceptions. I believe the earliest grammar of the Delaware language, which was compiled more than two centuries ago, presents the same, or closely analogous, grammatical features to the present idioms of the proximate Indian tribes. The Lithuanian language in the Baltic provinces of Russia is known to be in a grammatical condition as antique, in some respects, as the oldest Sanskrit.

[2] The date of the former is, of course, fixed by the Greek

this time—perhaps during the whole of it—Egyptian was an officially recognised language by the Greeks and Romans. It was scattered all over the country in inscriptions and in books; it was taught universally to the population. We ask what *a priori* probability or possibility is there of its having totally and completely changed?

But the positive and irrefragable evidence of facts above adduced disposes of the difficulty far more completely. The reader has seen that, with the aid of the ample vocabulary afforded by the Coptic Bible and Rituals, Champollion demonstrated the analogy, in itself as probable as it well could be.

The great increase in the number of exhumed documents, and in our consequent knowledge of the old language, may have allowed some later writers to speak slightingly of Coptic comparisons. Yet they should never forget that this was the real starting point, and still remains the sound and certain verification of their inferences.[1]

---

translations. As to the age of the Coptic MSS., cf. above, p. 137. There are bilingual inscriptions in demotic and Greek, published in *Lepsius' Denkmäler*, which seem a great deal later than the Rosetta and Tanis texts. If the Epistles of S. Antony really date from the third century A. D., the occurrence of Roman names written in hieroglyphics reaches almost down to that epoch; so that there is in some sense no gap at all.

[1] " Quorum impudentiam miratus essem," says Peyron of these writers, (*Lex. Copt.*, p. xi.), "nisi alios audissem de oeconomica

Some exaggerated statements concerning the fixity of Egyptian, or its changes, according to the Manethonian dynasties, cannot overthrow sound conclusions, though it may give scope for cavil in controversy.

In conclusion, Lewis thinks it marvellous that the Greeks and Romans should have neglected to have documents of such alleged importance translated and published. This observation shows that he had not penetrated beyond the surface of classical civilisation, and had failed to apprehend its defects. It also ignores the fact that the only literary kingdom of antiquity which valued the world's history as such, did order their translation. As soon as the Ptolemies consolidated their power at Alexandria, we know that they commissioned learned men, such as Eratosthenes, to perform this task. Unfortunately, with the general wreck of the great Alexandrine literature, these inestimable labours have perished all to a few wretched extracts. But Lewis should have rather thought it marvellous if

---

disputare, arithmeticae tamen ignaros." So Chabas, *Voyage d'un Égyptien*, &c., p. 5. "Les uns et les autres (Coptic and Old Egyptian scholars) doivent bien se persuader que l'étude un peu complète du Copte leur est absolument indispensable ; plus il avançeront dans la connaissance de cette langue, et de celle de l'ancien Égyptien, mieux il apercevront les analogies intimes qui attachent la langue dérivée à son type antique, et il leur arrivera, ce que m'arrive moi-même, à savoir ; qu'en lisant un texte copte on se le représente instinctivement en hiéroglyphique," &c.

any Greeks or Romans (with the exception of the Lagidae) had ever desired them to be translated. It was one great contrast between their civilisation and ours, that *as nations* they took no interest whatever in any history or antiquities save their own. No Greek state would have ordered such an undertaking, and the isolated Greek travellers, who visited the country, were at the mercy of the priests—probably the lowest of them—who told them truth and fiction almost at random.¹

As for the Romans, who could conceive their senate or their public taking the smallest interest in such matters? Consider the far greater importance to them of the Jews, as their opponents, and also as settlers in Rome. The sacred books of the Jews were easy of access and of interpretation, and yet their most learned historians remain in gross ignorance of the subject. Besides all this, the Roman State was peculiarly jealous of its citizens entering Egypt, which was valued as a storehouse of corn, not as a museum of antiquities. Educated Romans were debarred from visiting its remains, and Tacitus

---

¹ I see that Mr. Goodwin has fully appreciated this defect of the Greeks in his remarkable article on the *Story of Saneha* (*Fraser* for Feb., 1865, p. 186). "The Greek antiquaries did not go to work in this way. Few of them troubled themselves to learn the Egyptian language. They picked up stories here and there from communicative priests, and these, mixed up without

tells us that the Emperor Tiberius censured Germanicus for turning aside from state duties to attend to such trifles—a good example of the solemn bigotry and pompous ignorance lauded under the title of Roman *gravitas*.[1]

Such are the objections which Lewis could muster before the publication of the Canopus inscription.

---

any discrimination, were handed from one writer to another, without any one even caring to criticise, compare, or methodise them. To us at the present day this indifference of the cultivated Greeks and Romans seems strange." Cf. also M. Chabas' remarks in *Lepsius' Zeitschr.* for 1864, p. 98.

[1] Even the ponderous Bunsen grows eloquent on this subject. He says (*Egypt's Place*, &c., i., p. 165), "They understood the character of no people but in its defects; they loved no other people, and were loved by none, because they neither approached them in a humane spirit, nor expected to be received in the same; and did good to others, merely because they found it to their own advantage. . . . No genuine Roman, therefore, ever concerned himself with the history of other nations from any pure feeling of human sympathy, and as little from any zeal for the investigation of truth. The divine thirst for knowledge for its own sake, or for truth from a love of truth, never disturbed a Roman mind. The natural consequence is that the more respectable scholars of Rome appear ridiculously ignorant, or at best insignificant, beside the Greeks in the field of scientific research. . . . With all their patriotism, they had no respect for their species; and in spite of all their good faith and public integrity, they did not love truth, nor, consequently, with all their talent and all their education, could they love science. Thus far Pilate is their type, and his question their motto."

They are so superficial, and founded on so much ignorance, that I must apologise to the reader for delaying him with their refutation; yet it may conduce to the completeness of the present discussion, and may convince those as yet unacquainted with the fact, that a lawyer and a sceptic can be both inaccurate and dogmatical.[1] Time has, indeed, long since silently answered all his objections; for while they have fallen into oblivion, and his book now sleeps on forgotten shelves, the discovery which he slighted is making daily progress, and enlisting the attention of an increasing circle of thoughtful men.

---

[1] Here is a specimen of his accuracy; "Bunsen, however, states that the pyramids do not in general contain any sepulchral chamber, and *thinks that their destination is unknown*" (*Astronomy of the Ancients*, p. 341, note). This statement so astonished me that I took the trouble to verify his reference to Bunsen's *Egypt*, vol. ii., p. 389. This is the passage:—" Respecting the particular purpose for which the pyramids were designed, we have satisfactorily shown in the foregoing inquiry [one of great length, and accompanied by maps and ground plans] that they are exclusively gigantic covers of rocky tombs, built with great skill, &c., and that, as a general rule, they contain neither sepulchral chamber nor apartment." He adds that he cannot tell *why the Egyptians chose this particular method of honouring their deceased kings*—a thing not hard to understand, when we consider it as the gradual increasing of the stone protection to their early tombs. A farther study of Bunsen's work would have disclosed the explanation (iv., p. 651), whereby the author clears up to his own satisfaction even this last difficulty. The verification of the reference will, however, speak for itself.

ESSAY IV.

Cuneiform Inscriptions.

ὁ δὲ Δαρεῖος . . στήλας ἴστησι δύο, ἐνταμὼν γράμματα ἐς μὲν τὴν Ἀσσύρια,
ἐς δὲ τὴν Ἑλληνικά, ἔθνεα πάντα, ὅσα περ ἦγε.—HERODOTUS.

WE now proceed to the consideration of a discovery greater and more difficult than that of the Egyptian hieroglyphics. This latter was difficult enough, as has been seen from the previous Essay, but still it was mainly the work of one man, Champollion, who was not greatly aided by the speculations of his predecessors, nor have his successors done much more than amplify and explain the principles which he laid down in his Egyptian Grammar. It was also *one* language, and the pictures were real pictures. The discovery of the cuneiform writings, embracing, as it has done up to the present time, at least three distinct languages and two distinct species of writing, has exhausted the labour of many minds, and there are few works of forty years ago on the subject that are not now completely superseded. Of many different men each made his partial discovery, but recoiled baffled by the intricacy of the problem. There is, in fact, hardly any one who can be said to have kept in the van of the inquiry, and to have distinguished himself by several distinct contributions made at long intervals, except our own fellow-countryman, Dr. Hincks, sometime Fellow of Trinity College, Dublin.

The history of the discovery is one of the most curious in the annals of man. As early as the sixteenth century the ruins of Persepolis began to attract the attention of European merchants and travellers, and in 1621 Pietro della Valle copied a few of the characters inscribed on these monuments, and expressed his opinion that as the thick end of the letters was never at the right, but the left of the oblique characters, the signs must have been written from left to right.[1] This shrewd remark was perfectly correct, though the author knew nothing of the language, and could not attempt to decipher the characters.

From his day onward many visited and described the ruins. Built on a great platform, artificially constructed for the purpose, which commands a wide plain, and has a lofty mountain shaped like an amphitheatre at its rear, the stranger ascends the spot by a magnificent staircase, or pair of staircases, which separate in opposite directions, to meet at the summit. Here are the

---

[1] If the reader will turn to the specimens below, p. 175, he will at once perceive the gist of this observation.

gigantic remains of several palaces, great porticoes with winged bulls, and reliefs representing gods and princes. In the live rock of the mountain at the rear, tombs have been hewn, evidently to receive the occupants of the palaces, and all the rocks and walls are covered with the inscriptions called cuneiform, sometimes also arrow-headed, consisting of very simple elements, which are nothing but thin wedges and angles, ⟨wedge symbols⟩, but with these elements combined in wonderful variety. Similar designs were found in many other parts of the country, and it was not difficult to conjecture that forgotten generations of men had thus chronicled their deeds for the benefit of future ages.

But no record of the language or its import had survived, and the ignorant inhabitants of the neighbourhood looked upon the texts with greater awe than they did the winged monsters that loomed over the plain. They were to them symbols of magic import which, if duly pronounced, would unlock the hidden treasures guarded by the lions and the bulls. They had been engraved too with the greatest care and art, and there were yet to be seen, as on the Egyptian hieroglyphics, traces of the gold with which they had been adorned.[1]

Passing by notices of no value, we may well con-

---

[1] The reader who desires fuller information on the deciphering of old Persian may consult (1) F Spiegel, *Altpersische Keilin-*

sider the great traveller, Carsten Niebuhr (father of the historian), as the first man who threw any light on the method and order of the inscriptions. Agreeing with the belief of Della Valle, that the characters were written from left to right, he analysed the inscriptions with such care as to perceive that the three columns in which most of them were engraved, though at first sight very similar, and composed of the same elements, were yet different in their arrangement of letters or signs, that in fact the inscriptions were of a triple kind. He noticed several peculiarities in each, observing that they were always in the same order, the longest, but simplest, which contained about forty-two different signs, being on the right.

Carsten Niebuhr perceived that there were three different alphabets or characters, but was uncertain whether the languages were also distinct; he felt that in any case the sense of all three must be the same.

---

schriften, pp. 119-32; (2) J. Oppert, *Mémoire sur les inscriptions des Achéménides*, in the *Journal Asiatique* for 1851-2; (3) H. Rawlinson's great Essay (with the principal texts) in vol. x. of the *Trans. of the Royal Asiatic Society;* (4) J. Oppert, *Expédition Scientifique en Mésopotamie*, vol. ii., pp. 2-9; (5) J. Ménant, *Les Écritures cunéiformes*, second edition, Paris, 1864, pp. 49-99. From these high authorities the following exposition is compiled. The latter two works treat of old Persian merely as the necessary step to the deciphering of the Assyrian inscriptions; the work of Professor Spiegel is the most satisfactory, especially for the discoveries subsequent to 1836.

He also performed for the learned men of Europe the inestimable service of copying accurately and publishing, in 1764, several of these inscriptions. But even his acute mind could not fathom them any farther. He had merely shown that one of these systems of writing was far simpler than the rest, and directed the attention of the learned to its solution as the easiest.

Accordingly Münter, of Copenhagen, examining this character thirty years later (1798) saw that the diagonal bar (\), recurring constantly and at short intervals, must be the sign of the separation of words,[1] and he then proceeded to discover the vowels, by the frequency of their appearance as compared with consonants. This he did on the supposition that the language of the Persians was akin to our own, and of the Indo-European type, for in Semitic tongues, and in languages like the Egyptian, vowels are not generally written, but understood. This then was an investigation based on grammatical or philological grounds. He observed that certain groups, in most respects similar, varied in their terminations, and so was led to see in these varia-

---

[1] It was long thought to be the concluding sign, but M. Jules Oppert has shown that it was originally used as an initial sign, and that there are still extant some examples of this use. Cf. his *Inscriptions des Achéménides*, in vol. xvii. (for 1851) of the *Journal Asiatique*, p. 428.

tions grammatical flexions. By noting the frequency of recurrence, he actually discovered the signs for the vowels, but was unable to determine them individually, with the exception of A, which he really discovered. He also guessed B rightly, but without being able to give any satisfactory proof.

Such was the condition of the question, seriously considered, at the opening of the present century. But though we here avoid wasting time by detailing the absurd and ridiculous interpretations which were constantly being published, we are bound to mention the fact. For learned men had not before them, as we now have, the scanty grains of pure wheat winnowed and purified, but were puzzled and misled by a multitude of contradictory statements, the most absurd of which were, as usual, put forth with the greatest assurance, by men who pretended to have visited the spot, and have informed themselves better than their neighbours. To us these essays are obviously worthless, but in their day they must have had no small influence in misleading, and in retarding real progress.

It was, however, regarded as a settled point by archaeologists and historians at the opening of this century that these ruins were the remains of the palaces of the Achaemenid kings, who were known in the history of Herodotus as having carried on wars with the Greeks, and as having been the lords of Asia in the fifth and sixth centuries, B. C. Without the records of the Greeks, we should indeed have remained in total darkness on early Persian history. There is in Persian a celebrated work called the *Shah-nameh*,[1] or Book of the Kings, which professes to give an account of the past sovereigns of the country; but so completely does it differ in its names and dates from the Greek accounts, and so completely is it overlaid with fabulous details, that our fathers, who had not learned the art of criticising legends, rejected the whole as perfectly untrustworthy, and the pure and deliberate fiction of later Persian poets. The very names of Cyrus and Xerxes seemed to be forgotten.

The wretched fortunes of the country, first conquered and enslaved by the Greeks, then by the Arabs in the seventh century, A. D., might well account for this strange forgetfulness. Nor did the ancient sacred books, entitled the Avesta, written in the Zend dialect and preserved by the Parsees in India, seem to convey any better knowledge.[2] On Herodotus and on the books of Daniel

---

[1] This celebrated epic was apparently put into its present shape, from pre-existing materials, by Abu'l Kasim, surnamed Firdusi, about the year 1000, A. D., during the great reaction of Iranism against Semitism under the Soffarid, Samanid, and Ghaznevite dynasties. There is a splendid edition and translation of the work by M. Jules Mohl, Paris, 1838-60.

[2] The Comte de Gobineau has attempted to show in his fascinating *Histoire des Perses*, compiled in the country and chiefly

and Esther was based the only sound information that could be obtained on the subject. And among other valuable notices, Herodotus tells us that at the Bosporus, Darius set up two pillars of white marble, and engraved on them a list of the nations that had followed him, in Greek and in *Assyrian* characters. It appeared plain from this that the Persians used characters which appeared to the honest and careful historian identical with the Assyrian he had seen at Babylon. It also appeared that these kings were wont to set up inscriptions in different tongues, commemorating their achievements.

So much could be fairly gathered from Herodotus, and now a new observer, the famous orientalist, M. de Sacy, contributed his share, by copying and explaining inscriptions, engraved very lightly upon the same marble, by the Sassanid kings who lived at a much later epoch (the third century, A. D.) in the Pehlvi language, which is a mixture of Persian and Aramaic, and which is written in an alphabet perfectly understood. He showed that these Sassanid inscriptions were in the form: "*I, M or N, king of kings, son of X, king of kings, did thus and thus.*"

---

from oriental sources, that these legends, though greatly distorted, contain much valuable truth, even about the very personages that were believed to have been totally forgotten in the national version of Persian history He has not, however, sufficiently checked his imagination, and has consequently destroyed the scientific value of his work.

Such then was the historical and linguistic state of the question, when Grotefend read his memorable essay on the 4th September, 1802, at the Academy of Sciences in Göttingen. It has been remarked that at the very same meeting of this body Heyne described the first successes in reading the hieroglyphics of Egypt. The efforts of one man completed the latter discovery. Years and lives were to pass away before the other and greater riddle was solved. However Grotefend in his essay, going upon historical and not grammatical grounds (he was hardly an oriental scholar) asserted, first that the inscriptions were written not merely in three alphabets as C. Niebuhr had thought, but in three languages.[1] He next determined the direction of the writing from its form. Turning to the simpler column, where the letters had been numbered, he compared several of the inscriptions copied by Niebuhr, and found them to correspond accurately for the most part. One group (⟨⟨⟨𝌀 ⟨⟨ 𝌀 ⟩⟨- ⟩⟨⟨ 𝌀𝌀 ⟩⟨- ⟩)[2] recurred very frequently, and he agreed with previous scholars (Münter and Tychsen) that this group

---

[1] Curiously enough, this is still the practice of the Shahs of Persia, who rule over equally heterogeneous subjects, and therefore issue their decrees in Persian, Turkish, and Arabic, each the near relative of one of the languages in the ancient trilingual inscriptions. Cf. Ménant, *Écritures Cunéiformes*, p. 4.

[2] This group was afterwards read KH SH A Ya TH I Ya.

probably meant *king*, a word which recurred perpetually through the Sassanid inscriptions in the phrases "king of kings," and "great king," and these phrases had the air of being ancient and traditional. This conjecture he supported by the observation that the word occurred twice in succession, almost always after the first word of the inscription, and the second time with a termination which might be the sign of the genitive plural, viz. :

〈〈〉〉 〈〈 𝍤 𐎹 𐎹 𐎹 𐎹 𐎹 𐎹 𐎹 𐎹 𐎹
K SH A Y*a* TH I Y

He observed that two of the inscriptions copied by Niebuhr not only agreed throughout in most of their groups, but that they differed in the same places. And the differences were these: the first group in each inscription was different. Let us call these groups X and D. Then followed the word supposed to mean king, in both, with other words apparently identical. But some way down in both inscriptions they again, and at the same place, differed in a single group. That beginning with X had the group D here inserted, whereas that commencing with D had a new and strange group in the corresponding place. But while the group D was followed in both places by the supposed sign for king, the new group was not so accompanied.

Grotefend now proceeded to draw his conclusions. He guessed that the inscriptions were a fixed formula, only differing in the proper names. If these inscriptions began, like those read by De Sacy, with the formula X, *the king of kings, son of D, the king of kings*, then it was evident that D was X's father. Let us make the matter plain by quoting the actual text :—

Inscription I.—〈〈𒀸 〈〈 𒀸- 𒀸 𒀸 〈〈 𒀸 \ (X), 〈〈𒀸 〈〈 𒀸 𒀸- 𒀸 𒀸 𒀸- \ (King ?), 〈〈𒀸 〈〈 𒀸 𒀸- 𒀸 𒀸 𒀸- 𒀸 ⊏〈 𒀸-𒀸 \ (of kings), &c., &c. . .

𒀸 𒀸 𒀸 𒀸- -𒀸 〈𒀸 〈〈 \ (D), 〈〈𒀸 〈〈 𒀸 𒀸-𒀸 𒀸 𒀸- \ &c. (king of kings?).

Inscription II.—𒀸 𒀸 𒀸 𒀸- -𒀸 〈𒀸 〈〈 \ (D), 〈〈𒀸 〈〈 𒀸 𒀸- 𒀸 𒀸 𒀸- \ (king?), 〈〈𒀸 〈〈 𒀸 𒀸- 𒀸 𒀸 𒀸- 𒀸 ⊏〈 𒀸-𒀸 \ (of kings ?) . . . .

𒀸 𒀸 〈〈 ⊏𒀸 𒀸 𒀸 𒀸 (V), (not followed by king of kings.)[1]

It seemed also probable that D's father, mentioned in the second inscription was not a king, for his name was not followed by that title. This last fact Grotefend verified by other inscriptions, so that it

---

[1] The first inscription is now read : KH SH*a* Y A R SH A. KH SH A Y*a* TH I Y*a*. KH SH A Y*a* TH I Y A N A M, &c. D A R Y*a* V U SH, &c. The latter ends with V I SH T A S P*a*.

could not have been a mere accident. If so D was the founder of the race, and the first king.

To whom then could this correspond? Cyrus is naturally suggested; but in the first place the group appeared to contain too many letters for Cyrus' name, and secondly it happened that Cyrus' father and son were both called Cambyses. This would not explain the third name, which moreover began with a different sign from the first. Indeed the length of the names appeared to preclude Cyrus as too short, and Artaxerxes as too long. Darius then must be the second name. His father, Hystaspes, was not king, and he was in that sense the new founder of the monarchy. Applying these principles, and taking to his aid the Hebrew forms of the names, Grotefend actually spelt out the names Daryavush, Khshayarsha, and Vishtaspa. He was in error as to the *y* and the *v*, which he read *h* and *a*; but he had actually hit upon the real clue. We are at a loss whether most to admire the genius or the good fortune of this wonderful discovery.

But by the strange fate which seemed to allow no single man so much glory, though Grotefend lived for thirty years afterwards, he added nothing to his first attempt, but a fortunate guess of the name Nebuchadnezzar, in one of the Assyrian inscriptions, and an unsuccessful effort to read the name of the winged god, who hovers over most of the kings in the reliefs. He only deciphered three letters, *u*, *r*, and *d*, correctly. It should indeed have been quite evident that when the first clue was obtained, the rest must be achieved by pure linguists, and by grammatical, not historical, analysis. It was however only in the year 1824, that Rask, of Copenhagen, who was an accomplished Zend scholar, turned his attention to Grotefend's Essay then just republished,[1] and observed that the groups supposed to mean *king of kings*, which had some letters in common with the proper names, must have a genitive plural ending, and that in Sanskrit and Zend this form is *ânâm*. He accordingly deciphered the *n* ⊨⟨, and *m* ⊢⫯⫯, and with their aid read the title *Achaemenid*, which corroborated the previous discoveries. The letter *m* appeared also in the title of the winged god.

This was Rask's contribution, and was most important in fixing the Indo-European character of the language. It was obvious that a knowledge of Zend alone could enable the rest to be achieved. In 1832-3 the great French orientalist, Eugene Burnouf, edited and was the first to explain satisfactorily portions of the ancient books of Zoroaster. So well did he perform the task that his text is now regarded by the Parsees in India as the highest au-

---

[1] In Heeren's *Ideen über die Politik &c der alten Welt*, (Göttingen, 1815.) M. Spiegel observes that the later edition of 1824 (quoted by M. Ménant) does not contain Grotefend's Essay in its complete form. Cf. *Altpers. Keilinschriften*, p. 120, *note*.

thority, and is invoked as decisive in theological and ritualistic difficulties. This book bore rapid fruits, and the French Orientalist proceeded to farther discoveries. In the year 1836 he published a most important treatise on two inscriptions obtained from the papers of the traveller Schultz. His studies in the Zend language, while they gave him immense philological advantages, actually interfered with his deciphering, for on the analogy of the old-Bactrian (or Zend) alphabet he assumed too many signs for vowels,[1] and did not leave enough for consonants. He nevertheless determined many additional letters correctly, and would doubtless have held a higher place in the history of the discovery, had not the splendid work of Christian Lassen of Bonn appeared in the following month.[2]

The work of Lassen, as well as that of Burnouf, was based on Grotefend's discoveries. But while accepting his main results as to the names intended by the writing, the special values given by Grotefend to the letters of other words struck Lassen as highly improbable, from his knowledge of

---

[1] This peculiarity of the alphabet in which we possess the Avesta, has been noticed by Spiegel (*Altbaktrische Gram.*, p. 14), who shows that in this respect the Armenian and Greek alphabets can be compared to it. It is moreover a very modern alphabet, probably of the fifth century, A. D.

[2] June, 1836. M. Ménant reverses the order of these publications (*Écritures cunéiformes*, p. 92), though he is most anxious to give Burnouf as much credit as possible.

Sanskrit and old Bactrian (Zend). He observed also that the alphabet of Grotefend, when applied to new words, produced monstrous and inarticulable forms, which could only be possible on the supposition that the inscriptions had been inaccurately copied. Nevertheless, Niebuhr was an observer of known accuracy, and other copies, such as Ker Porter's, perfectly corroborated him. Considering then that in the reading of the proper names, the system of Grotefend could only require a more exact specialising of the articulations, Lassen openly questioned the rest of the alphabet. But he not merely assigned to many of the letters new values; he remodelled the system of the alphabet, by affirming that, like the Indian alphabet, a short *a* adhered to all consonants, when no other vowel sign was appended. This accounted for words apparently written in consonants only. It was this discovery which gave Lassen a great advantage over his predecessors.

His researches were corrected by his two critics, Beer, and more especially Jaquet, whose contributions he himself acknowledged.[1] They both agreed as to ⟨⟨⊢ being *y*, and ⟨⊱⟨ = *h*, whereas Jaquet, in addition, determined ⊢⟨⟨ to be *r* before *u*, ⟨⟨⟩ to be *th*, and ⟨⟨⊢ to be *c*, together with some other improvements. These signs had been read differently

---

[1] *Zeitschrift für die Kunde des Morgenlandes*, ii., p. 165.

by Lassen. In 1845, owing to the more accurate copies of M. Westergaard, the first Persian linguist who ever copied the inscriptions, Holtzmann was able to determine two more letters, the *d* and *j*.

The researches of Sir H. Rawlinson lie so perfectly apart from the development of the study in Europe, that they need not here be particularised. He claims to have arrived at most of the results described, without knowing any of the works on the subject; but when his discoveries were published in Europe all that he said had been elaborated, except the determination of *t'*, *m'*, and two new signs for *n*, which he obtained by having access to inscriptions hitherto unknown. He will ever deserve the gratitude of the learned for his careful copies of the great Behistun inscription.

Two more discoveries completed the reading of the Persian alphabet. The first was that of Hincks, who, in the *Transactions of the Royal Irish Academy* in October, 1846, asserted that the supposed homophone signs were not really such, but indicated that a different vowel was to be attached to each. M. Jules Oppert, in a treatise published in 1847 appears not only to have discovered this principle independently, but also to have solved the remaining point of doubt, viz., that very often *n* and *m* must be supplied before consonants, though they are not written.[1]

---

[1] I perceive that M. Ménant (*Écritures cunéiformes*, p. 125)

This is, in brief, the course of this brilliant investigation. Without considering stray hints and indications, or even the merit due to accurate copyists, it will be seen that the genius of at least twelve men was required, and the lapse of forty-five years, to bring this great labour to a successful termination.

The language of the Zend Avesta being in fact the sister of that of the inscriptions,[1] and the modern Persian its daughter, the problem of translating them was not more difficult than that of reading Provençal by the aid of old Italian and French. There is no surer clue to the meaning of an unknown letter in a partially deciphered word, than a knowledge what sort of form we have to expect. It was this *philological necessity*, as it is called, that had determined the *m* and the *n* for Rask.

Nothing will illustrate better the history of the discovery than the name of the winged god Ormuzd, in old Persian *Auramazda*. The *a* was discovered

---

also attributes to him the discovery of the value of ⟨≣⊢ = *gu*, and to him and Rawlinson the discovery of ⟨⟨≣ = *nu*. The signs for *di, ku, zi,* and *ru,* were first given by Hincks, according to M. Ménant's instructive table.

[1] Learned men are not agreed as to which of these dialects is the elder. Oppert and Westergaard give the prerogative to Bactrian; Rawlinson and Spiegel to the Achaemenid inscriptions. Spiegel (*Gram. der Altbaktr. Sprache*, p. 4) notices the arguments on either side.

by Münter in 1798, the *u r* and *d* by Grotefend in 1802, the *m* by Rask, in 1824, the *z* by Lassen and Burnouf, in 1836.[1]

The language was thus ascertained to be old Persian, but of a different dialect from that of the sacred books of Zoroaster, and yet implying a knowledge of his religion. It followed that this teacher, and the books compiled in his name, must have come into existence at an epoch vastly anterior to what had hitherto been supposed.

But the historical documents at once attracted great attention.[2] The most important inscription as yet published and translated is that copied from a lofty rock near Behistun, or Bisitoun, by Sir H. Rawlinson, commemorating the life and acts of Darius Hystaspes, his conquests, and the nations under his sway. There are added bas-reliefs representing the great king sitting, with his feet on Gaumates (pseudo-

---

[1] Cf. M. Ménant, *Op. cit.*, p. 95.

[2] They have been several times edited and translated, first by Sir H. Rawlinson, M. Westergaard, and by M. Jules Oppert; but in the cumbrous and expensive transactions of Asiatic societies. They are published separately by Theodor Benfey, *die Persischen Keilinschriften*, &c., Leipzig, 1847, and by F. Spiegel (Leipzig, 1862), who has taken advantage of all the scattered essays and suggestions in the Asiatic periodicals, and whose very valuable edition I have followed. His book contains, in addition, a grammar of the language, and a glossary, compiled from the inscriptions.

Smerdis) the usurper, receiving a train of nine captive princes, who have their names inscribed over them. Over Gaumates is written: "This is Gaumates, the Magian; he lied; he said I am Smerdis, son of Cyrus." And so for the rest. The recurring formula is: " This is M. He lied; he said he was king of N." Last of the nine captives comes a tall figure, out-topping the rest, and attired in a pointed cap. "And this," says the incription laconically, " this is Sakukha the Scythian."

The inscription opens with a pious and solemn invocation to Ormuzd, ascribing to him all power and dominion, and proceeds to the genealogy of the king, and a full list of his provinces. It next tells us how he snatched the dominion from the usurping Smerdis. Then he recounts the revolt of Susiana. "I sent thither an army," he says, "and the rebel Atrina was brought in chains before me; I slew him." He speaks similarly of the other revolting chiefs. In the case of Media indeed he is more explicit. " Phraortes was brought before me; I cut off his nose, his ears, and his tongue. He was kept chained at my court, so that every one beheld him. Then I had him crucified at Ecbatana, together with his accomplices." Such was the punishment of Haman under Xerxes, the son of Darius, as told in the book of Esther. After all these interesting details, which are strictly corroborated by the notices of Herodotus, the great inscription proceeds thus:

"King Darius saith: These countries rebelled against my power. By lies they were separated from me. The men thou seest here deceived my people. My army took them, according to my orders. King Darius saith: Oh! thou that shalt be king hereafter, see that thou art not guilty of deceit. Him that is wicked, judge as he should be judged, and if thou reignest thus thy kingdom will be great. King Darius saith: What I did, I did ever by the grace of Ormuzd. Thou that readest upon this stone my deeds, think not that thou hast been deceived, neither be thou slow to believe them. King Darius saith: Ormuzd be my witness that I have not spoken these things with lying lips."

I have quoted from this remarkable record for many reasons. Its exact correspondence, especially in the many proper names it contains, with the names of persons and provinces described by Herodotus, are a convincing proof of the accuracy of the deciphering. It will give some notion of the style of the documents that have been preserved. It will also prove the accuracy of the accounts given by Herodotus and Xenophon of the character of the ancient Persians; in whom an honest love of truth, and hatred of lies was the prominent feature—a feature which we justly honour more than any other in a nation, but in which most oriental nations, and indeed the Greeks also, were wofully deficient.

The inscriptions of Xerxes are shorter, and have evidently less glories and less achievements to record; and those of the later kings, near the time of Alexander's invasion, show a decline not only in the power of the realm, but even in the language of the inscriptions. There are, too, in these later documents, fainter traces of that eminently religious spirit, which made the great Achaemenid kings the emissaries of a new faith, that gained its proselytes by fire and sword. In the pompous enumeration of their titles there is no mere official *Dei Gratia*, but in each a solemn and repeated assertion that all power and dominion is due to the grace of Ormuzd. This was the secret of their power.

There is but one more of these Persian inscriptions which I shall quote, inferior to none in interest, though its terms are brief and simple, and contrast singularly with the explicit ceremony, and the pompous majesty of the later kings. But it is surely well suited to him of whom the Hebrew prophet exclaimed, that he was the Lord's shepherd, and should perform all His pleasure. Near the site of Pasargadae, the first capital of the empire, there are found pillars and a winged figure, as of a god, graven upon them, with this legend: "I am Cyrus, the king, the Achaemenid.[1]

---

[1] There are considerable doubts as to the identity of Murghâb, the site of the inscriptions, with the ancient Pasargadae, at which we are told Cyrus was buried; so that these inscriptions were

It seems quite needless to say anything in verification of the discovery. There never was an hypothesis which justified itself more brilliantly than that of Grotefend. The *language* produced by the deciphering was exactly what must have been expected, from modern Persian, and from the analogy of old-Bactrian. The proper *names*, when read, correspond with names transmitted to us by Greek historians. The historical *facts* conveyed also agreed perfectly with the accounts of the Greeks. All this resulted from attaching one fixed value to each of forty-two phonetic sounds. The coincidence, therefore, that on a few vases the names of Xerxes and Artaxerxes were read independently in hieroglyphics and in cuneiform letters (by Champollion and Grotefend) was rather required as a corroboration of the Egyptian than of the Persian discovery. Yet in the days of the two great men I have named, every addition to the evidence for their bold inferences was precious, and made no small noise in its day.[1]

We have hitherto occupied ourselves with only

---

most probably not over his grave, but set up at one of his palaces, at some distance from his capital. Cf. on this question Lassen's article *Pasargadae* in Ersch and Grubers' *Encyclopaedia*, and Spiegel, *Altpers. Keilinschr.*, p. 72.

[1] See the account of these vases in M. Ménant's *Écrit. cunéif.* p. 118.

one, and that the simplest of the cuneiform characters, and this has told us the sense of all the three inscriptions, provided they were transcripts of the same text, as seemed very probable from Herodotus' statement. But the reading of the second and third columns presented the greatest difficulties. Though much shorter than the first, they appeared to have, not twenty or thirty, but several hundred different characters, and in many cases a single sign seemed to correspond to a whole word of the Persian. It was moreover not plain whether there were two more alphabets or only one. Yet all these difficulties ought surely to be soluble, for if, as was explained in the last Essay, proper names are the only certain guide from a known to an unknown character, the Achaemenid inscriptions teem with proper names, all of which must be transcribed into the new language.

The Danish Professor, Westergaard, was the first to enter upon the new investigation. By means of the proper names, which were already known in the Persian version of the trilingual inscriptions, he discovered that fixed signs corresponded to them in the middle column, and from a careful comparison, fixed the meaning of these signs. In fact the Persian version performed the same office that the Greek portion of the Rosetta stone had done in the case of the hieroglyphics. The results to which Westergaard was brought by this labour were very curious; the language he deciphered was like no Indo-European or Semitic idiom; for though the pronouns appeared somewhat Semitic, and the general structure was not unlike the Persian, the declinations seemed like Turkish, the conjugations seemed Tartar, and the vocabulary suggested all sorts of languages.[1]

And yet later researches corroborated his conclusions. Above all Dr. Hincks read a very remarkable paper at the Royal Irish Academy in 1846,[2] in which he tested and corrected Westergaard's results, and proved that his labour had not been spent in vain. And in this paper Hincks made one of his great discoveries, by showing that the signs in the second language, which some call Medo-Scythian (who wrongly suppose it the tongue of the Medes, and that they came from Scythia), represented not letters, but syllables, and that when its writers wrote such a syllable as *nap*, they wrote it either in one sign or in two (never in three), and the two signs would be *na-ap*, the simplest syllables being a vowel, or a vowel and consonant combined.[3] There was no

---

[1] See his matured views in the *Trans. of the Royal Danish Academy* for 1857, pp. 41-178.

[2] This acute and original memoir, probably one of the most brilliant ever produced by the Royal Irish Academy, was published in the twenty-first volume of the *Transactions*, part i., pp. 114-32, and pp. 233, *sq.*

[3] We have already seen above (p. 182) how the same principle

more fruitful discovery than this ever made in the reading of cuneiform inscriptions.

Both these learned men also perceived that though none of the cuneiform signs bore any resemblance to any known object, yet many of them were intended to serve as conventional pictures, and were in fact ideographs, and not phonetics. They also observed that the same signs were used sometimes as ideographs, and sometimes as phonetics; and that, just like the Egyptian signs which were already explained, the sound indicated by an ideograph, when used phonetically, was the first syllable of the name of the object depicted by it. Thus there was an ideograph for God, and the word for God in this strange language was *annap*; but if the ideographic sign was used phonetically, it represented the syllable *an*. This is in accordance with the transition, in all other writing, from ideographs to phonetics. They further observed determinative signs, added to the groups to indicate their meaning; and of some of these the meaning was clear, while the sound was uncertain. There are two complicated groups, which are proved by comparison to mean *horse* and *camel*. They have before them a sign which determines the group to mean *animal*, and after them a sign to show it is ideographic, but

---

enabled Hincks to banish the supposed *homophones* from the old Persian alphabet.

the proper pronunciation of the names has not yet been determined.[1]

Though most of the inscriptions found in this language are translations of the acts of the Persian kings, the nature of the dialect is of the deepest interest, and suggests the most curious problems. Of the languages now extant, it was at first asserted to have some remote affinity with the Turkish, and with the Hungarian—in fact with the languages of the nations who burst forth from their homes in Upper Asia, and broke up the remains of the Roman Empire. Historically this is possible. Cold and dismal as are now these barren steppes; though Siberia is to us almost the emblem for desolation; yet for centuries, from these now deserted regions, wave upon wave of nations once burst into the civilised world. But linguistically, there is as yet no clear evidence of the relation of the second Achaemenid language with any known tongue. Hincks positively denied its Turkish or Scythian complexion. Upper Asia, moreover, was the cradle of nations; and this much only is certain, that the Assyrians borrowed from one of them their

---

[1] It is worth while to give these words, if only to show the extreme cumbrousness of this graphic system :—

𒀭𒀭𒀭𒀭(𒀭𒀭𒀭)𒀭 this word signifies *horse*.
𒀭𒀭𒀭𒀭(𒀭𒀭𒀭)𒀭 ,, ,, *camel*.

I have placed in parenthesis the ideographic groups, of which the

system of writing—the greatest symbol of civilisation—at an epoch not later than 2000 B.C.; and therefore the Siberian steppes may have contained a primitive culture, of which no other traces have yet been found, and which is only now rising into a dim twilight from the depths of the night of ages. Their system of writing was indeed far from perfect; it represented syllables and not letters; it preserved the ideographic stage, though also using the phonetic, and mixed them in perplexing confusion, just like the Egyptian; but who could have imagined that among the few races of the world, which have ever attempted to record their thoughts in a system of signs, we should find what many are pleased to consider the barbarous Scythians or Susians?[1]

Let me add that this latter opinion concerning the ancient Scythians has been accepted by moderns

---

sound is unknown, and which was the real indication of the animals. The initial group belonged to all animals, the final group to all names which were ideographically written.

[1] It is but fair to add that if Dr. Lottner's view be correct, that the second cuneiform language was that of Susiana, these remarks require modification. The resemblances to other Turanian languages, as they are vaguely described, are also called in question by sceptics. The whole controversy, as to the origin of the nation whose language forms the second column in the inscriptions, has been fairly summed up by Spiegel (*Eranische Alterthumskunde*, vol. i., pp. 381-7). He does not, in my opinion, allow weight enough to the influence which these inventors of the cuneiform system must have had on the Persians. ..

on very weak authority. In his *Histoire des Perses*, compiled from Oriental sources, the Comte de Gobineau shows[1] that the Chinese, Persian, and Indian traditions concerning these northern nations are quite consistent, and assert Hyrcania to have been covered with flourishing cities and rich harvests. The Iranians also asserted their original home to have possessed midsummer days equal in length to two winter days.[2] This would imply nearly 48° of northern latitude—a district now strictly Siberian, and sparsely inhabited by Turkoman hordes.

Despite the brilliant investigations of M. de Saulcy, M. Jules Oppert, and the continued researches of Westergaard, a great deal yet remains to be done in this branch of the subject. These scattered Asiatic dialects are by no means so thoroughly understood as those of the Aryan and Semitic types; and there are, besides the transcripts deciphered by Westergaard, other texts found in Susiana, in Armenia near Lake Van, and elsewhere, which reveal to us at least two strange dialects, that yet await the wand of the philological enchanter to call them into life.

But we must revert to the history of the discoveries. The labours of Westergaard and Hincks proved that the second column was indeed a translation of the first, from which it appeared certain

---

[1] Vol. i., p. 294.
[2] Cf. Spiegel's (translation of the) *Avesta*, vol. i., p. 62.

that the third column would contain the same sense also. But what was its language, and in what character was it written? The careful investigations of the learned proved, (1) that the graphic system was the same as that of the second column, for out of 109 signs in the second system they could identify 97 in the third; and (2) it was discovered that the language was yet quite distinct, and that it presented difficulties which totally baffled those that at first approached it. As these difficulties seemed to be greatly increased by more recent researches, so the importance of the language in the third column suddenly rose into the foremost place by the discoveries of Botta and Layard in Mesopotamia. These explorers found the sites and ruins of Nineveh and Babylon; and among the remains that were exhumed were thousands of inscriptions on brick and on sculptures—not in three languages, but in one, and that evidently the third language of the Persian records. This proved what had long been suspected, that the language was Assyrian—the speech of Nebuchadnezzar and Sennacherib—and that when deciphered it would give us, not merely an additional version of the acts of Darius and Xerxes, but the annals of an older Empire, and of a still more remarkable epoch in the history of man.

It is not the design of this Essay to attempt a description of the great ruins examined by

Botta, Layard, and Oppert. Their accounts have been published, and are easily accessible. The finest specimens of the architecture and other fine arts of Assyria are also to be seen in the British Museum, which most readers have opportunities of visiting. I shall confine myself to the inscriptions on these remains, and the system of writing employed in them — a subject which has hardly been treated in any popular English book, so far as I know.[1]

In the first place, it was plain, from the trilingual inscriptions, that this writing was, in part at least, ideographic; for one sign corresponded in many cases to a whole word of Persian, and especially to such words as *king* and *god*, which might fairly be represented by a symbol. It was also plain that it was read from left to right, because the signs were squeezed and crowded at the right extremity of many lines, while this never was the case at the left end; and again, some words could be easily read by phonetic principles, comparing them letter for letter as they occurred in the various proper names. This was done by MM. Löwenstern,

---

[1] The most readable accounts of the progress of the discovery are (1), Jules Oppert, *Expédition scientifique en Mésopotamie*, vol. ii., pp. 1, *sqq.*; and the following works of M. Joachim Ménant, viz., (2), *La Lecture des textes assyriens*, in vols. iii. and iv. of the *Revue archéol.*, new series (1861); (3), *Les Écritures cunéiformes*, Paris, 1864, pp. 164, *sq.*; (4),

Botta, and De Saulcy, long before the Behistun inscription was published. To M. De Saulcy—a fearless and independent worker, who never kept back his information in order to secure a reputation for himself, and who valued the progress of his science higher than his own glory—was due the first *bonâ fide* translation of an Assyrian text. M. Botta[1] had led the way by determining 𒀸𒐕 as the sign of the plural, 𒈾 as that of the suffix of the first person, besides the groups for *king* and *people*, and many other similar points of importance. But M. De Saulcy's *Memoir on the Inscription of Elvend*, in September, 1849, was the first systematic translation.

Dr. Hincks established, in 1850, the syllabic character of the signs—a point obscurely apprehended by De Saulcy, and even afterwards by Sir H. Rawlinson, but which was in truth the basis of all farther progress, as it exploded the theory of *homophones*, by showing that different vowels were applied. It was not till 1851, when the fortress was,

---

the same author's great treatise in the *Mémoires présentés par divers savants à l'Académie d'Inscriptions*, &c., vol. vii., Paris, 1868. These treatises show a marked progress, and the last named is by far the most complete and satisfactory, scientifically speaking. For ordinary readers, and as containing the history of the Persian and Scythic deciphering also, the third work is the shortest and the cheapest, and suitable to any library

[1] *Journal asiatique* for 1847.

so to speak, already stormed, that Sir. H. Rawlinson published[1] his great Essay on the Assyrian part of the Behistun inscription. This long text not only brilliantly corroborated the previous results, but added such a list of proper names that ninety remained in the unmutilated parts of the Assyrian copy. This was surely a great stock. Had Champollion been given ninety Egyptian names, instead of those of Ptolemy and Cleopatra, how quickly could he have proceeded!

But while Assyrian scholars had a great advantage here, it was counterbalanced by great perplexities. In the phonetic part of the language they could proceed well enough, but when they came to ideographs, they had not the clear and well drawn image, of which any one might see the meaning, but a set of conventional signs, which suggested objects to the Assyrians, but which had long since lost all similitude in any eyes but theirs. In fact, so far removed are these signs from pictures, that the hieroglyphic origin of the system was not proved till there were monuments discovered in an archaic style, drawn in plain lines, and which evidently were but little altered from the original sketches of the objects. Ker Porter even said there was a strictly hieroglyphic inscription at Persepolis, but unfortunately no copy of it

---

[1] *Journal of the Royal Asiatic Soc.*, vol. xiv., part i.

has yet reached Europe. **There is,** however, **a very** curious document on a brick in the British Museum, published by **Sir H. Rawlinson, where** three objects, now **of unknown use,** are drawn, **with their** single **cuneiform equivalent after** them. It was, in fact, **a direction to** the Assyrians what the equivalent meant; and although the three objects are different, the cuneiform equivalent is the same in **each case.**

This brings us to **the second great difficulty,** first discovered by **Sir H.** Rawlinson **in translating** the great inscription of Darius, that **many of the** signs, even when used phonetically, **were polyphonic**—that is, had several distinct values. **Not only were men** in doubt whether they were **to be** used ideographically **or** phonetically, but when it **was** settled **that they were mere** syllables, their **value was uncertain.** Thus the sign ⟪ was found in some proper names to **mean** *man*, in some *nis*. At **last an example was** found **in** the transcription **of the word Achaemenid, where in the** same word, **and in** two succeeding syllables, the same **sign was put** for *man* **and for** *nis*.[1] It was not enough then to ascertain **one meaning for a syllable;** often **four or five** different sounds were represented **by it.**[2]

$$\text{'}\mathord{\mathrm{\prod}}\ \ \mathord{\mathrm{\models}}\ \ \langle\!\langle\ \ \langle\!\langle\ \ \langle\!|\!-$$
a – χa – man – nis – si

[2] If, as was just now stated, we find three different objects

How was this difficulty to be overcome? It was conquered, not by trilingual inscriptions, but by the vast number of copies of the same Assyrian sentences, found on the bricks of Nineveh and Babylon. Among these there are often twelve or fifteen identical in sense, and in most of the characters; but differing in that the polyphonic sign is in some transcribed into its phonetic elements, and thus its sound is determined.[1] The sign for *man*, for example, is replaced by the simple signs for *ma* and *an*, which never vary, and it is thus determined. For after long and tedious investigations it was found that although almost all the signs were polyphonic, they never represented two different *simple* syllables, that is, syllables composed of two letters. If a sign then means a simple syllable, it can mean no other simple syllable.[2] If this were not the case, the writing would have been as unintelligible to the Assyrians as to us. The many and various tran-

---

represented by one cuneiform sign, probably it would have three different pronunciations, according as it was applied to them in turn.

[1] These varying copies of the same text may be compared to the varying copies of the Egyptian Funeral Ritual, by which homophones were discovered. But the problem was inverted. In Egyptian several signs represented the same sound; in Assyrian one sign represented several sounds.

[2] This law has been most clearly stated and explained by M. Joachim Ménant in his great Treatise on Assyrian, published by the French Academy. Cf. also his *Écrit. cunéif.*, p. 296.

scriptions in different places of such names as Nebuchadnezzar and Nabopolassar have been of great use, and so scholars are at last able to construct tables of the different sounds for these polyphonic signs.

And yet there are difficulties greater than this. It is perplexing enough to hesitate between several sounds; it is still worse to hesitate between an ideographic and a phonetic value. The Egyptians lessened the difficulty by adding very clear determinative signs, such as the open mouth, or the walking legs, or the speaking man. The Assyrians condescended to no such explanation. Again, the Egyptian ideograph was like the object it represented, and above all, if the picture phonetically represented a syllable, it was always the first syllable in the name of the object depicted; so that when Champollion found the names preserved in Coptic, he was able to obtain the phonetic values of the signs. But in the present case the language was lost altogether, and so was the image of the original object; but this was of little consequence, for when men came to compare the ascertained phonetic values of the ideographs with the Assyrian or Semitic names of the objects they suggested, they were found not to correspond at all.

This most curious fact will be best illustrated by a comparison of the proper names in the trilingual inscriptions. So long as the Assyrians were transcribing Persian names, they used phonetic characters. Darius and Xerxes meant nothing more to them than they do to us. But when they came to write down the names of Assyrian chiefs, mentioned in the history of Darius, they recurred to their more favourite way of describing them by ideographs; for among the old Semitic nations especially, proper names preserved their meaning in full vigour, and were not mere conventional sounds to indicate individuals. The reader will remember how carefully the old Hebrew names in Scripture are explained, and their derivations and reasons added. So it was with the Assyrians. Babilu was *the house of God*, Nidintabel *the gift of Bel*, and Nebuchadnezzar, which they pronounced Nebuchodrossor, meant *Nebo protects the crown*. Such ideas could be well expressed by ideographs, and in fact for oft-recurring names this was a short and compendious form, as compared with their very clumsy syllabic system. Accordingly such names as Nebuchodrossor are generally represented by a set of ideograms—in this case of god, and of a crown, and of protection. But when the name was first found written in this way, men applied to each sign its known phonetic value, and they read, not Nebuchodrossor, but *An pa sa du sis*. There could be no doubt about the name, or the intention of the syllables; as in other inscriptions these ideographs were replaced by the proper phonetics of the name. Here then was the result. The signs when used as sounds, had nothing at all to say to the signs when used as pictures. How was this possible? How could their name for God be *Ilu*, and its sign be used for *an*?

A comparison with the Scythian or Median inscriptions showed how this incongruity arose. It disclosed the strange fact that the least civilised of the three nations, as was supposed, had nevertheless been the originators of cuneiform writing, and that the whole system had been borrowed by the Assyrians from these Susians or Scythians, who had completed it at an age more remote than the earliest accounts we possess of Babylon. So, for example, the sign for God was borrowed both as such (ideographically), and also as representing phonetically the syllable *an*, and used in a language where the two meanings were completely estranged. For in the original language *an* was merely the first syllable of *Annap*, which meant God. But in Assyrian God was *Ilu*.

Let me endeavour to make these facts plainer by an illustration. There are still an important set of ideographs in our graphic system, and these are our numerals. The sign 5 means ∴, however pronounced, whether by the Englishman *five*, by the Frenchman *cinq*, or by the German *fünf*. There is also a habit in geographical books of designating square miles by a little figure □, and towns by ⊙. Suppose now that we had preserved the habit of using these ideographs in names, and that we had a town called *Ten-mile-town* (as we have an Irish town called Five-mile-town), which we wrote down in this way, X-☐-☉. But also suppose that we had borrowed these signs from the French in two ways, both to represent ideographically the number 10 and the mile and the town, and the first two also as phonetic signs for *di* and *li* (the first sounds of *dix* and *lieue*). And let me suppose that in spite of spelling, the sign for *di(x)* was used in writing all words when the *sound* was wanted, such as *inXcent*, *inXpendent*, X-☐-*a* (Delia), and so forth. In these cases the sign X would be used phonetically, while in such terms as X-☐-town, and X-fold, it appeared ideographically.[1]

Let us suppose farther that our civilisation had decayed, that our language and history had been forgotten, that our cities lay in ruins, and that thousands of years hence the learned of some newer race began to study, as we do now, the history of the past; and in doing so that, through the genius

---

[1] I may add, for completeness sake, that the sign X is dreadfully polyphonic; for besides the meanings I have imagined, it means the sound *x*, and also ideographically the process of *multiplication*. These complexities I omit in the text, lest my illustration should defeat its object, though they make the example much more perfect. If the sign X were used to represent the phonetic values *ten* and *ex* promiscuously, a decipherer, on meeting conX(t)ion, would hesitate between *connexion* and *contention*, and would be greatly perplexed with XXT (*extent*); and yet these very difficulties have been encountered in Assyriology.

of some second Grotefend, and the accidental preservation of monuments, a knowledge of the French language had been with difficulty attained. Let us suppose that in trying to proceed from the French language to a knowledge of ours, they had found some bilingual inscription, in which the sign X occurred constantly in various words, among which was the proper name X-☐-a (Delia) ; while the other words (inXcent, &c.,) would be *translated* from French, this last would be *transcribed*. And from a knowledge of the French language, they would at once read X-☐-a correctly, and discover that we had borrowed these signs from the French, and that we used them for the sounds of *di* and *li*.

But when they came in some other inscriptions to X-☐-☉, and tried to read it, they would find that the natural reading *Di-li*-town was in sound strange, and unlike English in character, perhaps even quite at variance with other transcripts of the name which were written out by letters. What would men conclude? Evidently that we had borrowed these signs, not only as phonetics, but as ideographs, and that they must have recourse to other means to ascertain how we pronounced the idea X, and what was the idea meant by ☐, as well as its pronunciation. If they found another copy of the inscription, written *Ten*-☐-*town*, they would discover the right sound of X, or they might find it written out in the case of *tenfold* and transfer the sound to the word under dispute;

and if they found an old map of Dublin, and saw the sign □ with *square* written inside it, they would imagine they had made a great discovery, and think that the word should be read *X-Square-town*. And it would be supposed, of course, to point to the fact that this puzzling old place had ten squares within its precincts. But then suddenly a new document might turn up, where it was written *X-mile-town*, and then there would be a great conflict between the man who discovered the meaning *square* and the discoverer of the new inscription; and it would seem so absurd to call a place Ten-mile-town (for what place could have been so long except London), that most men would side with the *square* hypothesis, and it would only be after many corroborations that the real sense of the ideograph would be definitely settled.

This illustration will give some idea of the *sort* of difficulty produced by the Assyrian ideographs. But no single illustration could possibly embrace the enormous complications, the endless varieties, the confusion produced by the many hundreds of signs used in this strange system, some ideographically, some phonetically, some polyphonically, with apparently no guide to unravel the confusion.

It was only after this illustration was worked out, that I became aware of an actual living instance of the whole process at the present day, an instance which has verified all the hypotheses of the cuneiform decipherers, and retorted all the ridicule directed against them upon their critics. The Japanese, Coreans, and several other adjoining nations, who speak a different language from the Chinese, borrowed the cumbrous graphic system of the latter, as soon as they came in contact with them. A great part of the Chinese system is ideographic. In his *Archives paléographiques*,[1] M. Léon de Rosny, one of the highest authorities on such questions, has addressed to M. Jules Oppert a remarkable letter, summing up the numerous points of analogy between the method used by these nations in borrowing a graphic system, and that of the Assyrian writing. The Japanese borrow the Chinese ideographs, and generally pronounce them quite differently. When there are many meanings for one ideograph, they add a phonetic sign giving the final sound of the word intended. They sometimes, however, use the Chinese ideographs as mere phonetic signs *representing the sound of the Chinese name of the object depicted*, as if for example, we were to borrow the sign 4 from the Germans, and use it to write the sound *fear* (vier). It is impossible to conceive a more striking corroboration of the alleged eccentricities of the Assyrian writing.

---

[1] Cf. 2ᵐᵉ *Livraison*, pp. 90-100. I omit many interesting details.

It may be well to state briefly, in conclusion, what were the *means* by which these difficulties are said to have been overcome ; and as in the case of the hieroglyphics, what *test* we have that they are really overcome. The means employed by learned men are four. (1) The trilingual inscriptions gave them not only the sense of several long passages in Assyrian, but a list of ninety proper names transcribed in the character. (2) As Champollion ascertained the variations in hieroglyphics, by comparing the various versions of the Book of the Dead, so a careful comparison of a great number of versions of the same words differing in signs, and of different words containing the same signs, explained the difficulties about polyphony. And it may here be added, that this same comparison led Dr. Hincks to the discovery that Assyrian (like Scythian) was written in syllables, and that where previous explorers had thought they found homophones, there was really a variation in the vowel. There were, for instance, not several signs for the sound *b*, but these signs represented *Ba*, *Bi*, *Bu*, &c. He thus discovered, by the variations in the writing of the same name in different places, that Nineveh, Babylon, and other cities differed in dialect, and these differences have now been laid down and explained. (3) There were discovered at Babylon a number of little grammatical documents on bricks, called *syllabaria*, where a list of characters is given, with the phonetic sound explained in simple syllables at one side, and its sound, when used ideographically, at the other. The graphic system required explanation to the people themselves, for it was used not in sacred matters alone, but also for ordinary purposes. And strange to say, far from feeling ashamed that they could invent no better system, or being conscious of its defects, the king who publishes these instructive tables, declares that the graphic system was given by the grace of the gods, and is explained by him as a boon to his people. Nevertheless, the learned men of our day have discovered occasional blunders in some of these tables, and have, by comparison with existing inscriptions, shown that even the Assyrians could not thread their way without error through so difficult a task. (4) A great source of help, increasing rapidly with our knowledge, is the distinctly Semitic character of the Assyrian language.[1] Whatever doubts may be felt about

---

[1] This point has been satisfactorily demonstrated by Hincks' articles on the Assyrian pronouns and verbs, in 1854-5, and the Assyrian grammar of Jules Oppert, first published in the *Journal asiatique*, in 1860. It has been demonstrated too in the face of the theory of Luzzato that the language was Sanskritic (*Le Sanscritisme de la langue assyrienne*, Padua, 1849) and of the negative scepticism of M. Renan, first announced in his *Histoire Comparée des Langues sémitiques*, p. 71, *sq.*, and afterwards in three papers in the *Journal des Savants* for 1859.

the parentage of the Egyptian language, the Scripture statement that Assur was descended from Shem is certainly correct. The roots, the declensions, the conjugations, all show a distinctly Semitic type, so that now many readings of polyphonic syllables can be rejected as producing combinations foreign to Semite instincts. And still more often, unknown or uncertain signs can be guessed, because a certain articulation corresponds with the grammatical analogies of the Hebrew, Aramaic, and Arabic, with which Assyrian is so closely connected. It is very difficult to put this point so as to make it weigh with untrained minds; but to men who have studied the character and complexion of any class of languages, especially the Semitic, the argument from the affinities of sister dialects must ever have the greatest influence.

So much concerning the means of the discovery. As to the tests of it—the proofs that all these discoveries are genuine and trustworthy—this very fact, which we quoted as a means of deciphering and explaining cuneiform texts, can be also now cited as affording a proof of the genuineness of the discovery. Let the reader remember that this Semitic character of the language was not anticipated, it was not the result of a foregone conclusion. On the contrary, it is not many years since an essay was written by the Italian scholar Luzzato, to prove that the Assyrian approached the Sanskrit in type.

What then is the honest result at which we have arrived? There are found three columns of parallel inscriptions. Men guess the proper names, and find one of the inscriptions written in an ordinary alphabet. Then the others are read, with the aid of one hundred proper names transcribed in each column, and the perfectly unexpected result is, that one of the languages discovered can be proved the sister of a tongue (Old Bactrian) spoken near the country of the inscriptions at an early period, and the mother of the tongue now there spoken. The second language (as if to prove that there was no system of accommodating the interpretation to preconceived theories) turns out like hardly any known language, with but stray words and processes like Turkish and Hungarian, so that its parentage is as yet uncertain. The third column turns out Semitic, in spite of the attempts to prove it Aryan, and so tallies with the Scriptural statement that Assur was descended from Shem, for in Assyria itself this language is reproduced in thousands of documents.

The reading also of all these languages by the now received processes gives a consistent and satisfactory sense, corroborated historically by Egyptian and Jewish records.

Does the reader require farther proof? If so, he can have it. Even in Grotefend's day there were bilingual inscriptions on vases which Grotefend and Champollion deciphered independently, and read, in cuneiforms and hieroglyphics, the name of Xerxes; and lately, as was noticed in the last Essay,[1] the remarkable discovery of pillars set up by Darius, when he cut through the Isthmus of Suez, proves that the Persian language as deciphered translates the Egyptian, as deciphered quite independently.

Once more, Sir H. Rawlinson found a bilingual inscription which came from Phoenicia, not in Persian and hieroglyphics, but in Assyrian and Phoenician. Now Phoenician is a language well understood both in characters and structure. The document is a private contract in Assyrian, to which a Phoenician is witness, and trustee of the settlement, and there was added, while the clay of the tablet was yet soft, an abstract of the acts in Phoenician, giving the names of the contracting parties and other details. All these are found to correspond with the Assyrian inscription when read according to the received methods. This series of tests, when considered conjointly, forms a proof which no scepticism can possibly resist or gainsay.

---

[1] Page 153.

PART II.

CARICATURE OF A BATTLE DEPICTED ON A WALL AT MEDINET-ABOU.

(From the Turin Satiric Papyrus.)

ESSAY V.

Language and Literature of Ancient Egypt.

Ἔρχομαι δὲ περὶ Αἰγύπτου μηκυνέων τὸν λόγον, ὅτι πλέω θωυμάσια ἔχει
ἢ ἄλλη πᾶσα χώρη καὶ ἔργα λόγου μέζω παρέχεται πρὸς πᾶσαν χώρην·
τούτων εἵνεκεν πλέω περὶ αὐτῆς εἰρήσεται.—HERODOTUS.

THE reader who has taken the pains to follow the process of deciphering the old Egyptian language in a previous Essay, will not be content to part from the subject without learning what has been gained by this labour. I propose, therefore, to give a short sketch of the language and literature written in hieroglyphic, hieratic, and demotic characters, confining myself to a mere literary description of the documents, as a discussion of the historical inferences they suggest would be in fact to write a complete history of ancient Egypt. As to the language we shall not here attempt any analysis of its grammar, but rather seek to establish its connexion with other known tongues, and its position in the linguistic table of human speech.

§ 1. *Character of the Language.* — It is well known that in seeking to determine the affinities of a language the names of objects are not the resemblances of most value. Every nation borrows such words easily from its neighbours. Sometimes even the majority of the words of a language are not its own. For example, a great part of the English language consists of Norman French, yet the tongue is distinctly Saxon. So also modern Turkish has borrowed a great proportion of its vocabulary from Arabic and Persian, and yet Turkish is in no way a Semitic language. For both the English and the Turks retain certain classes of words, which nations are not in the habit of borrowing from their neighbours, such as pronouns and numerals. These are in use at the first formation of a language, and are therefore sure to be fixed prior to any intercourse among different nations. But besides the indication of these words when separate, a language can be known (as to origin) by its inflexions, by the way in which it forms its cases and its numbers, and conjugates its verbs; for even when the root is borrowed, it is treated according to methods which each people frames for itself, and which it seems never to abandon.[1]

If we examine the old Egyptian language from

[1] Professor Max Müller goes so far as to say, in the first vol. of his *Lectures on the Science of Language*, that a *mixed language*, that is to say, with inflexions and grammar compiled from different languages, *is impossible*. It is, however, generally held by learned men that the Pehlvi language of Persia, which came into

any or from all these points of view, we shall, I think, be led to the conclusion that it is related, though remotely, to the Semitic family of language, of which Arabic, Hebrew, Aramaic, and Assyrian, are the recognised branches.

This conclusion falls short of that held by two of the greatest authorities—Lepsius and Schwartze—who believe it to be equally cognate to the Indo-European family, and who postulate a time when these distinct groups of tongues were united. From this common stock they believe the Egyptian language to have sprung, anterior to other separations, and by this means they account for the alleged similarities to both families, especially in those numerals which appear remotely alike.[1] "The Egyptian language," says Dr. Lepsius, in his latest exposition of the theory, "points indubitably to the fact that the Egyptian race is of the same original stock not only as the Semitic, but as the Indo-European

---

use under the Sassanid kings, circ. A.D. 300, is compounded in grammar, as well as vocabulary, of old Persian and of Aramaic, two languages of totally distinct families. This case may possibly be unique, and the language appears in any case to have been only a literary dialect, suggested and developed in an age of artificial taste and general decay.

[1] Cf. R. Lepsius, *Zwei sprachvergleichende Abhandlungen*, Berlin, 1836, Schwartze, *das alte Aegypten*, vol ii., passim. See also Lepsius, "*Ueber die Annahme eines Steinalters in Aegypten*," in his *Zeitschrift* for July, 1870, p. 92, from which the following passage in the text is translated.

nations. It is a part of the Hamitic group, to which belong in addition the Libyan tribes scattered over North Africa, the ancestors of the Tuarik, Hausa,[1] and other of the Atlas tribes, as well as also the Ethiopians, ancestors of the Bischari, Galla tribes, &c. These three great Noachite families of nations, as they may be conventionally designated—which were distinguished from the beginning by a deeper capability of culture, and which became the exclusive actors of the world's history, as they yet are and ever shall be—went forth from a common home in Asia like a new wave upon the substratum of an earlier population already spread over the face of the globe. The comparison of their language, in concordance with their geographical position, teaches us that the Hamitic race was the first of these to leave its Asiatic cradle. Of the Egyptian again the Upper Egyptian branch necessarily invaded the Nile valley before the Lower Egyptian which pressed after it. But the Ethiopic preceded both, and before them all went the Hamites that dwell round Habesch, [afterwards] colonised by Semites from Arabia. All these immigrants brought from their original home their language already developed, with its flexions, and with its indication of grammatical genders—a pregnant distinction separating them from all non-Noachite languages. They doubt-

---

[1] Dr. Lottner assures me that this language has no relationship to the others mentioned, or to Semitic.

less also brought with them a higher degree of social culture, by which they had already been raised far above the hunting stage of the wild primitive races with their rude flint weapons. We cannot indeed determine what time elapsed since the immigration of the southermost Africo-Asiatic people into the Nile valley down to that of the North Egyptian race, nor again from this down to the building of the temple of Phtha in Memphis, and the commencement of written chronological state-annals and calendars, under or soon after Menes, in the sixth millenium from the present day ; but [though we cannot fix it accurately] it is surely to be reckoned with more probability according to thousands, than according to hundreds of years."

This seductive theory, though also maintained with much ability by Bunsen in his ponderous work on Egypt, appears to me to rest upon too many hypotheses. I cannot find, after a careful examination of the evidence, either that an original unity of the Indo-European and Semitic faculties of speech is proved, or that the Egyptian language bears any structural likeness to the former, if we discard the few verbal analogies on which that unity is assumed. It is not difficult to discover remote resemblances if we start with a preconceived theory as to the unity of language ; but apart from this influence, any unprejudiced student will find the Egyptian and Aryan varieties of speech so profoundly apart in genius, in complexion, and in form of thought and expression, that a greater difference could hardly be conceived among *grammatical* languages.

When we come to compare Egyptian with the Semitic family, the case appears very different. Not only is there a great analogy between their graphic expression, which omits many vowels, and writes the words as it were in skeleton, but the actual coincidences in vocabulary are so numerous as to be hardly explicable by intercourse, and by exchange of names. Several hundred such coincidences are collected by Bunsen,[1] and there are few sentences of old Egyptian which do not contain words reminding us of Hebrew or Aramaic. If the Vicomte de Rougé is right, the farther back we trace Egyptian, the stronger this likeness appears.[2] He also asserts it to be chiefly shown in syntax.

The close resemblance in the pronouns has long been remarked. *I* in Egyptian is *anuk*, in Hebrew anoχi. *You* is *entuk*, almost the same as in biblical Chaldee. The form for *he*, which is *entuf*,

---

[1] I am not a sufficient linguist to criticise this list, or to say how many of the derivations are doubtful. The reader will find it in Bunsen's *Egypt's Place*, &c., v., pp. 748-73. Dr. Ebers says (*Aegypten und die Bücher Moses*', i., p. 45) that he has found 300, but postpones his precise conclusions, pending the completion of Brugsch's Dictionary and other evidence.

[2] *Mémoire sur l'inscription du tombeau d'Ahmés*, p. 195.

is fuller than that of any Semitic language; but I fancy these shorter forms have not reached us in their original condition. *We* was probably (as in demotic) *aunen*, and similar to the Arabic. With regard to pronominal suffixes, not only is the principle of the Egyptian language that of the Semitic, but in some cases the particular suffixes are the same. I shall not cite the numerals, as the similarities with Aryan numerals make the whole question uncertain, but shall merely note one more detail. The feminine termination in Egyptian is *t* or *th*, which is well known to have been the older feminine ending in Hebrew.

These and other such analogies, especially in pronominal suffixes, appear to indicate that Egyptian has a real affinity to the Semitic languages, though it is certainly a very distinct language, and not connected by the close bonds that unite Hebrew, Aramaic, Arabic, and Assyrian with one another. Many great linguists have maintained this view, which is certainly the most reasonable and best supported by the facts. It agrees also with part of the former theory we have mentioned, and is in so far maintained by Lepsius and Bunsen. It has been specially defended by Benfey, Ernst Meier, P. Bötticher, Carl Lottner, F. Müller, and the Vicomte de Rougé.[1] It would, however, be unjust to the reader

---

[1] Cf. Meier, *Hebräisches Wurzelwörterbuch* (appendix), Bötticher, *Wurzelforschungen*, de Rougé, *loc. cit.*, &c., &c. From a delicate analogy drawn between the Hebrew and Egyptian modes of

to recommend it without stating that several important writers have protested against the insufficiency of the evidence, and have denied that any such affinity has been really proved. When I mention under this class the great names of Pott, Ewald (of late less positive), and Renan, he will see how difficult it is to establish any certain conclusion on this obscure problem.[1]

In spite, however, of these objections, which are, indeed, becoming fainter of late years, I am persuaded that the Semitic affinities of Egyptian will yet be shown clearly by a closer analysis of the language. Many interesting inferences would naturally follow concerning the prehistoric and forgotten life of the primitive Egyptians. Ancient as were their records, they preserve no recollection whatever of any immigration, and consider themselves as sprung

---

expressing *times* (in the sense of repetition), it is obvious that the authority of M. Chabas is on the same side. "Entre l'égyptien," he says, "et les dialectes sémitiques il existe plus de rapports qu'on ne s'imagine généralement." *Mélanges égypt.*, i., p. 25. It must be repeated, at the same time, that the resemblance is but remote and general, nor is there any greater resemblance between Assyrian, which is I suppose the oldest form (historically) of Semitic speech known, and Egyptian, than between the latter and the Aramaic dialect. Dr. Ebers indeed asserts that Aramaic (or Chaldee, as he calls it,) has the greatest number of affinities with Egyptian. Cf. his *Aegypten*, &c., i., pp. 43-46.

[1] The curious student will do well to consult Renan's *Histoire comparée des Langues sémitiques*, pp. 80-89, where some of the

from the gods of the country and indigenous to its
soil.¹ Yet here, as in the case of the Greeks, who
laboured under the same delusion, it is probable,
I would almost say certain, that they came from
the common home of all the Semites, somewhere
in Asia. Not only their language, but their physical type points to this conclusion—a physical type
as distinct from the African in the oldest monuments as it now is. By one of those strange laws
of nature, no series of invasions or conquests seem
able to destroy, or even to modify, the Egyptian
type beyond certain narrow limits. All competent
physiologists who have examined the mummies ana-
tomically assure us that the modern Fellahs are un-

---

above-named authorities are correctly cited, as far as I have been
able to verify them, and where the evidence is fairly discussed.
Renan's extraordinary obstinacy in not recognising the Semitic
character of Assyrian destroys, in my opinion, the weight of his
sceptical doubts in the present instance.

¹ M. Ed. Naville, in the Preface to his *Textes relatifs au mythe
d'Horus* (Paris, 1870), thinks that the allusions to Horus invading Egypt from the south may point to a pre-historic immigration, and civilisation of Egypt from Ethiopia. This theory is
however so completely contradicted by all the other evidence we
possess, that it cannot possibly be maintained on such isolated
grounds. The invasion of Horus must therefore point to some
later fact, perhaps to the restoration of his worshippers, who
had retired into the south after the expulsion of the Hyksos.
I see that Dr. Ebers (*Aegypten und die Bücher Moses'*) believes some of the Egyptians to have come indeed originally
from Asia, but to have entered Africa from South Arabia, and so
to have colonised the Nile valley in one sense from the south.

mistakably their direct descendants.[1] M. Brugsch has an interesting discussion on the gradual change of type shown in the Egyptians by their monuments.[2] They appear to have come from Asia stouter and shorter than they became in time through the action of the climate. But when he states that the end of the twelfth dynasty is the turning point, it must be remembered that there is a considerable gap and confusion during the Shepherd occupation which followed soon after, and that the type in the New Empire may have been changed by new infusions of Asiatic blood and by mixture of races.

The fact that the linguistic resemblances apply to all the recognised Semitic dialects equally, some of them reminding us of Aramaic, some of Hebrew, and some of Arabic, is likewise of much importance. It coincides with the belief suggested by other facts

---

[1] A parallel case on a smaller scale is that of the Irish, who have absorbed many settlements of foreigners, and have only been modified in language. It would seem as if the *Atavism* of (comparatively) indigenous races was stronger than that of vagrants. The anatomical evidence on the origin of the Egyptians has been collected by G. Ebers, *op. cit.*, i., pp. 46-54. All craniologists agree that the type differs from that of the negroes. Prof. Czermak has given a most accurate account of the dissection of two mummies (*Sitz. ber. der Wiener Akademie* for 1852, p. 427). Every feature separates them from African, and unites them with Caucasian, races. The details are copied by Ebers in full.

[2] *Histoire d'Égypte*, p. 70.

that Egyptian was, so to speak, not a sister, but an aunt of these languages, separated from the mainstock at an earlier period. It was not till I had arrived at this conclusion independently that I became acquainted with Dr. C. Lottner's important papers on the subject, published in the *Transactions of the Philological Society* for 1861. The learned author opens up a new ground of comparison, that of the Berber, Saho, and Galla languages adjoining the Egyptian in Africa. These languages have an unmistakable affinity with Egyptian; they are also declared of one origin with Semitic tongues by all competent linguists, and they afford in many cases the intermediate forms between Egyptian and the proper Semitic dialects. Owing, however, to the great gulf that separates these languages from Semitic, Lottner proposes to call them not dialects of one family, but *sister families* of languages. These conclusions have been further illustrated and corroborated by the researches of Fr. Müller.[1] The comparative tables of forms given in his work appear to me perfectly decisive on the original unity of all these languages. The same conclusions are to be found in the learned work of G. Ebers.[2]

Thus the hieroglyphics may yet be compelled,

---

[1] Published in the linguistic part of the splendid *Account of the Cruise of the Novara* (Vienna, 1867), pp. 53-70.

[2] '*Aegypten und die Bücher Moses,*' i., p. 43 (Leipzig, 1868).

after surrendering their proper meaning from beneath its intricate disguise, to inform us farther of ancient truths, of which the writers were themselves ignorant, for they had forgotten their own origin. The noble type of the Egyptians, their intellectual gifts, and the pure ideas that exist in their religion might have led us to suspect some connexion with the higher races of the globe. But the structure of their speech was an evidence which they could not appreciate, and which owes its recognition to the researches of modern science; for just as accent must betray our birth place, just as his Sibboleth betrayed the Ephraimite, and his speech Peter the Galilean, so the processes of language must convict all nations of their stock and parentage.

I must decline entering farther into the linguistic aspect of Egyptian, which is not the province of an historian, but rather of the scholar who has made comparative grammar his special study. For us it is enough to weigh carefully the evidence adduced, and take the details assured by the independent researches of professed Egyptologists. What has been said above was merely an introduction to a sketch of the contents and style of those Egyptian documents which have been exhumed and translated.

Such a sketch cannot pretend to any completeness. For the papyri are scattered through many collections; they have not been all edited or translated, and such as have become accessible are the subjects of scattered monographs and essays, chiefly devoted to historical and linguistic discussion.[1] With the exception of Brugsch's *Histoire d'Égypte*, which embodies the documents discovered up to the date of its publication (1853), there is, so far as I know, no general collection whatever, and the student must seek for them through the proceedings of learned societies, and the antiquarian periodicals published in France, Germany, Holland, and Italy. The only journal indeed specially devoted to Egyptology, and conducted by MM. Lepsius and Brugsch, concerns itself about linguistic and archaeological details, and does not afford the general student the information he requires, by translating and explaining the documents of interest from a literary point of view. By far the most available information of this kind will be found in the numerous admirable articles published from time to time in the *Revue archéologique*, in the *Mélanges* of M. Chabas, and in

---

[1] Speaking of the similar condition of Assyriology, M. Joachim Ménant observes: "Il est certain que cet empressement que chacun a mis à communiquer promptement le résultat de ses observations a tourné au plus grand profit de la science : c'est la preuve de l'indépendance des premiers essais (viz., the fact that the discoveries are often of doubtful anthorship) et c'est peut-être une des causes les plus directes de la rapidité des progrés qui se sont accomplis pendant ces dix dernières années : je crois avoir déjà compris que la nature des choses imposera long-temps encore ce mode de publication." *Écritures cunéiformes*, p. 11.

the *Essays* of Mr. Goodwin on Hieratic Papyri,[1] and the various papers of Mr. Birch. But these latter valuable papers, the only reliable English publications which I have met, have appeared in scattered journals, or are now many years written, though sundry new Egyptian treasures have since seen the light. It will therefore not appear presumptuous in a weaker hand to attempt the same subject with the increased resources now available, though it is indeed a bold undertaking for any but a professed Egyptologist.

§ 2. *Chronology of the various Graphic Systems.*— A few words will be useful by way of an introduction to this part of the subject, summing up the conclusions of the learned on the chronological limits during which the four distinct graphic systems were employed, in which old Egyptian has unfortunately been concealed.

At what date in the world's history the old full HIEROGLYPHIC[2] writing was developed, no man can tell. The monuments of the third and fourth dy-

---

[1] Viz., in the *Cambridge Essays* for 1858, in the *Revue archéologique* for 1860 and 1861, and in *Fraser's Magazine* for February, 1865. The French article is particularly valuable in giving a connected sketch of the London, Leyden, and Berlin papyri, not elsewhere to be found (*Rev. Arch.*, N. S. ii., pp. 228-34). MM. Pleyte and Rossi's publication of the Turin papyri, when completed, will supply a serious gap.

[2] The following are among the inscriptions which have not

nasties prove that it was then perfectly understood, and freely used. A monument dedicated by king Sent, of the second dynasty, to the memory of Shera, apparently his grandson, is in the Ashmolean Museum at Oxford. Egyptian tradition ascribed to writing a divine origin prior to Menes, and spoke of his immediate successors as the authors of books.

All these things point to a very early discovery indeed, not less than 3500 years before our era, and probably much older. Though other shorter methods were afterwards devised, this pictorial representation of the language, especially in the linear variety, never lost its dignity and importance in state documents and inscriptions, and in religious compositions. Regarded at last as a sacred character, and accompanied by transcriptions in demotic

---

only been published, but also translated and grammatically explained, by MM. Birch, De Rougé, Chabas, and others, so that they will be useful to the student as a chrestomathy:

(1) *Inscription du Tombeau d'Ahmès.* Paris, 1852.
(2) *Statuette naophore du Vatican.* Rev. arch. for 1851.
(3) *Stele in honor of the god Chonsu.* Journal asiat., 1856-8.
(4) *Inscriptions des Mines d'or.* Chalon sur Saône, 1862.
(5) *Inscriptions de Toutmès iii.* Rev. arch. for 1867.
(6) *Mémoire sur les attaques dirgées vers l'Égypte, &c.* Rev. arch. for 1867.
(7) *Die Pianchi stele, Münch. Akad. Abhandl.* for 1869.

To specify all the texts published, or the inscriptions translated, would be endless. I have only cited the latest versions of those above enumerated.

and in Greek, it was still used in the dedications of temples by the Roman emperors, whose names are expressed in the old royal rings down to Decius,[1] and possibly even later, down to the usurpation of the kingdom of Egypt by Achilles, who was put to death at Alexandria by Diocletian in the year 296, A. D. It is not improbable that the rude reorganization of the whole country, in consequence of its insurrection, by the cruel emperor, may have been accompanied by a persecution of the national religion, and a consequent proscription of the sacred writing.[2] The spread of Christianity at the same time in Egypt, owing to the sympathy of the Egyptians with fellow-martyrs, and their dislike of the persecutor, must have secured the disuse of the character. For it teemed with mythological allusions and figures disgusting and sinful to the early Christians.

We are equally unable to fix the first use of HIERATIC[3] writing, which was evidently determined

---

[1] Cf. Lepsius in his *Zeitschr.* for 1870, p. 25.

[2] Cf. Lenormant, *Rev. Arch.*, vol. xxi., p. 106. His reading of the name Achilles does not, however, seem to me at all certain.

[3] General descriptions of the hieratic papyri in the various museums and collections are not easily to be found. The following indications (chiefly confined to foreign publications) may therefore be not unwelcome to the student:

(1.) *Berlin. Les papyrus du Musée de Berlin,* F. Chabas, Chalons sur Saône, 1863; and in *Lepsius' Zeitschr.* for 1864, p. 100,

by the literary wants of a reading and writing age.
There are, it is true, long documents in linear hieroglyphics; but the demand upon the scribes' time was
too enormous even for the old Egyptians, and a
cursive hand was substituted in writing lengthy
documents on papyrus. The great body of Egyptian *literature*, in the stricter sense, has reached us
through this character, the reading of which presents great difficulties, and is only to be determined
by resolving it into its prototype hieroglyphics.
That this writing was in use before the time of the
shepherd kings, and under the old empire, is not
proved by any probable inference from the allusions

sq.; Mr. Goodwin's *Story of Saneha* in *Fraser's Mag.*, for February, 1865, and his essay in the *Rev. arch.*, N. S., vol. ii., containing a short sketch of the first four papyri in the collection, which are remarkable as belonging to the days of the Old Empire. The papyri themselves are splendidly reproduced in Lepsius' *Denkmäler*, part vi., pl. 104, *sq.* A very ancient papyrus in the possession of Dr. Lepsius has not yet been published. M de Rougé identifies the writing with that of the Prisse papyrus.

(2.) *British Museum.* Mr. Goodwin's papers on hieratic papyri in the Cambridge Essays for 1858, and the *Revue archéologique*, N. S., vols. ii. and iv. I may add M. Chabas' *Voyage d'un Égyptien*, &c. (Berlin), 1860, and M. Lauth's *Moses der Ebräer* (appendix i.) on the Pap. Anastasi, i.: the Vicomte de Rougé, in *Rev. arch.* for Oct. 1852, on the Pap. d'Orbiney, and in the *Recueil de Travaux relatifs à la philologie égypt*, &c. (Part i., Paris, 1870), &c., on the Pap. Sallier iii. Mr. Birch (*Rev. arch.* for 1859), and afterwards M. Chabas (*Mélanges*, vol. iii., *Spoliation des Hypo-*

to royal authors in Manetho, but by the actual preservation of several hieratic papyri of the old empire, some at the Museum of Berlin, another presented by M. Prisse to the Bibliothèque Impériale, and which purports to have been a collection of moral treatises of far older days, made in the time of the eleventh dynasty. The writing is large and clear, and far nearer to the original hieroglyphics than the later papyri. Nevertheless, it was then a perfectly distinct, and well-developed writing, so that it must have come into use long before the time of Abraham, and not less than 2200 B. C.

---

gées), have translated the Pap. Abbott, and M. Maspero the Hymns to the Nile in the Sallier Papyri. Mr. Birch, and afterwards M. Brugsch (*zwei bilingue Papyri*, Leipzig, 1865), have treated the most important Rhind papyri. Mr. Birch has also discussed (*Zeitschr.* for 1868, p. 108) the Rhind geometrical papyrus, and some of the Salt pap. in Chabas' *Mélanges*.

(3.) *Leyden.* M. Chabas' masterly sketch in Leemans' magnificent *Monuments du Musée des Pays Bas.*, ii., pp. 61-80, supplemented variously in his *Mélanges*. M. Lauth (appendix ii.) has translated fully (perhaps too fully) one of the most important, that numbered i., 344, *verso*. M. Pleyte's *Études égyptologiques*, (Leyden, 1866-70) are also very valuable.

(4.) *Paris.* Beyond the official catalogue, I know of no general description of the papyri, which seem not so valuable a collection as those already mentioned. The Pap. Prisse has been partially treated by M. Chabas (*Rev. arch.*, 1858, and *Zeitschr.* for 1870), but has received its first complete (though somewhat problematical) translation at the hands of Dr. Lauth, in several remarkable articles to be found in the *Sitzungsberichte der Münch-*

Under the kings of the new empire, and about the
date of the exodus of the Hebrews, it received its
greatest development, and had no rival till the
seventh century B. C.,[1] when the great social revolution in the reign of Psamtik (Psammetichus) brought
the demotic character into fashion. For centuries
after, however, it still occurs, sometimes alone, as
in the Papyrus Smith, which is a medical treatise,
with on the back a calendar prepared for the year
114 B. C.; sometimes with a demotic transcription

ener Akademie for the years 1869-70. The judicial Pap. Rollin
has been fully discussed by M. Devéria (*Jour. asiat.*, 1868), and
the Rollin collection in general by Chabas in *Lepsius' Zeitsch.* for
1869, p. 100, *sq.*

(5.) *Turin.* The papyri of this great Museum are now in process of publication by MM. Pleyte and Rossi. Three numbers
have appeared, containing hymns, lists, and letters. M. Devéria
(*Jour. asiat.*, 1866-7) has translated the judicial papyrus, and M.
Chabas (*Spoliation des Hypogeés*, pp. 5-47) has ably criticised his
defects. The catalogue of the dynasties has been best discussed
in Lepsius' *Königsbuch*. M. Lieblein (*deux papyrus hiératiques*,
Christiania, 1868) has commented on some curious lists and
accounts.

(6.) *Egypt.* The collections in the Museum of Boulaq are
just being published by M. Mariette. (Cf. Maspero's review of
the 1st volume in No. 29 of *The Academy*). Mr. Harris' collection,
of great value, especially in relation to Ramses III., has not, so
far as I know, been described. M. Chabas has published its
magical treatise. The Smith papyri at Luqsor are chiefly medical, with an interesting calendar. All the works above cited will
be again referred to in their proper places.

[1] The oldest demotic papyrus we possess is one in the Turin

added, as in the Rhind bilingual papyri, which date from the reign of Augustus.[1]

From Psamtik downwards DEMOTIC[2] was **used to transcribe** hieroglyphic and hieratic papyri and **inscriptions into** the vulgar idiom, **till** the second century A. D.; when **the** dictates of expediency and of simplicity, which must have been **felt by the** literary world of Alexandria long before, were reinforced by the authority and earnestness of Christian prejudices. We can almost watch the **transition from** the obscure and difficult demotic **to the sensible** Coptic alphabet. **We** have demotic **words** transcribed in Greek letters; we have **pure** Coptic

---

Museum, which dates from the forty-fifth year of Psamtik's reign, viz., **620 B. C.** (Cf. **Brugsch,** *Gram. dém.*, p. 200). We can **hardly assume** this to have been necessarily one of the earliest **specimens, especially as it differs** clearly from hieratic, for which reason I have left a margin which might **be extended to** 750 B. C.

[1] These remarks will qualify the statement of Mr. Goodwin (*Cambridge Essays* for 1858, **p. 227**) that hieratic was supplanted **by demotic** about 600 B. C. M. Devéria (in the *Journal asiatique* for **November,** 1867, **p.** 416, *note*) states that the medical treatises of the Pap. Smith date from the Ramessid epoch; **but** Dr. Eisenlohr, who saw them in the spring of **1870,** ascribes them **(hesitatingly) to the** same age as the calendar. (Cf. *Zeitsch.* for 1870, p. 167). Mr. Birch states (*Introd.*, &c., p. 276), that hieratic was as old as **the** fifth **dynasty, and lasted** till the days of the Antonians. I do **not know on** what **precise** evidence he assigns these limits.

[2] On **the materials** accessible in Demotic and Coptic, cf. above pp. 101, *sq.*, and 133, *sq.* I may repeat that many demotic texts

written in the demotic characters, and we have demotic written in Greek letters, with the non-Greek sounds preserving their original signs. This was in reality the Coptic alphabet. With some conventional changes, it uses the Greek letters as far as they will go, and supplies the remainder by simple and consistently-used demotic symbols. Would that the Egyptians had condescended to this piece of common sense centuries earlier! COPTIC, the exclusive character used in Christian Egyptian literature, was the last garb in which the language was clothed.[1]

If we proceed to inquire how far the languages written in these different characters agreed, it appears that hieratic was only a cursive writing of the language found in the hieroglyphics. There were indeed many affixes and particles ordinarily spoken, but left out in the more cumbrous method, which are added in the less tedious hieratic writing, and which are said to make the style of these papyri much more difficult. But it is probably for that

---

are reproduced in Lepsius' *Denkmäler*, and that the most important text yet discovered (the *Romance of Setna*) has been translated in the *Revue archéol.* for 1867-8.

[1] The Christian Egyptians would, of course, object to the older characters as of heathen association. But secular treatises were written in Coptic, though no sacred literature was written in demotic. There are medical and judicial documents mentioned in Zoëga's *Catalogue*.

reason a better representation of the tongue of the old Pharaohs.[1]

Demotic, on the contrary, denotes a rise of the vulgar tongue of the country into literary use, and has been treated in a separate grammar by M. Brugsch. I suppose, as in most other countries, the conservative instincts of the priests and scribes bound up old forms with religious associations, so as to embalm the literary dialect, and preserve it from decay. Meanwhile the common people, having no such check, modified their speech with that secret instinct which linguists have everywhere perceived, but find it so hard to explain. Yet it may be regarded as a remarkable sign of the social revolution, attested by historians to have taken place under Psamtik, that this popular dialect then began to be written in serious documents. The graphic art having been everywhere, and in Egypt particularly, surrounded with sanctity and mystery by the priests who first used it, we can imagine the holy horror of the profession when they were obliged

---

[1] Cf. Chabas' *Mélanges*, i., p. 116. Mr. Goodwin also notices (*Rev. arch.* for 1860, p. 235) the abusive employment of determinatives common in hieratic. The sign which was properly meant to indicate the *sense*, often indicates the *sound* of an object quite different from that really intended by the writing. They were often attached to *phrases*, as well as words. Cf. Chabas in *Zeitsch.* for 1869, p. 55.

to admit the vulgar translation beneath their clumsy and now unintelligible hieroglyphics.[1]

Coptic marks a farther development or decay of the language ; for, though there has been found part of a funeral ritual written in demotic characters, but in the pure Coptic language, yet this is noted as an exception. The explicit division of the language into three literary dialects probably took place in this period. Although it appears that some evidence of their existence has been found in demotic,[2] and though ancient documents tell us that the men of Abou and Athou could scarce understand one another, Champollion has shown with his usual acuteness that in the old Egyptian the same sign was used for the letters which replace one another in the Coptic dialects.

§ 3. *Method of the Present Essay.*—The reader will perhaps be surprised that the consideration of these several species of writing is not here treated

---

[1] Cf. the elegant observations of M. Maspero, in his *Études démotiques* (quoted above, p. 103) on the character of the language written in demotic character.

[2] Cf. on this question Brugsch, *Gram. démotique*, pp. 8 and 81. He was the first to show any linguistic evidence for the dialects prior to the Coptic stage, and thinks they may have been distinct long anterior to the Ptolemies. The discovery was only made through varying Greek transcriptions, the demotic writing itself containing no vestige of different pronunciations. Cf. also Champollion, *Précis*, p. 367, and on the dialects, the observations in a former Essay, pp. 134, *sq.*

separately, along with an account of the literature preserved in each. We are all accustomed to a chronological history of literature, which is in other cases absolutely necessary, in order to show the gradual development of different species of composition at different epochs, and the action of historical causes upon the mental expression of successive ages. To this universal law the literature of Egypt, so far as we now know it, presents a remarkable exception. Though the characters were changed, and the language underwent some modification, the literature, in all its main features, remained the same. The novel, or secular work of amusement, may have predominated in the great literary development of the Ramessid epoch, after the expulsion of the shepherds. Historical accounts of Egypt, such as the work of Manetho, were doubtless stimulated by the learned patronage of the Ptolemies; Christian literature, homilies, and church rituals invaded Egyptian in its Coptic stage; but nevertheless the same type and impress appear in every epoch. Not to speak of the Book of the Dead, of which copies have reached us, dating from the earliest to the latest ages (and in all the graphic systems, with the exception of the Christian Coptic), we can point to other species of composition, which reappear in almost the same form throughout all Egyptian history. Magic formulae, moral treatises, medicinal receipt books, magisterial records—these are preserved to us from all dates; nay, even in Coptic, where the heathen deities are merely supplanted by saints and angels.[1]

This curious but characteristic circumstance will explain the reason why the present sketch is not chronological, but logical, and divided, not according to seasons, but subjects. Its materials are indeed so scanty, and so many epochs of Egyptian history are as yet complete literary blanks, that the former method is almost impossible. But, scanty as are our relics, their striking uniformity, and the fact that even among them repetitions and allusions to the same persons are not uncommon, will suggest to the reader that possibly no other literature would be so adequately represented by so small a number of fragments. In the magical and moral departments, I almost fancy additional discoveries would add little to our knowledge—in novels or historical

---

[1] Intelligent Greeks, like Plato, were greatly struck by this extraordinary uniformity. He says (*Laws*, p. 656, E.): "To this day no alteration is allowed in either of these arts [painting and sculpture] or in music at all. And you will find that their works of art are painted and moulded in the same forms which they had ten thousand years ago; this is literally true, and no exaggeration; their ancient paintings and sculptures are not a whit better or worse than the work of to-day, but are made with just the same skill." There is here a curious mixture of truth and error. No doubt the oldest statues we have discovered are artistically almost the best, but the canon of proportions was distinctly modified at different periods.

romances the variety is greater, and it is in this direction that the literary historian of Egypt must long for more light and for more diligent search.

Most unfortunately, even the scanty documents rescued from the tooth of time are not all accessible, and many of them are lying idle in private collections. Whatever reaches the museums of London, Leyden, Berlin, or Turin, is immediately examined, and generally published and explained by able scholars; but the magnificent collection of Mr. Harris of Alexandria, that of Mr. Smith, an American gentleman resident at Luqsor, and doubtless many other such treasures, are yet almost completely unknown.

§ 4. *Religious Literature.*—It is very easy to determine with what branch of Egyptian literature we should begin our sketch. Important as is the religious literature of any nation, in Egypt it assumes tenfold prominence. There was never a people so extraordinarily δεισιδαίμων. The whole of their life, their government, their society, their art, was interwoven and sustained by religion. And yet there is no study more obscure for modern scholars. It is easy enough indeed to construct theories upon it, but very difficult indeed to reconcile all the facts with any theory. Their great mythological system, replete with a hierarchy of deities, at first sight proclaims them of all men the most polytheistic. But a more careful examination of their literature, especially of their solar hymns, leads us to perceive that under all the luxuriance of gods nothing more may have been meant than to bring out in symbol and in allegory the various qualities and manifestations of one great God, uncreate, eternal, and omnipotent. Some of the more important passages affirming this exalted doctrine will be quoted presently, and the reader will be able to judge for himself.

Whatever the truth may be, I am strongly disposed to question a commonly received opinion, that the simpler doctrine of one God under many forms was an occult belief of the learned, and that the great complication of the Egyptian Ritual was invented or intended for the vulgar. The simpler and higher religion appears to have been preached in the solar hymns, which are not difficult, and not intended for a select few, but published and in popular use, whereas the greatest profusion of distinct deities is brought forward in the so-called Funeral Ritual, which is expressly asserted, and probably intended, to be obscure and deep, and only intelligible to the initiated. This fact corresponds with the general evidence of history, that refinements and complications of theology are seldom understood or appreciated by ordinary men, and that the subtilties invented by schools of priests and monks do not reach beyond the inner circle, where they are certain to arise among a class who devote all their time and learning to explain the inexplicable. All the evidence we possess tells us that during the Pharaonic times the priests took no trouble to teach the complications of their theology to the people, nor did they instruct them in the special adventures or prerogatives of the various gods. This is, in fact, our greatest difficulty in comprehending their real meaning. The names of the gods are but casually mentioned, mostly in stereotyped phrases, and no further clue is given for comprehending their nature.

From this point of view, the temples of the Ptolemaic era, which have but lately occupied the attention of the learned, promise to give us unexpected light. For the temples of Esneh, Edfu, and Dendera are covered with mythological paintings, accompanied by illustrative texts explaining the myths concerning the gods. Whether it be that the Egyptian priests then felt that the people were abandoning the faith of their fathers, and that nothing had been done to make it rational or to explain its import,[1] or whether, as I should conjecture, the loss of political power, and perhaps of judicial and administrative functions, which they possessed under the Pharaohs, turned their intellects to religious

---

[1] Cf. Ed. Naville, *Textes relatifs au mythe d'Horus*, Introd. H. Brugsch, *die geflügelte Sonnenscheibe*, in the *Göttingen Transactions*, vol. xiv., p. 179, and A. Mariette, *Notice, &c., du Musée de Boulaq*, p. 302.

speculation, the **fact is certain, that** these comparatively modern temples **tell us vastly more of** Egyptian theology **than all the** older monuments. But **let us turn from** these reflections to our texts.

§ 5. *The Funeral Ritual.*—I shall separate the religious Literature of Egypt, in accordance with **the** distinction above implied, into *theological* and *devotional* treatises; and of the theological, **by far the** most prominent, though **by no means the most** interesting to the general reader, **is the Book of the** Dead, also called the Funeral **Ritual,** but **most properly** the Book of the Manifestation (of the **soul) to** Light.[1] The earliest copy we possess is in hie-

---

[1] Almost every museum in Europe has specimens of it, and many have published facsimiles. The following are the principal authorities on the Ritual:—(1). Dr. Hincks' Catalogue of the Egyptian MSS. in the Library of Trinity College. This is the earliest description attempted. (2). Mr. Birch's complete translation of it in the 5th volume **of Bunsen's** *Egypt,* with **a valuable** introduction. (3). M. de Rougé's Preface to his hieratic text, Paris, 1869-70 (not yet completed). Besides these general accounts, there are several valuable monographs on parts of it, viz., (4). M. P. Pierret's translation of the 1st chapter, with M. Devéria's comments, in *Lepsius' Zeitschrift* for 1869 and '70. (5). In a paper published by the *Société archéologique de Langres* (*Memoires* for 1863), M. Chabas has also commented on the 6th chapter. (6). M. Lefébure's **work** on the Solar Hymns in the 15th chapter (Paris, 1870); (7). De Rougé, *Études sur le Rituel*, &c., in the *Rev. arch.* for 1860, analysing the 17th chapter. (8). There are also some interesting remarks on the very ancient 64th chapter in M. **Chabas'** *Voyage d'un Égyptien,* pp. 43-6; and (9). M. Pleyte (*Études égyptologiques*) has **exhaustively treated**

ratic writing of the oldest type, and was found in the tomb of a queen of the eleventh dynasty, which flourished long before the shepherd invasion, and can hardly be placed later than 2500 B. C. Yet even in this ancient copy, the work is regarded as of the most venerable antiquity. Certain chapters are referred to kings of far anterior dynasties, and the sense had already become obscure to the writers, who add many notes and rubrics, and sometimes two diverse readings, without attempting to decide between them.[1] The latest trace of it is in fragments contained in demotic papyri, which are as to language in pure Coptic,[2] and must therefore have been written shortly before the disappearance of the heathen character in the second century A. D. Many

---

the great 125th chapter. The best editions of the whole text are Lepsius' *Todtenbuch* (in linear hieroglyphics), from a Turin copy, and M. de Rougé's *Rituel funéraire* (in hieratic) from the Paris papyri.

[1] See Mr. Goodwin's article in *Lepsius' Zeitschr.* for 1866, p. 53. In the old copy described there are two versions of the 64th chapter, ascribed to King Menkera of the 4th dynasty: this shows that in the 11th dynasty it was already so old and venerable, that the copyist did not know which to prefer. Cf. Goodwin, *loc. cit.*, p. 56.

[2] This is the assertion of M. Brugsch (*Abhandl. der Morg. Gesell.*, vi., p. 150). In a curious article, entitled *die Thierfabel unter den Aegyptern* (*Munich Sitz. ber.*, 1868, ii., p. 50), M. Lauth asserts that the liturgical parts of this papyrus are only isolated prayers and invocations, and not the Ritual. He translates the rest as a dialogue among beasts.

intermediate exemplars, both in linear hieroglyphics and in hieratic, are found in the Museums of Berlin, Leyden, Turin, London, and Dublin.¹ The work in its complete state consists of 166 chapters, of which a good many were added in the great days of the New Empire in the sixteenth century B. C. and after.²

But the main body of the work is uniform throughout. It is a very lengthy and mystical account of the adventures of the soul after death, and of all the dangers it must undergo from the attempts of hostile deities, with directions how by the use of theological knowledge, and by being able to recite the names and titles of innumerable gods, the soul could reach the halls of Osiris. Here it was to be judged by Osiris and the forty-two assessors,³ who took cognisance of the forty-two mortal sins of the

---

¹ To one of our own Fellows, the late Dr. Hincks, belongs, as I have said, the credit of having been the first to attempt a connected sketch of the Ritual, in his *Catalogue of Egyptian MSS. in the Library of Trin. Coll., Dublin*, 1843. These MSS. have since been collated by M. Devéria, whose death (during the siege of Paris) is a great loss to Egyptology. His collations of various Rituals have not been published.

² M. de Rougé thinks the completion of the Ritual was not accomplished till about the time of Psamtik. Lepsius (*Todtenbuch*, p. 17) seems to imply that it was completed at a much earlier date.

³ It was from some confused report concerning this chapter of the Ritual that Diodorus was led to state that the Egyptians

Egyptians. If able to establish its claim,[1] the soul was sent to the abodes of the sun, to live in blessedness. The principal point to be observed in the contests of the soul with the powers of darkness is that it identifies itself with Osiris, and assumes as far as possible his attributes. This feature we shall again meet in the magical literature. The following brief analysis is gathered from M. de Rougé's and Mr. Birch's Introductions.

The first fourteen chapters are concerned with the ceremonies at the funeral (as is plain from the vignette), and include a priest reading from a roll, public mourners, and relations. There is also a calf gambolling before its mother—a symbol of the new life of the deceased. The 15th chapter contains several hymns to Ra (the sun) in different capacities. The 17th is a most important theological chapter on the future privileges of the dead. After various preparations and invocations there come

---

held trial over their dead *before* burial—a story often repeated in modern books.

[1] *If justified* is the usual acceptation. M. Devéria, however, contends that as no definite accusers appear, the declarations of the soul are merely a strict examination of conscience. This is, in fact, the only chapter in the Ritual where the soul is not identified with Osiris, and even called *the Osiris of M or N*. As Osiris cannot be said to be justified, so M. Devéria shows from a collation of many passages that the expression so translated (*maá-xeru*) must be active in sense, and means *truthful*, or *making good his word*, (*véridique*). This quality is bestowed by Thoth, the Lord of persuasion and of words, on Osiris, and is

(26-30) chapters on the preservation of the heart, which the Egyptians regarded as the seat of life, and therefore essential to a future existence.[1]

The next group (31-42) concern the conflicts of the deceased with the various monsters in the lower world. These chapters instruct him in the sacred *formulae* by which he can overcome them. Among the evil beasts appear chiefly serpents. The deceased identifies each of his limbs with one of the deities, so as to escape this danger.[2] Then follows (43-53) a description of all the tortures and punishments of the damned, which he must avoid, and (54-65) an enumeration of the blessings attending on virtuous souls. The 64th chapter, in particular, is very ancient, and seems complete in itself, as if it had been composed before the longer development of the Ritual.[3] Chapters 66-75 are about the luminous transformation of the soul. This appears

---

peculiarly appropriate, seeing that the salvation of Egyptian souls depended on *declarations* of religious knowledge. Cf. *Recueil de Travaux relatifs à la philologie égyptienne*, vol. i., p. 10.

[1] De Rougé thinks they distinguished two hearts—*Hati* and *Het*, the former as the principle of life, the latter the mere substance. This, if true, is another evidence of the strange multiplication of internal principles in old Egyptian philosophy.

[2] Cf. Brugsch *Gram. dém.*, p. 202. The Demotic Funeral Pap., in Paris, of Nero's reign, begins thus:—"Ton âme vit longtemps et rajeunit à toujours, &c. (Line. 6), Que son âme aille aux cieux, et qu'elle fasse la transmigration sur la terre jusqu'à jamais."

[3] Cf. Chabas' *Voyage*, &c., p. 44.

to conclude the necessary performances of the righteous soul.

The next division (76-88), describes the various transformations which the righteous soul can assume at pleasure either as a hawk, or (79) in the form of the chief of the princes—and this chapter is accompanied by the vignette of a prince—or of a lotus, or of Phtah, or (85) in the form of a soul without entering into its (earthly prison?) "for there can happen no ill to him that is instructed." 89-124 comprise a variety of subjects, or of repetitions without any ascertainable connexion. The famous judgment of the dead is in the 125th chapter, and will be quoted presently. When judged, Thoth commands "that his heart be restored to its place." The next chapter describes a lake of fire, in which the soul is purified, as in purgatory, by four apes. Then follow adorations and directions to the soul entering the sun boat with its companions.

Chapters 140-1 contain great litanies, with lists of names of gods, by the proper recitation of which the deceased would advance rapidly, and assume any form he pleased. Then come an enumeration and description of the several gates and habitations into which the souls of the blessed might enter (144-50). It is remarkable that in the 148th chapter Osiris, under the form of a bull, is accompanied by seven cows, his wives, a feature which reminds us of the dream of Pharaoh, the friend of Joseph, in the book of Genesis. I need only specify, in conclusion, the group of chapters (155–60), which concern the objects that were to be deposited on or with the mummy, and that the last three chapters (163–5) are specially stated to be an appendix, added most probably at a later time. They are also full of mystic terms, apparently borrowed from strange languages.

There are *rubrics* (literally) placed at the head of many of the chapters, stating the special advantages to be derived from an accurate knowledge of the succeeding chapters. It appears probable from their form that the original intention of the Ritual was rather to be learned by heart during life, than placed beside the body after death. In time, however, superstition substituted this barren form for the older moral duty, and so the papyrus roll, once the vehicle of Divine knowledge, became an irrational amulet. But lest the reader should imagine that such devices show any peculiar mental weakness in the old Egyptians, I append a very modern parallel—a prayer found on the person of a poor woman who died in one of the Dublin hospitals last year, and which seems to be strangely analogous in its rubrics to the Egyptian Funeral Ritual.

"*A most important prayer.*—The following prayer was found in the grave of our Lord Jesus Christ in the year 1505, and sent from the Pope to the Emperor Charles, as he was going to battle, for his safety.

They who shall repeat this **Prayer every** day, or hear it repeated, or keep it **about them, shall** never die a sudden death, nor be drowned **in water, nor** shall they fall into the hands of their enemies, nor shall they be overpowered in any battle, nor shall poison take any effect on them; and it being read over any woman in labour, she shall be safely delivered, and be a glad mother; and when the child is born say this Prayer, and lay it on his or her right side, and he or she shall not be troubled with any of the thirty-two misfortunes. And if you see any one in fits, lay this on his or her right side, and he or her (*sic*) shall stand up and thank God; and they who laugh at it shall suffer. Believe this Prayer for truth, for it is as true as if the Holy Evangelist had written it; and they who repeat it every day shall have three d. warning before their death."[1]

It is evident that the Ritual was full of mystery to the Egyptians themselves, and was probably not plainer to the priests of the Augustan age in Egypt than the *Carmen Saliare* was to Horace.[2] From a

---

[1] I add a few extracts from the prayer:—

"O Holy Cross of Christ, ward off from me all sharp repeating words! O Holy Cross of Christ, ward off from me all dangerous weapons! O Holy Cross of Christ, protect me from all my enemies! O Holy Cross of Christ, ward off from me all dangers and give me life always, &c., &c."

[2] *Epp.* ii., 1, 86.

literary point of view, I could only find three chapters which in our eyes have any merit. The first is the declaration of the soul in the Hall of the two Truths, that it is free from sin and defilement. I quote selected passages of it from Mr. Birch's and M. Pleyte's translations.[1]

"O ye Lords of Truth! let me know you. I have brought you truth. I have cleansed away for you (all) sins. I have not privily done evil against mankind. I have not afflicted the miserable. I have not told falsehoods in the tribunal of Truth. I have had no acquaintance with evil. I have not done any wicked thing. I have not made the labouring man (or superintendent) do more than his task daily. I have not been idle. I have not been immoral. I have not been weak. I have not done what is hateful to the Gods. I have not calumniated the slave to his master. I have not caused hunger. I have not made to weep. I have not murdered. I have not given orders to smite a person privily. I have not done fraud to men. I have not eaten the sacred bread in the temples. I have not injured the images (or offerings) of the Gods. I have not torn scraps from the bandages of the dead. I have not committed adultery. I have not defiled the water of the God of my country.[?] I have not cheated, I have not falsified measures. I have not

---

[1] Bunsen's *Egypt*, vol. v., pp. 252-3, and Pleyte's *Études égypt.* 4me *Livraison*, pp. 66, *sq.*

thrown the weight out of the scale [?]; I have not cheated in the weight of the balance. I have not withheld milk from mouths of sucklings. I have not hunted wild animals in their pasturages. I have not netted sacred birds. I have not caught the fish which typify them. I have not stopped running water. I have not separated the water from its current. I have not put out a light at its [proper] hour. I have not robbed the Gods of their offered haunches. I have not turned away the cattle of the Gods. I have not stopped a God from his manifestation. I am pure! I am pure!"

This chapter is peculiarly interesting on account of its moral tone, as contrasted with the mystical theology of almost all the remainder. It gives us an accurate list of the (42) sins and virtues prominent in the most ancient Egyptian society. The second is the 155th chapter, relating to the preservation of the body from corruption, which concludes as follows[1]:—

"Hail, my father Osiris! Thy limbs are with thee; thou dost not corrupt, thou dost not turn to worms, thou dost not swell, thou dost not stink, thou dost not decay [?], thou dost not change into worms. The Eye of Shu has not decayed away—I am! I am! I live! I live! I grow! I grow! I wake in peace. I am not corrupted, I am not

---

[1] *Op. cit.*, p. 314.

suffocated there. I grow tall. My substance is not dissipated; my ear does not grow deaf; my head and neck do not separate; my tongue has not been taken away, it has not been cut out; my eyebrow is not plucked out. No injury is done to my body, it neither wastes nor is suffocated in that land for ever and ever!"

The third is the collection of hymns to Osiris in the 15th chapter, which will be noticed hereafter.

What relation was conceived by the ancient Egyptians between the immortal soul and the preserved mummy has not yet been satisfactorily explained. There is no clear evidence, as far as I know, of any ultimate reunion between them,[1] nor that the preservation of the mummy is absolutely necessary to the life of the soul. In the Rhind bilingual Papyri[2] the eulogy on the deceased lady ends with these words: "Osiris opens his mouth to say: this good woman, whose heart is wise, may she be counted as one of the chosen that serve Osiris; may her soul be restored to youth with their souls, and may her body endure in the depths." This prayer evidently contemplates a separate eternity for soul and body.

---

[1] I do not know what M. de Rougé means by saying (*Rituel*, p. xv.), "Le texte (of chap. 89) se termine par la promesse d'une éternelle union entre l'âme et le corps." Mr. Birch's translation (*Bunsen*, v., p. 228) gives exactly the opposite sense. Cf. also MM. *Pierret and Devéria in* Lepsius' *Zeitschr.* for 1870, p. 1, *sq.*

[2] Ed. Brugsch, p. 30.

Yet it is commonly held throughout Egyptian religious documents that the soul can and does revisit the body. The 89th chapter of the Ritual (Birch's trans.) is entitled, *The Chapter of the Visit of the Soul to the Body in Hades.* The Romance of Setna, lately discovered by M. Brugsch, is based on a similar supposition, and details the adventures of two souls revisiting the scenes of their earthly life. We have many representations on engraved stones of this favourite subject. The concluding note to the chapter of the Ritual in question states :—" If this chapter be known, his body is not injured ; his soul does not enter into his (its ?) body for millions of years."

If we connect this passage with the belief, common throughout the whole Ritual, that while the soul goes through many metempsychoses or transformations, the great thing to be avoided was *a second death*,[1] by which they meant a second birth in an earthly body ; then the Ritual appears intended to enable the soul to pass from one spiritual form to another, just as it pleases. But a second inclusion in a body would be its greatest misfortune. The chief difference between a man's mummy and his body appears to have been this, that he could go to and from the one, but not the other. Possibly, however, the importance of preserving the mummy is this: as long as the soul could claim the bodily habitation which it had once

---

[1] Cf. Chabas, *Voyage*, &c., p. 44.

possessed, it was safe from the danger of being forced into another body. But if the mummy were destroyed, such a result might ensue. This is, I suppose, the meaning of the note to the 89th chapter of the Ritual, which states that with a knowledge of this chapter the soul will not be compelled to enter *any body* for millions of years. The existence of its former body in a preserved state seems to save it from some unexplained necessity of being provided with another body.

It is, however, very unsafe to base any theological argument on the Ritual until the age of the several chapters is accurately determined. There are, I think, many traces of inconsistent theories to be found in it. MM. Pierret and Devéria, in their interesting discussions on the first chapter of the Ritual, show some reason to believe, from the theories of Hermes Trismegistus, and of Jamblichus, that the word *sahou*, commonly translated *mummy*, is not to be identified with it; but that as in all nature life springs from death, so there was in the mummy the seed of a new envelope or receptacle of the soul, formed gradually, and depending on the preservation of the mummy.[1] If this view be correct,

---

[1] There is no doubt that *Sahou* is used not for mummy, but for living *Manes* of ancestors, in the 27th chapter of the *Prisse Papyrus*, cf. Lauth's translation, *Munich Sitz. ber.* for 1870, ii, 2, *appendix*, p. 24.

it at once explains the importance attached to embalming in Egypt.[1]

But although the advantage of preserving the body is not clear, the whole tenor of the Ritual, in its earliest form, shows that the Egyptians, from the very commencement of their civilisation, believed firmly in the immortality of the soul, its judgment after death, and its ultimate happiness or misery in accordance with the deeds of its life. How Moses, who was learned in all their wisdom, never adopted this belief, is indeed curious, and will require some theory even more ingenious than Bishop Warburton's to explain it.

---

[1] In the *Notice des principaux monuments exposés, &c., au Musée à Boulaq* (p. 46, and also pp. 108, 112), by M. Auguste Mariette, M. de Rougé's views are very dogmatically sustained, but the evidence is rather assumed than stated. "Après ces détails, le but essentiel que les Egyptiens se proposaient d'atteindre en donnant à leurs sépultures ces grandioses proportions est facile à distinguer: tout y est combiné pour assurer la conservation du corps et sa durée. C'est qu'en effet là réside le pivot de toutes les croyances égyptiennes sur la destinée de l'homme après sa mort. Pour l'Égypte, la vie humaine ne finit pas au moment où l'âme se sépare du corps ; elle se continue dans l'autre monde. Après des combats plus ou moins terribles, qui toutefois ne mettent à l'épreuve que la piété et la morale du défunt, l'âme proclamée juste est enfin admise dans le séjour éternel ; mais l'heure dés félicités sans bornes ne viendra que quand le corps aura été réuni au principe éthéré qui l'a déjà une fois animé. Alors commencera cette seconde vie que la mort ne pourra plus atteindre. L'homme alors, identifié à Osiris, sera éter-

The preparation of these books of the Dead seems to have been a regular trade with the Egyptian priests. They were written and illustrated with vignettes, &c., in various styles, proportioned to the rank of the deceased, or perhaps rather according to the price his relatives chose to pay for the book. It was placed in the coffin with the dead, for the Egyptians, as we have seen, could not

---

nellement juste et éternellement bon. Il sera celui qui cherche à faire le bien et qui l'aime. Quant aux réprouvés, à ceux qui, par leur conduite sur la terre, n'ont pas mérité d'entrer dans la demeure des bienheureux, ils subiront toutes les tortures de l'enfer; ils deviendront des êtres malfaisants: ils aimeront à faire le mal. Chose singulière, ils seront des esprits ayant pour nuire à l'homme tout le pouvoir qu'ont les autres pour lui être utiles. A ceux-là une seconde mort, c'est-à-dire l'anéantissement définitif, est réservée. Le secret de la grandeur des sépultures égyptiennes est dans ces croyances. Il faut qu'à un jour dit le corps soit prêt à recevoir l'âme qui viendra l'animer de nouveau. Ces momies que nous poursuivons d'une si indiscrète curiosité attendent une seconde vie qui ne sera pas, comme la première, sujette à la douleur, et qui ne finira pas. Les belles tombes que l'on admire dans les plaines de Thèbes et de Saqqarah ne sont donc pas dues à l'orgueil de ceux qui les ont érigées. Une pensée plus large a présidé à leur construction. Plus les matériaux sont énormes, plus on est sûr que les promesses faites par la religion recevront leur exécution. En ce sens, les Pyramides ne sont pas des monuments de la vaine ostentation des rois; elles sont des obstacles impossibles à renverser et les preuves gigantesques d'un dogme consolant."

S

shake off that strong association, which has led many nations to imagine some sort of connexion subsisting after death between soul and body. But solemn as was their duty, and awful, we may suppose, as was the vengeance threatened upon a careless or frivolous transcription of the sacred book, the scribes could not, even in religious Egypt, keep up their attention during the labour of so long and tedious a piece of writing; and as the books were to be sealed up, and never seen again by the relatives, they are often written with the greatest carelessness, words and letters being left out, or gross faults in orthography committed.[1] They seem indeed to have been often kept ready-made, for the name of the deceased appears in different ink or handwriting from the rest of the book, and is inserted in a blank left for the purpose. The hieratic copies are, however, usually written off, names and all, in the same hand.[2]

It is, I think, to be regretted that the fashion of

---

[1] In the last days of paganism in Egypt there were even tombs ornamented with unmeaning hieroglyphics by men who knew not their import. Cf. Mariette, *op. cit.*, p. 46.

[2] From the blunders found in the linear hieroglyphic copies after the nineteenth dynasty, which can frequently be shown to have arisen from substituting a wrong hieroglyphic which is represented in hieratic by the same symbol as the right one, M. de Rougé acutely infers (*Rituel*, p. i.) that the hieratic texts were at this period the models used, and therefore of higher authority.

filling all the tombs and the coverings of the mummies with fragments of this Ritual displaced, about the time of the twenty-sixth dynasty, the older habit of a biographical sketch of the deceased, with simpler prayers to the gods to grant him a happy immortality. Many precious historical details and dates have been gathered from these epitaphs. They did not wholly fall into disuse, for the bilingual Rhind papyri of the year 11 B. C., found in the coffin of a person of importance, though full of mystic symbolism, yet describe in eulogistic terms his own qualities, and those of his wife. There are also other theological treatises describing the metamorphoses of the gods, and the lamentations of Isis, found in the tombs of priests and priestesses.[1] But as before observed, all these older books imply so much and explain so little, that we are at a perpetual loss to discover the meaning of the sentence or the point of the allegory. In the Ptolemaic temples, on the contrary, the myths have been far more thoroughly and systematically illustrated, and when learned men have collected and published the immense profusion of pictures and texts found at Edfu, Esneh, Dendera, and other such temples, the obscurities of the Ritual will doubtless be sensibly diminished.[2]

---

[1] Cf. Mr. Birch's learned Introduction in Bunsen's *Egypt*, v., p. 120.

[2] "Les inscriptions des temps des Lagides ont cet avantage

These texts, which are inscribed on the walls in hieroglyphics, are the only other class of composition which can be strictly classed as theological. They describe such myths as that of the winged disk, or the adventures of Horus in avenging his father Osiris,[1] with occasional historical allusions of great value. They seem in all cases to have adhered strictly to the ancient traditions of their fathers, and are in this respect, though comparatively recent in date, quite trustworthy. Just as the temples themselves, though of late structure, are now found to have been built on the site and with the plans handed down from gray antiquity,[2] so the moral structure of

---

qu'à travers les jeux de mots, la recherche d'esprit, j'oserai même dire les calembours dont elles sont chargées, on y rencontre une variété de renseignements sur lesquels les temples d'époque Pharaonique restent constamment muets. En un sens, Edfou est moins discret qu'Abydos et que Karnak, le profane y a un plus libre accès. La porte du sanctuaire est entr'ouverte, l'oeil peut y penetrer." Mariette, *op. cit.*, p. 46.

[1] Cf. Brugsch, *Die geflügelte Sonnenscheibe*, in *Göttingen Transactions*, vol. xiv.; and E. Naville, *Textes relatifs au Mythe d' Horus*, Paris, 1870; see also his letter to M. Brugsch in Lepsius' *Zeitschr.* for 1870, p. 123.

[2] This was the remarkable discovery of M. Dümichen, who found a history of the first foundation and successive restorations of the temple of Dendera in a secret passage. Cf. his *Bauurkunde der Tempelanlage von Dendera*, Leipzig, 1865. Cf. the still more remarkable case in M. Mariette's *Notice, &c, of the Boulaq Museum*, 3rd ed., p. 207, where King Chufu of the fourth dynasty restores an old temple.

their worship, like the material, adhered with conservative tenacity to beaten paths.

§ 6. *Devotional Treatises.*—I turn with greater pleasure to the *Devotional Hymns*. These, as might be expected, cannot be separated very strictly from the other theological works, as the invocation of deities has generally been combined by the human race with dogmas and creeds. The 15th chapter, for example, of the Ritual is properly a series of hymns to Osiris as the greatest of deities, closely similar in style to those quoted below. But, nevertheless, the distinction is more than ever important in Egyptian literature, if it were only to point out the two sides of Egyptian religion. The great body of the Ritual lays no stress on moral conditions, and the 125th chapter, above quoted, is a remarkable exception to this rule. The Ritual rather promises salvation to the soul that possesses the right faith, that knows the correct names and titles of all the deities—that can explain the Divine mysteries when required. 'The deceased,' says Mr. Birch,[1] 'is the victim of diabolical influences, but the good soul ultimately triumphs over all its enemies by its γνῶσις, or knowledge of celestial and infernal mysteries.' And as the moral character of the soul is not prominent, so the moral attributes of the gods are postponed to their mystical forms

---

[1] *Introduction to the Ritual, Bunsen*, v., p. 136.

and titles. This side of the Egyptian religion corresponds to that party in our own Church who avoid all moral teaching, and occupy themselves exclusively with doctrines, such as Justification and Election.

But there are also a number of devotional hymns, addressed to the sun, or to the god of Egypt considered as such, and these hymns abound in lofty and pure sentiments.[1] Above all, it appears from

---

[1] The following are the available commentaries and translations of solar hymns that I have been able to discover:

(1.) E. de Rougé, *Une statuette naophore du Vatican*, *Rev. archéol.* for 1852, pp. 53, *sq.* The latter part of the article is on the unity and self-generation of the Deity.

(2.) E. de Rougé, *Hymne de Taphéroumès*, to be republished in his *Chrestomathie* from the *Moniteur* for 7th March, 1851.

(3.) F. Chabas, *un Hymne à Osiris*, *Rev. archéol.* for 1857, pp. 64 and 193. The second article is the clearest and most satisfactory account of this side of the Egyptian faith I have met.

(4.) F. Chabas, in *Leemans' Monuments*, &c., ii., p. 65, gives various notes and translations of solar hymns in the Leyden collection.

(5.) F. J. Lauth, *Moses der Ebräer*, Munich, 1868 (appendix ii). He gives a complete translation of the great hymn on one of the Pap. Anastasy (i. 350 of Leyden.)

(6.) E. Lefébure, *Hymnes au Soleil dans le* xvme *Chapitre du Rituel*, Paris, 1870, a very excellent work.

(7.) F. J. Lauth had already translated them in his article, *Obelisken und Pyramiden*, published in the Munich *Sitz. ber.* for 1868, pp. 99-105.

(8.) S. Birch's translation of the same hymns, in *Bunsen's Egypt*, &c., vol. v., pp. 167-71.

many of them that in spite of the numbers of the
deities and their separate attributes, they were all
regarded as manifestations of the one great Creator,
himself uncreate and the father of the universe.[1]
Thus one of these hymns, written in a papyrus of
the Ramessid era preserved at Leyden, exclaims:[2]
"Glory to thee, who hast begotten all that exists,
who hast made man, who hast made the gods, and

(9.) G. Maspero, *Hymne au Nil*, Paris, 1868, which, though addressed to the river, gives it the solar attributes.

(10.) F. Chabas, in his *Papyrus magique Harris*, has also translated some remarkable hymns, which I know from M. de Rougé's review, *Rev. arch.*, N. s., vol. iii, p. 420.

[1] M. Lefébure (*chap.* xv. *du Rituel*, p. 12) considers that even the Ritual plainly shows the Egyptian religion to have been the worship of the sun regarded as the Creative Deity, combined with that of Osiris as the Mediating Deity. Around them other gods are grouped either as servants or as attributes. Phtah, the great god of Memphis, and Amon of Thebes are rarely mentioned. "Il est probable," he adds, "que ces Dieux naquirent sans légende dans les collèges des prêtres, comme les abstractions dans le cabinet d'un savant, et eurent prise sur l'âme ni par la crainte, ni par l'amour. Leurs noms, d'ont l'un, Phtah, signifie ouvrir, et l'autre, Amon, cacher, indiquent bien l'effort abstrait de l'esprit qui cherche, derrière les symboles où s'arrête le vulgaire, l'invisible auteur de la création." Being, as he calls them, *dieux locaux et philosophiques*, they only obtained a place in the Ritual by being identified, the one with Osiris, the other with Ra, the sun.

[2] Cf. Chabas' description of Leyden Papyri in *Leemans*, ii., chap. 3.

all the beasts of the field; who makest man to live, who hast no being second to thee.¹ Lord of generation, thou that givest the breath of life, that makest the world to move in its seasons, and orderest the course of the Nile, whose ways are secret. . . He is the light of the world; he shooteth in the green herb, and maketh the corn, the grass, and the trees of the field. . . . He giveth to sons the dignity of their fathers." They regarded the sun in fact as the conservator not only of the laws of nature, but of those social arrangements which they knew had raised them above all neighbouring nations. "He hath made this earth with his hands," says another solar hymn, translated by M. Chabas, " its water, its air, its vegetation, all its flocks, its fish, its birds, all its reptiles, and all its quadrupeds. The world delights when he riseth on the throne of his father; he shineth on the horizon, and chaseth away the darkness."

I select from Dr. Lauth's translations the following additional passages which are very striking.²
" The assembly of the gods rises from the sea; the

---

¹ Cf. Hor. *Od.*, i. 12.
  Unde nil majus generatur ipso,
  Nec viget quidquam simile aut secundum.
A sentiment often repeated in these hymns.

² The curious nature of the composition has been ingeniously explained by Lauth (*Moses der Ebräer*, p. 32). The poet getting ired of long accounts, which are still found on the other side of

wanderers rise up before **thee, Lord of lords, that** establishest thyself. He is the Lord; all beings behold His rays, which cause their faces to shine. The men that **attain unto** His light honour His light; all the plants **and trees** shoot forth for joy in Him. . . . **The** beasts multiply before Him; the birds slip forth from their nests; they praise Him in due season; they revive through His sight every day, and praise Him for His fire. **The god destroys them not, holy** in His being, incomparable in His mercy. **He is the** great god that ruleth the company of **the gods.**

"Secret in being, withdrawing Himself from measurement, giving laws to men **that** are not gainsayed, piercing with His eyes, removing the mist; He is free from the weakness **of creatures ;** His words fulfil themselves in season, opening the chambers according to His heart; the approach of them that have not **yet** prayed is known to Him; he that cometh to Him with praise is joined **to Him in a** moment of time.

"He is honoured more than the gods. **He** moveth Himself aloft, He sinketh to the depths. **No**

---

the papyrus, turned to a poetical treatment of his figures, and suits each of them to some attribute of the gods, just as the letters of the alphabet are used in the *akrophonic* psalms. By the aid of puns on the names he succeeds in going through all the numbers from 1 to 10, and then the tens and the hundreds, probably up to 1000.

god knoweth His real form. His image is not painted on walls; there is no evidence of Him in the temples. He giveth strength more than the need, which yet layeth hold of all; He is greater than man can think, mightier than man can know. Sudden destruction cometh upon him that speaketh not rightly His divine name, mysterious. No god revolts against Him. His name is considered secret, like His secret being."[1]

What I already remarked about the identity of the different deities is also easily proved from these hymns. In one addressed to the god Horus among the Leyden papyri, he is adored under the special title of Thoth, the divine inventor of writing. He is called "The king of writing, the lord of words, the founder of the house of books," among other epithets; and this agrees perfectly with the passage translated elsewhere by M. Chabas,[2] which says of the sun, "He is Phra, when he speaks; Thoth, when he writes." So the same hymn opens with this address:—"Hail to thee, Osiris! Lord of the lapse of time; King of gods, of many names, of holy trans-

---

[1] Lauth, *op. cit.*, pp. 100-3.
[2] *Rev. arch.*, o. s., xiv., p. 80. So Jamblichus, in expounding the Egyptian religion (*de Mysteriis*, sec. viii., cap. iii., ed. Gale), ὁ γὰρ δημιουργικὸς νοῦς, καὶ τῆς ἀληθείας προστάτης, καὶ σοφίας κ. τ. λ. ʼΑμῶν κατὰ τὴν τῶν Αἰγυπτίων γλῶσσαν λέγεται. συντελῶν δὲ ἀψευδῶς ἕκαστα καὶ τεχνικῶς μετʼ ἀληθείας Φθά, . . . ἀγαθῶν δὲ ποιητικὸς ὢν ʼΟσιρις κέκληται.

formations, of mysterious forms!"[1] I have multiplied these quotations in order to impress on the reader the profoundly interesting fact that, with all their complicated mythology, there was deep truth and purity in the faith of the old Egyptians. One more declaration, more precious than the rest, cannot but interest the reader: "God is the sun himself incarnate; His commencement is from the beginning. He is the god who has existed of old. *There is no god without Him.* A mother hath not borne Him, nor a father begotten Him. God-goddess, created from Himself, *All the gods* have existed as soon as *He began.*"[2]

The invocations end with some such formula as this: "What thy father Seb hath ordained for thee, so be it according to his word"—no real inconsistency with the foregoing doctrine; for though Seb stood in

---

[1] Cf. Jamblichus *de Myst.*, sec. viii., chap. 3. He seems very well informed as to Egyptian belief, as might be inferred from his having assumed the name and position of an Egyptian priest. S. Hippolytus (*Refut. Haer.*, iv. 43) seems not at all so accurate, but knew the point about self-creation.

[2] Cf. Chabas in *Leemans*, ii., p. 74. "Ces deux dernières phrases," he adds, "sont la formule la plus nette et la plus simple de la théologie égyptienne, telle qu'elle était enseignée au plus haut degré d'initiation. Un dieu unique, investé de la puissance de produire, c'est-à-dire de deux principes, mâle et femelle ; il s'est créé lui-même avant toutes choses, et l'arrivée des dieux n'est qu'une diffusion, qu'une manifestation de ses diverses facultés et de ses volontés toute-puissantes."

the same relation to Osiris as Kronos to Zeus in the Greek mythology, the speculations of the Egyptians on the paternity and maternity of the absolute and self-created Deity were indeed very curious, and have engaged the attention of Egyptologists. The sun-god was held to have had no father, but to have generated himself, being both the husband and son of his mother Neith, the vault of heaven, perhaps more vaguely space, or eternity. For this mother of the sun-god was always placed in the background, as something unintelligible, like Plato's matter, and perhaps merely as a necessary supposition or starting point in creation. This is implied by the inscription on her statue quoted by Proclus.[1]

Many interesting corroborations of the old Egyptian monotheism are to be found in other hymns than those addressed to the Trinity *Amon, Ra,* and *Phtah.* Two examples will here suffice.

---

[1] *In Timaeum*, i., 30., τὰ ὄντα, καὶ τὰ ἰσόμενα, καὶ τὰ γεγονότα ἐγώ εἰμι, τὸν ἐμὸν χιτῶνα οὐδεὶς ἀπεκάλυψεν, ὃν ἐγὼ καρπὸν ἔτεκον, ἥλιος ἐγένετο. On the other hand the self-generation of the Deity was strongly and even coarsely put forward. In the Leyden hymn he is called *taurus matris,* husband of his mother; in another *qui maechatur in seipso,* and so forth; by Jamblichus he is styled τοῦ αὐτοπάτορος, αὐτογόνου, καὶ μονοπάτορος θεοῦ (*De Myst.,* sec. viii., cap. 2). The whole subject is ably discussed by the Vicomte de Rougé, *Mémoire sur la statuette naophore du Vatican, Rev. archéol.* for April, 1851, pp. 53-60. See also his review of M. Chabas' *Papyrus magique Harris,* and quotations from similar hymns in *Rev. arch.* N. S., iii., p. 420.

First, in the hymn to the Nile, in the collection of the British Museum, published by M. Maspero, this deity is identified with the one omnipotent spiritual Creator. "He is not carved in stone, he is not seen in the images of the gods, nor are prayers offered before him, no man knoweth his abode, vain are images of his form."[1]

Secondly, a stronger confirmation of this monotheistic tendency will be found in the fact noted by M. Chabas,[2] that among the hierogrammates, or literary class, who specially worshipped Thoth, the god of eloquence, of learning—in fact, of intelligence—it was common to consider *him* also as the one uncreated God, concealed behind numerous symbols. There are extant hymns which attribute to him the creation of the world and of light, *before that the sun came into existence.* This last idea is peculiarly interesting, both as showing a controversial attitude of the literary class towards the popular belief, and as proving a strong monotheistic instinct; for otherwise Thoth would have been set up side by side with Ra-Osiris.

I cannot refrain from digressing for a moment to note the close correspondence of the literary faith of Egypt with that of Moses, who had been educated in it. A Turin papyrus says of Thoth: "He hath

---

[1] Cf. Chabas' *Inscriptions des mines d'or*, p. 7.
[2] *Mélanges égyptologiques*, i., p. 118.

made all that the world contains, and hath given it light *when all was darkness, and there was as yet no sun.*" The creation of Light before that of the Sun, a curious feature in the book of Genesis, is closely analogous.

After all this evidence for monotheism I am bound to add that the only known attempt to introduce it *formally* into Egypt failed. Amenophis IV., (circ. 1500 B. C.), a monarch peculiar even in his type of face, not only attempted to abolish the worship of all gods save that of the sun, but even transferred his residence to a new capital, where the architecture would not suggest the popular polytheism. The ruins of this city have been explored by Dr. Lepsius, at El-Amarna, who found the walls covered with peculiar *floral* decorations, and with hymns to the sun, that seem to have been sung with rich musical accompaniments.[1] They are of considerable literary merit, and often descriptive, viz. :—" The beasts leave their lairs, and walk upon their feet, the birds rise from their nests with joy, and spread their wings, flying in the splendour of the solar disk." This remarkable reformation lasted, it appears, only a generation, and passed away. Bunsen[2] speaks of this king as " the weak-minded bigot who tried to introduce the adoration of the

---

[1] Cf. Brugsch, *Histoire d'Égypte*, p. 118.
[2] iv., p. 656.

sun's disk, instead of the ideal worship of Ra," but I fear he gives the popular creed too high a place. The facts appear to indicate that monotheism, though believed by the priests, and perhaps felt by the people, was not the first guiding principle in their religion. Even the Greeks, who were *bonâ fide* polytheists, often speak of the Deity as One.

The hymns conclude with the dedication by the individual who offered them up, or had them inscribed on stone, as follows :—" Oblation to Osiris, who dwells in the West, Lord of Abydos. May he grant the performance of its transformations, the enjoyment of the celestial Nile, the coming forth as a living soul, the light of the solar disk at the pole of heaven, a reception among the faithful, &c., &c., to the guardian of the flock of Amon, even to Amonmes, the truthful (*maâ-xeru*), the son of the lady Hent." It is well to call special attention to this noble species of funeral offering. The glory of God occupies our attention almost completely. The memory of the offerer is secured by a mere brief dedication at the close. Does it not contrast favourably with many modern epitaphs, where the moral character of the deceased is lauded, not merely above his own merits, but above the merits of almost any mortal?

Yet even these have ample parallels among Egyptian inscriptions. The reader has observed the bold and precise statement of its own purity made by the soul before the judges in the Hall of the two Truths. There are an abundance of sepulchral monuments with inscriptions in the same strain, which are addressed to mortals. It was usual, especially under the Old Empire, for the deceased to speak in his own person, and commemorate all his virtues and his public services. 'I honoured my father and my mother. I succoured the afflicted. I gave bread to the hungry; I gave drink to the thirsty, and clothes to the naked. I sheltered the outcast. I have offered to the gods their dues, and funeral oblations to my ancestors. I treated the great and the poor alike. My doors were open to the stranger. I was a man wise on the earth, and my heart ever loved God. I was a brother to the great, a father to the afflicted, and never did I sow hatred among men. In my day the district which I governed suffered no want, even though there was a famine in the land.' Such are the declarations we meet. There is little trace of humility or any sense of unworthiness in these declarations.

There are, however, many noble exceptions to this offensive self-righteousness. In the hymns addressed to Thoth, the special god of the literary class, all the honour and the power gained by his servants are specially attributed to his favour, and not to their own merits. 'Come, O Thoth,' says one of them,[1] 'writer of the books of the gods, &c., &c., be my protector. Make me skilled in thy works, for they exceed all other works. He that gives himself up to them is found fit for high places. Many have wrought, **and it is** thou who hast wrought for them. **They** stand before the king ; they are rich and great through thee. For thou art their guide—the guide of every man that is born of woman. Come then to me, and be my guide. I am the servant of thine house. Grant me to speak with thy power to all the earth. **Yea,** the multitude will say: His greatness— it is Thoth that hath made it.' I may add that the Egyptians **also** saw through **and despised the pride** of riches as contrasted with the pride of honesty. **This** appears from the injunctions of Ptah-hotep: '**If after** having been humble thou become great, and the chief man of thy city in wealth, let not riches make thee proud, **for** the author of all good things is God.'[2] This noble utterance is well sustained **by** another passage[3]:—' Speak nothing offensive to the *great Creator.* Even if the **words are** spoken **in secret, the heart of a man is no secret to him that**

---

[1] From the Anastasi collection, **translated** by M. Chabas, *Mélanges,* i., p. 119.

[2] This is M. Dümichen's translation, in his *Felsentempel von Abusimbel,* p. **23,** verified by Lauth, *Munich Sitz. ber.* for 1870, ii., **2,** *appendix,* p. **136.** M. Chabas only attempts the first clause.

[3] Section **25 of** Pap. Sallier 2, Goodwin, *Essay,* p. 274.

T

made it. If the words are spoken boastfully, he is present with them, though thou be alone.'

The Rhind papyri, to which I have already alluded, do not speak in the first person, but were composed by order of the relatives, and placed in the tomb with Sauf and his wife Tanur. Their panegyrics are therefore not so characteristic. But here there is such an admixture of mysticism, that they might fairly be characterised as a sort of compromise between the fantastic funeral Ritual and the plain, moral, self-righteous inscription.

I may add that, as their moral notions were plain and precise, so the rewards they expected hereafter were of the same description. Plenty of eating, drinking, and sleeping,[1] were their prospects—a heaven not higher than that of the old Germanic race, and justifying M. Lefébure in calling them *positivistes d'outretombe*.[2]

Strange to say, among these practical views, we meet not unfrequent allusions to the absorption of the soul in the sun, or to the world regarded as the body of the sun-god, which point plainly enough to the most abstract and refined of all doctrines—Pantheism. Bunsen in vain denies the distinct tend-

---

[1] Giving in marriage does not appear.
[2] Cf. also M. Chabas' translation of a *stele* at Turin in *Lepsius' Zeitschr.* for 1870, p. 164.

ency of these utterances.¹ 'There is not a shadow,' he says, 'of the abominable materialistic doctrine of absorption of the soul into the universe: on the contrary, the soul living with God is in a state of consciousness of divine life; the soul continues to have an organ (body), as Osiris has his body in the sun.' But though this statement is false, I am nevertheless convinced, as M. Lefébure is,² that the general tone of the Egyptian religion was not pantheistic. The worship of ancestors, as Bunsen has remarked, which was always so popular in Egypt, plainly contradicts it. Both the novels discussed in the sequel are totally inconsistent with it. That individual thinkers adopted it would be almost certain, even without texts, from the analogy of all other philosophic nations; but those parts of the Ritual which preach it are, I think, chiefly glosses, and may perhaps some day be traced to some particular age, or school of thought, perhaps even to a few isolated thinkers, on whom high office may have conferred the authority to insert the doctrine in religious services.³

---

¹ iv., p. 664.   ² *Op. cit.*, p. 14.

³ I may add that it is particularly difficult to convict the old Egyptians of pantheism, seeing that they multiplied internal principles in so extraordinary a manner. At least four distinct natures appear (besides the body) in the Ritual. That some one of the elements came from the Deity or Universe, and would

§ 7. *Ethical Treatises.*—The three great moral duties implied by all the religious documents—piety to the gods, charity to all men, and veneration of deceased ancestors—are farther developed in several *Moral Treatises*, which, like the religious, date from the earliest as well as the latest epochs, and show us clearly the nature of good education among the old Egyptians. They have been handed down to us in three forms: first, that of the regular moral treatise, either in a connected discourse, or in disjointed proverbs—the latter a very favourite form of ancient and primitive ethics; secondly, the epistolary form, under the garb of a private letter from a teacher to his pupil, but evidently intended for general use; thirdly, there is said to be a specimen in the form of dialogue, representing a conversation between a father and his son, but the publication of this interesting papyrus, though promised in the year 1868 by Dr. Brugsch,[1] has hitherto been delayed.

---

be reabsorbed, was a doctrine held by some of the Greeks also. But this does not prove pantheism. Δύο γὰρ ἔχει ψυχάς, says Jamblichus (viii., § 6, p. 162, Ed. Gale), ὡς ταῦτά φησι τὰ γράμματα, ὁ ἄνθρωπος, καὶ ἡ μὲν ἐστιν ἀπὸ τοῦ πρώτου νοητοῦ μετέχουσα, καὶ τῆς τοῦ δημιουργοῦ δυνάμεως, ἡ δὲ, ἐνδιδομένη ἐκ τῶν οὐρανίων περιφορᾶς, εἰς ἣν ἐπεισέρπει ἡ θεοπτικὴ ψυχή. He says that one of these souls, being determined by the periods of the κόσμος, is not free; but the other, which they conceived to be an igneous principle, frees us from fate, and gives ἄνοδος πρὸς τοὺς νοητοὺς θεούς.

[1] Cf. his Letter in *Lepsius' Zeitschr.* for 1868, p. 128.

In the form of treatises or collections of proverbs we have the moral reflections which taught the practical side of the Egyptian religion from all ages of their history. The very oldest intelligible hieratic book which we possess is the moral treatise of the magistrate and prince Ptah-hotep, our copy of which, contained in the MS. called the Prisse papyrus, now in the Paris Bibliothèque, may have been prepared as late as the eleventh dynasty, but the author asserts himself to have reached a ripe old age under Assa, the last king of the fifth dynasty.[1]

The strange archaisms of the first part (which is assigned to the third dynasty) have hitherto baffled all Egyptologists who prefer induction to conjecture, and the two translations offered by Mr. Heath and Dr. Lauth cannot be safely quoted. The central part of the papyrus, apparently a distinct work, has had its writing carefully erased, and its surface smoothed. It is a good specimen of what German erudition sometimes attempts, that Dr. Lauth has devoted much time and ingenuity to ascertain the title and character of the author of the *erased treatise !*[2] As to the moral maxims really translated

---

[1] Cf. Lauth, *op. cit.*, p. 54.
[2] *Munich Sitz. ber.* for 1870, vol. i., part iii., p. 245. The most reliable authorities on the Prisse papyrus are (1) M. Chabas in the *Revue archéol.* for 1858, p. i, '*Le plus ancien livre du monde*,' and a farther article in *Lepsius' Zeitschr.* for 1870, p. 82. The first results arrived at by this acute and cautious Egyptologist have

from the latter portion of this most ancient of books, the most remarkable point is their perfect coincidence with such remnants of morals as are preserved to us from all the other epochs of Egyptian history. The collection of proverbs in the Leyden papyri, which is of the Ramessid era, and the instructions of a demotic papyrus (in the Paris Library) which dates from the Ptolemies, differ in no fundamental point from the wisdom of the founders of Egyptian greatness. They do not even show a development. The ordinary private and social qualities which make a man respectable are enumerated and enjoined. There is, perhaps, in the Prisse papyrus a little more stress laid on filial obedience than there was afterwards. In those old conservative days it is almost regarded as the sum of all virtue, and the sure road to all earthly happiness.

The reader will be glad to see full extracts from so curious a work; and though I am bound to add that the earlier version of M. Chabas differs in many details from Dr. Lauth's, yet the general agreement

---

been sustained by him in his later article; and he discredits the versions, especially of the former treatise, by M. Lauth and Mr. Heath. M. Chabas' translation was tested and corrected by (2) Mr. Goodwin in his *Cambridge Essay*, pp. 276-8. (3) M. Dümichen's allusions, above cited, are also valuable. (4) Dr. Lauth's complete (I fear too complete) translation of the second treatise (*Munich Sitz. ber.* for 1870, ii., part 2, *appendix*) appears to me of real value.

as to the subject of the document, and its instructions, is such as to convince any inquirer that not only the broad sense, but even most of the details of prince Ptah-hotep's moral discourse have now been fully ascertained. The fragments translated by M. Dümichen[1] show that he agrees closely with Dr. Lauth.

The main body of the treatise, including chapters 3–37, contains various wise instructions concerning men's conduct in society, connected by no closer link than their practical usefulness. We shall therefore postpone their consideration to that of the opening and concluding chapters, which concern the pains and privileges of old age, and the duty of obedience in youth (1, 2, 26–7, 38–44). This is the division of Dr. Lauth.

The work opens with an interesting complaint on the miseries of old age, which I shall quote in full. 'Instruction (or prayer) of the magistrate Ptah-hotep, under his majesty Assa, king of all Egypt. Ptah-hotep says: O Osiris, great Lord, to become old is a shuddering, extreme evil, the last curse, a second childhood. His couch (or weakness) affords him torment every day; his eyes become dim, his ears dull, his strength passeth away. The mouth speaks no more, it hath no words. The heart grows hard, and remembers not yesterday (*or* feels no joy);

---

[1] *Der Felsentempel von Abusimbel*, p. 28.

his bones ache in turn; the good is changed to evil; every taste vanishes. Old age makes a man wretched in every way; his nose is closed, and cannot breathe; it is labour to him either to stand or to sit: this is the condition of the decrepid man.'

The parallel from Shakspeare will occur to all[1]:—

> Last scene of all
> Is second childishness and mere oblivion;
> Sans teeth, sans eyes, sans taste, sans everything.

Older literature affords no less accurate analogies; so Sophocles[2]:—

> Τό τε κατάμεμπτον ἐπιλέλογχε
> πύματον, ἀκρατές, ἀπροσόμιλον,
> γῆρας, ἄφιλον, ἵνα πρόπαντα
> κακὰ κακῶν ξυνοικεῖ.

But most of all the sad termination of the book of Ecclesiastes reproduces both in form and thought the sentiments of the older Egyptian sage:—' While the evil days come not, nor the years draw nigh, when thou shalt say: I have no pleasure in them. While the sun . . . be not darkened, nor the clouds return after the rain . . . [when all the limbs shall weaken and decay] and fears shall be in

---

[1] *As You Like It*, ii., 7.

[2] *Oed. Col.*, 1235, *sqq*. Cf. also Euripides' fine chorus, *Herc. Fur.*, 637, *sqq*. There are similar passages in old Chinese literature.

the way . . . and desire shall fail; because man goeth to his long home."[1]

'What,' continues Ptah-hotep, 'shall his fellow in age do? Shall I tell him the words of the experienced in the wisdom of olden time, and what was their knowledge of the gods? Prepare a model to destroy defects among men: prepare thou help. The divine majesty speaks: Teach him but the word of antiquity: so make him valued among the sons of the great, who come in and hear from him. Willing is every heart: what he says excites no satiety.'

It appears from this that the qualities now-a-days rather disliked in old men are considered by Ptah-hotep as their most valuable contribution to society. He is essentially Horace's

> Laudator temporis acti
> Se puero, censor castigatorque minorum.

He proceeds in the second chapter to expound his plan, and promise blessings and curses, according as his precepts are obeyed. 'He saith to his

---

[1] Eccl. xii., 1, *sqq.* It is to be regretted that this fine passage is almost unintelligible in our Authorised Version and is indeed in the original compassed with difficulties. The best commentary is that of Hitzig (Leipzig, 1855, p. 212), who makes, as usual, some ingenious emendations, such as pointing יְנָאֵץ (from נאץ) instead of the usual יָנֵאץ which is extorted from נצץ, and gives no good sense.

son: Be not proud of thy knowledge; take counsel with the learned or with the unlearned; the bounds of art are not fixed; no master is complete in his glory. Honour the good word more than emeralds, for these are found on the arms of slave women.'

Two chapters (26–7) in the body of the work are justly treated in connexion with this preamble by Dr. Lauth, as they discuss the proper reception of an aged sage, and the blessings attendant on such hospitality. The most characteristic promise is this: 'Therefore his reception promotes the life of thine house; thy *manes* also (ancestors), which are dear to thee, therefore continue to live.' It seems strange that the immortality of a man's ancestors should depend on his own morality.

The closing chapters (38–44) are all concerned with the virtue and advantages of obedience, and the evil results of disobedience, ending with remarks on the nervousness attendant on public speaking, and the means of overcoming it. The author concludes by observing that he himself by means of this rule of life has attained many honours, and the full age of 110 years. Then follows the note of the transcriber: 'It is finished: from beginning to end it agrees accurately with the writing found in the original document.'

As to the reflections on obedience, they are hardly worth quoting *in extenso*, being to us very trite and obvious. They commence by insisting on the conservative force in obedience, which hands down the same truths and the same social principles from father to son. The 39th chapter specially deals with filial obedience, repeating itself tamely enough. 'Fairer is obedience than all things, when it is rendered freely. Very fair is it when a son receives the word of his father; therefore shall his life be long in the land.' Chapters 40-41 show that all evils and errors arise from early disobedience, and the stiff-necked son is described as one 'who accomplishes nothing, who sees knowledge in ignorance, and virtue in vice . . . whose life is death and his food distortions of the truth.' On the contrary, (chap. 42), the obedient son is the avenger of his father. His old age is happy on account of his obedience; his word is a model to his children, renewing the teaching of his father; his actions are taught everywhere. All his children declare his words to be harvests of truth. Farther, they are regarded by all as quieting the masses, which do not cling to the old, despite of its excellence. 'Take not away from them one word; add not one thereto; put not one in the place of another. Beware of producing crude thoughts; study till thy words are matured. When anxious about speaking before the great (chap. 43), keep close to the words of thy master; speak as great things as possible, so that they who hear may say: Beautiful is all that comes forth from his mouth.' With additional promises of earthly rewards the book closes.

Turning to the body of the work, we can distinguish, amid various repetitions in a very desultory style, certain leading thoughts, which disclose to us a picture of social life 5000 years ago. Even then the ethical teacher regarded himself, not as a teacher of novelties, but as preserving and transmitting to posterity the wisdom of his ancestors. To him the past seems not less extended, or less civilised than it is to us; he does not hint at the ancestral ape, or the acorn-eating troglodyte. There are rather signs in the book that the writer apprehended or even witnessed the decay of an old conservative society, under which Egypt had flourished for centuries, and to which we owe the mighty pyramids, that have made her fame known even to the ignorant of subsequent generations.

I infer this, not merely from the perpetual recommendations of obedience which we have already cited, but from the stress laid upon (1) *rules of conduct in the presence of great men*, which occupy six chapters.[1] 'If you meet a lordly person in a bad humour, treat him with humility and deference. To oppose him would show total ignorance of the world. Be silent, no matter what

---

[1] 3, 4, 7, 8, 13, 31 of Dr. Lauth's translation.

violent language he uses, for it is very dangerous to contend with him.' Again: 'When you meet a great man, salute him most humbly, and do not annoy him by staring at him: a man is hated that does this. Address him not till he has spoken to you; for a great man can dispense bread as he likes, but an underling must take the position of a suppliant.' Again: 'If one great man send you on a message to another, act in concert with the wishes of the sender, and perform his message; take care not to change one word that might cause division among the great by damaging the truth. Gossip is abominable.' There are also directions for keeping watch at a great man's door. Two remarks are obviously suggested by these chapters, and I think only two—first, the servility recommended in the presence of the great; and secondly, the plain shrewdness which recommends it as likely to be of service in obtaining bread and advancement. These social arrangements are regarded by Ptah-hotep as of divine origin.

The subject next in prominence is decidedly the (2) *regulation of temper*.[1] The restraint already recommended before angry superiors is urged in not answering insults. By silence men avoid the excitement of a quarrel, and therefore the excesses which put them in the power of their advers-

---

[1] Chaps. 23, 29, 33, 36.

aries (chap. 23). There is no closer parallel than the fragment of Philemon:—

"Ἥδιον οὐδὲν οὐδὲ μουσικώτερον
ἔστ' ἢ δύνασθαι λοιδορούμενον φέρειν·
ὁ λοιδορῶν γάρ, ἂν ὁ λοιδορούμενος
μὴ προσποιῆται, λοιδορεῖται λοιδορῶν,

And so Menander:—

Τὸ δ' ὀξύθυμον τοῦτο καὶ λίαν πικρόν
δεῖγμ' ἐστιν εὐθὺς πᾶσι μικροψυχίας.

The last development of Greek social ethics thus attained to the earliest of Egypt. So also, if you meet a man after a quarrel, avoid his gaze, and remind him not of your dispute; and if you fall out with a relative (chap. 33), discuss your differences with him privately, reason with him kindly, and conciliate him: do not injure his public reputation. If you be a superior be not too strict, but indulgent (36).

Four chapters[1] are devoted to recommending (3) *honesty* in the administration of public business, in tilling the fields (where fences between neighbours did not exist), and generally (19, 20), as being necessary for peace, for a good conscience, and for prosperity.

(4.) *Benevolence* is also recommended,[2] especially liberality to servants, to mendicants, and to the

---

[1] 5, 9, 19, 20.   [2] Chaps. 17, 22, 30, 34.

poor generally. Chapter 30 is peculiarly interesting. 'If thou become great after being small, and gainest fortune by toil, and art therefore placed at the head of thy city, be not proud of thy riches, which are thine by the gift of God. Thy neighbour is not inferior to thee ; be to him as a companion.'

(5.) The *treatment of women* recurs several times through the work.[1] 'Love thy wife, and cherish her, as long as thou livest; be no tyrant; flattery acts upon her better than rudeness, and will make her contented and diligent.' And the author reverts to the subject (chap. 37), to recommend liberality in affording her dress to exhibit herself to her friends. ' But in the house of a relative or friend, where thou hast access to the female apartments, beware of meddling with the women. A thousand men are carried away to enjoy the pleasure of a short delusive moment. But a man attaineth unto death if he knoweth her. It is a passion which destroyeth a man altogether.'[2] Above all, any indiscretion with the wives of near relatives is to be abhorred as the most odious of crimes.

(6.) *Prudence and caution in council* form the subject of three chapters. Especially the learned

---

[1] Chaps. 18, 21, 32, 37

[2] Cf. Prov. vii., 26, *sq.* ' For she hath cast down many wounded: yea, many strong men have been slain by her. Her house is the way to hell, going down to the chambers of death.'

[3] 15, 24, 25.

man's slowness to speak is contrasted with the rashness of the soldier, whose pleasures are short-lived; when the conflict is over, he is like an oar thrown aside on the beach, whereas the cautious and quiet man will rule permanently. I need not dilate on the scattered precepts which lie outside these topics. Flatterers are commented on, and the vain expectation that our work will last after us, whereas even as it emerges, so it sinks again in the stream of time without leaving a trace.

We may conclude this lengthy review with a remarkable utterance (chap. 12). 'If thou art wise, bring up thy son to fear God. If he obey thee, walking in thy steps, and caring thy goods as he ought, then show him all favour. Yet thy foolish son is also thine own offspring; estrange not thine heart from him, but admonish him. But if he violate all thy commands and revile thee, strike him on the mouth; give not way to such an one.' The whole book is very like the Proverbs of Solomon—as much so as if his Egyptian bride had brought him a copy of it among her gifts. But it is the obvious morality of all human society, and has probably been repeated in every century of the world's history. Constant allusions to written ordinances seem to imply the existence of some acknowledged sacred books even at this period; so that the total absence of all allusion to future rewards and punishments is very remarkable. We should, perhaps, expect this omission in the Proverbs of Solomon, but not in the ethical teachings of an Egyptian author, whose Ritual had told him the immortality of the soul. I suppose here, as elsewhere, theology had so complicated religion as to dissociate it from morality. The ethical teacher was a layman, and seems to have avoided spiritual considerations.[1]

As was observed, there is no change in the morality of later Egyptian thinkers. The following proverbial precepts are selected among those translated by M. Pierret from the demotic moral treatise preserved in the Louvre.[2]

'Let not bitterness enter into the heart of a mother.

---

[1] Though I have not extracted passages from Dr. Lauth's translation of the first treatise, in which there is a great deal of conjecture, his Essay (*Munich Sitz. ber.* for 1869, vol. ii., pp. 530-79) is well worth reading. He agrees tolerably with the fragments previously rendered by M. Chabas. The main point treated appears to be the evil of gluttony in society—a vice so prevalent in after days as to be pictured in the tombs of Beni Hassan. The conclusion of the document asserts it to have been written under Huni and Snefru, kings of the third dynasty; yet even then not only are the palette and inkhorn used as signs, but reference is made to older books as authorities for several statements. If books were written before the third dynasty, how old must civilisation have been in Egypt? Cf. especially *op. cit.*, pp. 536 and 579. It appears that Dr. Lepsius has in his possession a papyrus of the same date, and perhaps even (Lauth, *op. cit.*, p. 534) by the same hand, which has never been published.

[2] Cf. *Recueil de Travaux*, &c., p. 46.

Slay not, lest thou be thyself in peril of being slain.

Be not the companion of a wicked man.

Establish not thy tomb above those that rule over thee.

Be it far from thee to deal roughly with thy wife, whose strength is less than thine; but be thou a protection to her.

Curse not thy master before God.

Redeem not thy life with that of thy neighbour.

Make it not thy sport to deceive them that are thy servants.

Let not thy son keep company with a married woman.

Establish not thy tomb in thine own domain.

Establish not thy tomb at the entry of the temple.

Walk not with a fool.

Tarry not to listen to his words.'

This proverbial advice is no doubt sound and excellent, and if not very deep is, at least, free from any bitter or satirical view of life.

If the moral treatises of any one period can be regarded as peculiar, it must certainly be the Ramessid era, where, though the principles are the same, we have much greater detail of illustration and of practical advice. The proverbial philosophy of the Leyden papyrus, like the earlier part of the

Prisse papyrus, speaks in parables, and brings home its truths by the aid of metaphors from common life. The fragmentary character and the want of aid from the context make these collections among the most difficult to translate.[1] The following specimens are given by Dr. Lauth and by M. Chabas.[2]

'If the Nile increases, no one can work. If a beggar is made rich, the magistrates will praise him. If thou make a man that knows not the *plectrum* master of the harp, he will not play to charm away melancholy. If a man has no knife how will he slay an ox? That man is happy who lives on his own labour. A ragged girl becomes possessor of a *trousseau;* she that looked at her face in water the possessor of a mirror.'

Again: 'All manner of jewels [enumerated] are found on the neck of slave women; honourable women and mistresses of houses are saying: Would that we had enough to eat!' This last observation appears to be a satire on the luxury and vice of contemporary society.

But the instructions conveyed in letters of this period are more interesting, as they concern particular cases and recommend special professions in life.

---

[1] Dr. Lauth (*Munich Sitz. ber.* for 1870, ii. 2, *appendix*, p. 17, *note*) promises a complete translation of this papyrus, and also of the *Instructions of Amenemha* from the Sallier papyri.

[2] *Leemans*, ii., p. 69

I do not wish to touch here on the epistolary character of these papyri, which will be considered hereafter, but on their moral tone. Being all the compositions of literary men, they naturally laud their own profession as the highest, and its first condition, diligence, as the greatest of virtues. They contain not only encouragements to study, but also sharp reproofs of idleness, and a special castigation of its lower forms. Doubtless the great complications of the graphic system, as well as of the more learned mythology, made the preparation for a scribe's profession almost as arduous as that of a civil servant now-a-days.

Many exhortations to study have been preserved. Here is a specimen :—' O scribe, give not way to sloth, or thou shalt be soundly chastised. Let not thy heart turn aside after pleasure, or thou wilt let the books fall from thine hand. Practise eloquence, and dispute with those that know more than thou; accomplish the work of an educated man. Yea, when thou art stricken in years, thou shalt find it to thy profit. A scribe cunning in all manner of work becometh great, therefore separate thyself not from it. Spend not thy days in wantonness, or thou shalt be stricken. The ears of the young man are on his back—he hears when he is beaten. May thy heart attend to words, for thou wilt find it profitable to thee. The beasts are taught to perform their work, the horse is tamed, and the hawk

trained. Such is the power of education. **Neglect
not books, do not loathe them.**'[1]

But to the idle and the dissolute, the **admoni**tions are very outspoken. Here is the eleventh letter of the Pap. Sallier, i., in the British Museum, which has been translated **by** Mr. Goodwin[2]:—
'Whereas it has been told me that thou hast forsaken books, and devoted thyself **to pleasure** [?] ; that thou goest **from tavern to tavern,** smelling of beer, at the **time** of evening : if beer gets into **a** man, it overcomes his mind. **Thou art like an oar** started from its place, which is unmanageable every way ;[3] thou art like a shrine without its god,[4] like **a** house without provisions, whose walls are found **shaky.** Thou knowest that wine is an abomination, that thou hast taken an oath that thou wouldst not put liquor into thee. Hast thou forgotten thy resolution ?"[5]

The most complete discussion of the **comparative**

---

[1] This passage is quoted **from** Chabas' *Mélanges*, i., p. **117.**

[2] *Cambridge Essays* for 1858, **p. 253.**

[3] So the disbanded **soldier is described in the Prisse Papyrus** (chap. **25) as an oar cast** away, and left on shore.

[4] **This is** the remarkable metaphor repeated in the **New Testament ('** Ye are the temples **of the Holy Ghost'), and which** could only be found in a nation of very lofty and spiritual aspirations.

[5] I have culled these sentiments, and omitted such sentences as Mr. Goodwin does not vouch for. The **rest** of the letter contains no new **idea of interest.**

merits of the scribes and other professions is, however, that contained in the second part of Pap. Sallier 2, which consists of twenty-nine sections, but which has been too briefly expounded by Mr. Goodwin.[1] The document has, as usual, the form of instructions given by a father to his son, and enumerates (a) the hardships of other callings, (β) the advantages of a literary profession, (γ) its moral requisites.

The artificer must work at night, and strain his arms to fill his belly. The embalmer has his fingers filthy, and his clothes defiled; the shoemaker is bad at walking. The dyers, that carry on their labours in a pool, are neighbours to the crocodile: but the products of literature are *eternal as the rocks*. The assertion of the omniscience of God, and cautions against lying, manifest a high moral tone. The 'instructions of Amenemha I.' in the same papyrus are not moral, but almost entirely biographical details as to his own achievements, which are intended as a model for his son. They need not, therefore, come into consideration here.

It is not difficult from these materials to form a clear picture of Egyptian morals. The very ancient documents which have been discussed show that most of the same social principles which now regulate society not only were in force twenty-five or thirty centuries before Christ, but were

---

[1] *Cambridge Essays*, pp. 272-4.

regarded even then as of venerable antiquity, and of established **authority** through the practice of earlier generations. Obedience, prudence, sobriety, self-restraint, affection at home, and courtesy abroad—these and other virtues served men as they do now, and were esteemed accordingly; and if these blunt ethical teachers show a want of refinement in the plainness of their language, and the self-assertion of their deserts, they avoided that excessive refinement which seeks hidden motives for apparent moral worth, and which, under the guise of exalting the Deity, maligns the **real** goodness of His work.

§ 8. *Magical Books.*—It is, however, at first sight strange that *Magic* and **its** mysteries should have laid such firm hold on these prosaic and home-spun moralists. The two conditions of mind seem at first sight contradictory.[1] Yet there **is no** evidence that Egyptian magic was confined to the lower classes, or that it did not exist in primitive times, and **only** arose in the decay of the nation. The truth is **that** all through the many centuries of Egypt's life, **along**

---

[1] Perhaps they are so to Aryan **races, the Semites** having always been the great propagators **of magic, even in the West.** So Firdusi describes **the frightful millennium of the reign of** Zohak, **in** the mythical antiquity of Iran, **as a time** 'when morality **was despised,** but magic held in honour'—a contrast which **would** have appeared quite unintelligible to an Egyptian. Cf. Firdusi, *Ed. Mohl.,* vol. i., p. 69.

with her religion, and her morals, Egypt had her magic also.

It was this tendency which is chiefly displayed in the Ritual. There, as we have seen, the moral side is very scantily represented; and it is by the aid of formulae and of incantations that the soul is to overcome the spiritual adversaries that will attempt its destruction. As therefore the moral treatises were naturally connected with the practical part of the Ritual, so the magical literature will illustrate and explain the mystic and formal parts.

We are amply supplied with specimens of magical literature. They are preserved in the papyrus of Mr. Harris, which M. Chabas has translated, in the Ramessid papyri of the Leyden museum, in demotic fragments in the same museum, as well as in that of Paris, and even in Greek papyri.[1] But it appears that, as in other countries, when the solid sciences, the arts, and the political greatness of Egypt waned, men gave more attention to superstition and to charlatanism. Thus, for example, the earliest medical treatise we possess displays but few charms and incantations compared with the later, in which they are placed side by side. The latest demotic treatises

---

[1] The superstitious turn of the Egyptians is indeed sufficiently proved by the remarkable calendar in Sallier Papyrus 4, commented on by M. de Rougé, *Revue archéol.*, 1854; and by Mr. Goodwin, *Cambridge Essays*, p. 275.

are the most ignorant and irrational of all. It is then not without a certain historical significance, that the last indigenous king of the country, Nectanebos II., is only known to history as a magician. No higher occupation now remained for his effete kingdom.[1] The preservation of this particular branch of literature, even in the Christian times of Egypt, shows how this side of the Egyptian mind affected those who came into contact with it; and I believe that in the mystic systems of Alexandria there will yet be found a vast deal more of old Egyptian influence than has been suspected.

The principles adopted in the magic ceremonies of the Egyptians were uniform, and are described by M. Chabas as follows:[2]—

There is first the mention of a mythological event, almost always relating to some of the conflicts between Osiris and Set, or the good and evil powers in nature; secondly, the conjuror identifies himself with a deity whose powers and attributes he assumes by means of the incantation; then follow, lastly, injunctions and threats against the object to be conjured. This plan is followed in all the epochs from which magic treatises have survived.

Let us reflect for a moment on the moral ideas im-

---

[1] See the article on the Leyden Pap. 67, in C. J. Reuvens' *Lettres à M. Letronne*, pp. 76-8.

[2] *Leemans*, ii., p. 64.

plied in these forms. A profound sympathy with the great struggle between good and evil pervaded every portion of Egyptian life. The fasts and feasts, for example, in the Sallier calendar, are all determined as commemorations of a victory or apparent defeat of Osiris in his great battle with the Wicked One— in fact, on the very same principle that the holidays of our own Church are determined; and the fear of bad fortune on certain days was a superstition indeed, but a superstition founded on the belief that God would punish the disrespect and want of sympathy of men with his Labour of Love, and his benevolence on their behalf. Again, the identification of the man, in such a difficulty, with a Deity whose power he assumes, is one of the most interesting features in the Egyptian mind, and if I mistake not, one of the great secrets of their national success. This has in all ages marked the difference between the brutal savage and the more refined Aryan and Semite, that the latter have ascribed to invisible agency the direction of the affairs of men. The consequent belief that the Deity was co-operating in their labours, and even acting in and through man, has enabled them to carry out with confidence what seemed impossible to mere human strength. We may ridicule the travesty of this noble conception in the magic formulae, drawn up for *M the son of N*, and sold at a trade price; but do we not see in it a mere exaggeration of the fundamental idea of the Ritual, which represents the deceased saved from the powers of Hell by assuming the purity and righteousness of Osiris? It is the very language of the apostle—' Put ye on the Lord Jesus Christ;' of many metaphors of Scripture; and of our popular preaching; and if we do not by any means enter so thoroughly into the idea as the old Egyptians, yet the fundamental principle is the same.

We are too fond of treating with contempt the faith of ancient nations, because the *object* of their worship appears to us clothed in unworthy forms, and portrayed with gross and material qualities. But surely, in the absence of a direct revelation, it is rather the *principle* of worship which should be regarded; and if we consider Egyptian religion from this fair point of view, we cannot but infer even from their lowest superstitions, that, whatever may be the theories about Chamite civilisation and its material character, facts prove the Egyptians to have been a people of highly intellectual gifts, and of deeply spiritual faith.

Numerous quotations from this branch of literature will not be demanded, as they are now chiefly of a philological value, and their literary interest must always be secondary.

Most of the formulae in the Leyden papyrus are directed against diseases supposed to be produced by the entrance of an evil spirit into the body, just as in so many cases of sickness in the New Testament. And if in the Middle Ages men sought to exorcise Satan out of the body of the sick, so in the magic treatises with which we are concerned, the disease is identified with Baal or Set, the wicked gods of the shepherds who had once ruined Egypt, and they were cursed until they should relinquish their grasp.[1]

In the same way a division of the Ritual (including chapters 31-42) is devoted to *exorcising* by means of formulae the crocodiles, serpents, and other wicked animals that oppose the deceased.[2]

A very interesting hieroglyphic inscription on a pillar in the temple of the god Chonsu, which has been translated by Dr. Birch and the Vicomte de Rougé, shows that this belief was received in the days of king Ramses XII. (in the eleventh century B. C.). The daughter of the king of Bouchten, an Asiatic kingdom not yet determined,[3] had been married to Ramses. Her younger sister, Bent-entrest, was attacked with grievous internal pains. Her father sought help from the famous physicians of Egypt. The king called together his College of physicians, and said : ' Now show me a man of intelligent heart, a master of skilful fingers, from

---

[1] Cf. Chabas in *Leemans*, ii., p. 63.
[2] Cf. De Rougé, *Rituel*, pref., p. viii.
[3] Possibly Ecbatana.

among you.' But the spirit was too powerful for a mere physician. The god Chonsu, being solemnly transported to Bouchten, at once expelled it.[1]

So in the Lee papyrus, and in one of the Rollin papyri, which contain fragments of a judicial prosecution, the accused are charged with having employed magical arts to obtain access to the hareem of king Ramses III., in order to promote a conspiracy against him.[2]

There was, in fact, hardly any condition of life which does not appear to have sought assistance from magic. In one of the Leyden papyri there are magic rites and sacrifices to be performed at certain seasons of the year, to avert the plague and destruction of crops; there are also numerous little rolls of papyrus inscribed with magic formulae, and used as amulets to protect the wearer from sickness or death.[3]

The two cases with which the Harris papyrus and the Leyden collection conclude are not the least remarkable. The former is a formula intended to

---

[1] Cf. for longer details Brugsch, *Hist. d'Égypte*, p. 206. The whole inscription has also been fully treated by M. de Rougé in the *Journal asiatique*, 1856-8. See particularly his complete translation in the last article (Sept., 1858, pp. 221, *sq.*).

[2] Cf. M. Devéria's article in the *Journal asiatique* for November, 1867, pp. 412, *sq.*

[3] It has been shown above (p. 249) that the Funeral Ritual was intended to afford a similar protection to the dead.

give a watch-dog magic power against thieves and wild beasts. The latter was found attached to a little image of a lady, and consists in a deprecatory address of a husband to his deceased wife. He fondly thought that death had relieved him effectually of the lady, but was grievously mistaken. In some unexplained way, but very probably in dreams or apparitions, the lost wife was in the habit of revisiting him. He reminds her that he had been a good husband, and recals some of the events of their wedded life as evidence. Despite of her troublesome visitations, he calls her 'a perfect and living spirit.'[1]

I shall conclude this part of the subject by quoting the remarkable imprecation with which one of the Leyden formulae concludes.[2] 'The heaven,' it proclaims, ' shall be no longer ; the earth shall be no longer ; the five supplemental days [of the Egyptian year] shall be no longer; no longer shall there be offerings to the gods, the lords of Heliopolis. There shall be failure in the

---

[1] This highly interesting papyrus, sketched out by Chabas (*Leemans*, ii., p. 79), has, so far as I know, never been translated.

[2] M. Reuvens, in his learned and interesting *Lettres à M. Letronne*, pp. 11, *sq.*, and p. 41, comments on a Greek invocation of Mystic Love, in the Leyden Pap. 75, which reproduces all the same features. He shows, in particular, how accurately the treatise *de Mysteriis*, attributed to Jamblichus, repeats the same ideas.

heaven of the South, disaster in the heaven of the North; lamentations shall be heard within the tombs. The sun shall no longer shine, nor the Nile increase, but shall diminish at his season' [of inundation]. Such was the most frightful picture which the imagination of the old Egyptian could paint of the collapse of the universe. Most characteristically it considers the sustenance of the living secondary to the worship of the gods and the repose of the dead.

§ 9. *Medical Literature.*—The consideration of magic leads us naturally to consider the medicine of the Egyptians; for in all imperfect stages of civilisation these two have been connected, and at times hardly separated. The earliest notices of the Greeks are indeed, in Egyptian matters, very late authorities; but it may still not be amiss to remind the classical reader that the poems of Homer express themselves very strongly on the point:

[Αἴγυπτος] τῇ πλεῖστα φέρει ζείδωρος ἄρουρα
φάρμακα, πολλὰ μὲν ἐσθλὰ μεμιγμένα, πολλὰ δὲ λυγρά,
ἰητρὸς δὲ ἕκαστος ἐπιστάμενος περὶ πάντων
ἀνθρώπων, ἦ γὰρ Παιήονός εἰσι γενέθλης.[1]

This passage concludes a curious description of a *mental* opiate administered by Helen to her company, when they were burdened with sad memories of other days. But though the anatomical knowledge displayed in Homer's descriptions of wounds is said to

---

[1] Hom. Od., iv., 229-232.

be considerable, the notions of medical and surgical treatment in his day were so crude that his praise of the Egyptians has but little weight.

The testimony of Herodotus is more explicit. He says that the science was divided into several branches, relating to eyes, teeth, intestines, and obscure diseases, and practised by specialists.[1] In the Egyptian prescriptions I have not found any mention of diseases of the eyes or teeth; but the facts that ophthalmia was always prevalent in the country, as it is even in the present day, and that there are mummies *whose teeth are stopped with gold*, not only corroborate his statement, but seem to prove that the silence of the extant medical papyri on these diseases arises from the reason alleged by Herodotus. They were discussed in special treatises by oculists and dentists, and none of these treatises have yet been found. For the same reason there is no mention of properly surgical treatment, though we can see from the bandaging of the mummies that no devices of modern surgery surpass in neatness or comfort those of the old Egyptians.

Some facts related by the historian afford independent evidence. Amasis had sent to Cyrus an oculist at his request, just as we already saw

---

[1] Cf. ii., 84: Ἡ δὲ ἰητρικὴ κατὰ τάδε σφι δέδασται. μιῆς νούσου ἕκαστος ἰητρός ἐστι καὶ οὐ πλεόνων. πάντα δ' ἰητρῶν ἐστι πλέα· οἱ μὲν γὰρ ὀφθαλμῶν ἰητροὶ κατεστέασι, οἱ δὲ κεφαλῆς, οἱ δὲ ὀδόντων, οἱ δὲ τῶν κατὰ νηδὺν, οἱ δὲ τῶν ἀφανέων νούσων.

that the King of Bouchten applied long before to
Ramses XII. for a medical man skilled in intes-
tinal complaints. Darius also, when he sprained his
foot so badly that a bone (which Herodotus calls
the *astragalus*) was displaced from its socket, is said
to have then had in his household Egyptian sur-
geons, who were in the highest repute.[1]

But all these scattered notices sink into insigni-
ficance since the discovery of the medical papyri or
prescriptions of the old Egyptians themselves.[2] Of

---

[1] Herod., iii., 129. Νομίζων δὲ καὶ πρότερον περὶ ἑωυτὸν ἔχειν Αἰγυπτίων τοὺς δοκέοντας εἶναι πρώτους τὴν ἰητρικὴν τούτοισι ἐχρᾶτο. When the historian proceeds to say, οἱ δὲ στρεβλοῦντες καὶ βιώμενοι τὸν πόδα κακὸν μέζον ἐργάζοντο, it appears that the swell-
ing was so great as to make it difficult to tell whether a bone
was broken or not, and that the Egyptians treated the injury
as a fracture, which they endeavoured to *set*. At all events,
these men used a well-known principle in surgery, and probably had artificial aids (στρεβλοῦντες) for drawing bones into
their places. M. Mariette's evidence, however, shows that
bone-setting was not in common use during the eleventh dynasty.
For in his instructive catalogue of the antiquities in the Boulaq
museum, he describes (p. 243) a mummy of that date with its
thigh bone broken, and the ends overlapping, and so grown
together again naturally. He says such things are common, but
has not told us whether the specimens are all of ancient date.
Strangely enough, the two greatest wars in Herodotus' history—
the invasions of Egypt and of Greece—are said by him to have
been brought about by the machinations of doctors exiled by
their talents from their own country.

[2] The sources of information on the subject which I have been
able to collect are the following :—M. Brugsch (1), *Ueber die*

x

these by far the most remarkable is the papyrus of
Berlin, of which the date is well determined to be
the fourteenth century B. C. But on the fifteenth
page there occurs the following curious superscription : 'Commencement of the treatise on curing the
ouchet (inflammation?). It was discovered, written
in ancient writing, and rolled up in a case under the
feet of an Anubis in the town of *Sechem*, in the days
of his sacred Majesty *Tet* (or Thoth), the righteous.
After his death it was transmitted to his sacred
Majesty king *Sent*, the righteous, on account of its
importance. It was then restored to [its place
under] the feet of the statue,' &c., &c. Whatever
difficulties there may be in identifying the former

---

medizinischen Kenntnisse der alten Aegypter, in the *Monatschrift
für Wissenchaft u. Literatur* for January, 1853; and (2) *Notice
raisonné d'un traité médical*, &c., Paris, 1863, reprinted from his
Monuments, ii., p. 101. The older paper is more general, and indeed interesting. (3) F. Chabas, *Mélanges égyptolog.*, i., p. 55,
'*La Médecine des anciens Egyptiens*,' and (4) his notice of the
Leyden medical papyrus in Leemans, ii., p. 67; also (5) a letter
of M. Chabas to the Editor of *Literary Gazette* for April 19th,
1862 ; (6) a mere mention of Mr. Edwin Smith's papyri at Luqsor
in *Lepsius' Zeitschrift* for December, 1870, p. 165 ; (7) two
translations of the Coptic medical papyrus in Zöega's *Catalogue*,
one by M. E. Dulaurier (*Jour. asiat.* for 1843, p. 433), another
found among the papers of Champollion, and printed in the
Rev. arch. for September, 1854 ; (8) some notices in M. Pleyte's
Étude sur un rouleau magique du Musée de Leide, pp. 8, 60, &c.
(9) Dr. Birch's description of a newly-acquired medical papyrus (Brit. Museum) in *Lepsius' Zeitschr.* for 1871, pp. 61-4.

name, King Sent is well known to have been one of the second dynasty, which reigned long before the pyramids were built ; and if the treatise was old in his day, the statement of Manetho must be more than probable, when he tells us that the second king of Egypt, the immediate successor of Menes, composed works on anatomy. These data remove the origin of medicine among the Egyptians to an antiquity almost incredible. In no reasonable system is the reign of King Sent placed below 3000 B. C ; and if the science had long before that time reached the stage of definite treatises, where are we to place its first rude commencements? We have here one more argument for the antiquity of civilisation.

Turning to the contents of this very ancient chapter, the first subject which meets us is a definite anatomical theory. 'The head,' it says, 'has 32 veins [or canals], which draw the breath from it to the breast, and so transmit the breath to all the limbs.' Then follows a detailed description of these vessels, which go in pairs to each limb or part of the body. There seem to be only two allowed for the legs, and two for the arms, whereas the *occiput, sinciput, cervix,* and each ear, have two allotted to them. Special remedies are appointed to be taken for an attack in any of the separate veins. These remedies are almost all to be taken internally, and consist of carefully quantified prescriptions, in which milk of various animals, honey, salt, and vinegar play a prominent part.[1] The nature of many other substances mentioned has not as yet been determined. Morning and evening, while the patient was in bed, appear to be the approved time for administering medicines. We know not what the particular disease *ouchet* is, against which so many prescriptions were urged. It appears to have been such as to affect any part of the body, and was probably in general *fever*, the various species of the disease not being distinguished, and local affections being therefore treated as special manifestations of the same malady.

But apart from the particular disease or particular remedies, some striking features obtrude themselves upon our consideration in this ancient treatise. Not only is there a distinct anatomical theory at the basis of the treatment, but we notice a most remarkable absence of charms and superstitious observances in administering medicines. None of the later treatises elsewhere preserved (except the Coptic fragment) are so free from this fault. There are indeed two prayers at the end of the papyrus, intended to be addressed to Isis and Horus while the medica-

---

[1] There also appear various kinds of milk, urine and excrements, and directions for the application of raw flesh, lard, and hartshorn. Draughts, unguents, and injections are all prescribed. The milk of a woman with a male infant is preferred. Several stimulants are also used. (Cf. Brugsch and Chabas, *loc. cit.*).

ments were being mixed; but they seem the same for all, being, as it were, a concession to the popular belief, and not of any great importance in the writer's mind.¹ Considering that the later papyri are full of incantation and magic, this fact is of great importance, and a strong confirmation of the statement that the golden age of Egypt, the highest condition of its art and civilisation, was in its earlier days, 3000 years before Christ, when the pyramids were built, and when sculpture attained a perfection not subsequently equalled.²

The earlier pages of the document we are now discussing are also free from incantations or gross superstitions, and give a number of simple remedies

---

¹ I think the remark of M. Brugsch (*Monatschrift*, p. 46), that the earliest development of medicine in Egypt was effected by the priests, who treated it theologically, is devoid of evidence. The priests seem rather to have gradually got this power into their hands, in the course of that theological development of Egypt which crushed everything else in the country, embalming its civilisation, perhaps, but certainly killing it. M. Brugsch has not stated on what evidence he ascribes (contrary to tradition) the earliest medicine to the priests, except it be on the analogy of other nations—a precarious reason when our documents do not support it.

² This is established by the magnificent statue of King Shafra, now in the museum of Boulaq, and of which a copy has been made for the museum of Berlin. See the description in the *Rev. archéol.* for 1860, ii., p. 19, or in *Lepsius' Zeitsch.* for 1864, p. 58. Cf. also Mariette's *Notice, &c.*, p. 203.

for tumours, eruptions, boils, and bruises. The remedies are ointments, or doses compounded with honey, milk, salt, and many unknown herbs. But what is far more interesting to medical men is the diagnosis of the *ouchet* disease, which appears so formidable. The description is more like the Hippocratic records of cases than any other ancient document with which I am acquainted. The following are some of the symptoms :—' He feels indigestion, the mouth of his heart (*os ventriculi*) is sick, his heart is burning ; his clothes are heavy upon him—many clothes will not warm him ; the taste of his heart [apparently used for *stomach* throughout] is perverted, like that of a man who has eaten sycamore figs ; he is in a very costive condition ; and if he gets up, he is like a man prevented from walking."[1]

---

[1] As this Essay is not intended for medical readers, I have, of course, omitted or softened several symptoms. The reader will find them in Chabas' *Mélanges*, i., p. 60, or in Brugsch's second treatise, above cited. On the back of the papyrus there are two pages of symptoms and prescriptions added, relating to the signs of pregnancy and barrenness. This department appears to have been in a bad condition as a speciality. See the details in Chabas, *Mélanges*, i., pp. 68-70. Clemens Alexandrinus notices that there was a special hermetic medical book περὶ γυναικίων. We can hardly fancy medical practitioners being allowed to carry out some of the prescriptions proposed. It appears certain from the charms translated by M. Pleyte (*Étude sur un rouleau magique*, &c., Leyden, 1866, p. 171) that men attended confinements medically.

This observation of details, and attempt at rational treatment, far surpass the medical lore of Homer and the early Greeks.

It was not, in fact, till the development of Kroton in the fifth century B. C., that the Greek doctors attained any reputation. If I may digress for a moment into their history, it will afford a clue to the development of Egyptian physic also. We know that in Greece, as elsewhere, the earliest notions on the subject were those common among primitive nations, not so much of the actual possession of spirits, as of curing disease by charms, and by the invocation of higher powers. I do not believe that sound notions were attained by a study of disease, starting from such premises. But along with the medicine-men applying charms to the sick, there sprang up, owing to the athletic habits of the Greeks, a very different class of men, who found that no amulet or spell would secure victory at the games and festivals of Greece. These were the *trainers*, who prepared youths for athletic contests; and they started, not from *pathology*, but from *hygiene*. Their rational inferences were gradually applied to cases beyond their sphere, where some abnormal condition had arisen and must be remedied.[1] So it was that Kroton, which produced the

---

[1] Plato attributes the change to Herodikos. Ἡρόδικος δὲ παιδοτρίβης ὢν καὶ νοσώδης γενόμενος, μίξας γυμναστικὴν ἰατρικῇ, κ. τ. λ. (Rep. p. 406.)

best athletes, also produced perhaps the earliest school of rational doctors. And this school existed side by side with the old superstitious quackery, so that in the days of Plato, *men* were treated by physicians who made it their duty to expound the nature of their treatment and to justify it,[1] while women and slaves were doctored at home by means of the old absurdities.

It is not improbable that the same development took place in the history of Egyptian medicine. For we know that from early times they studied hygiene as well as pathology; and from hygiene rational Physic will arise far sooner than from the attempt to cure diseases as they chance to occur. In the face of these facts it is sad to find that from the date of our earliest authority on Egyptian medicine the rational side wanes, and the superstitious grows stronger and more predominant.

The next document which has been preserved is in the Leyden[2] museum; and though dating from

---

[1] There is somewhere an account of Gorgias' brother, who was a physician, bringing the rhetorician with him to *persuade* his patients; the reader may contrast with it, as Plato himself does, the treatment of the lower orders by the physician's slaves (*Legg.*, lib. iv., p. 720). The Greeks laid such stress on rational persuasion as to ignore the evil effects such discussions might produce on the patient.

[2] Numbered i., 346. The medical papyrus of the British Museum appears to be the same date, but mentions far older names.

the Ramessid era, like the last, is probably a century or two later. It has been very briefly described by MM. Chabas and Brugsch.[1]

There does not appear to be any new principle enounced in it, and its scientific value is even inferior to the older treatise. There is a great deal more magic and incantation in it. But still it appears from M. Chabas' account (though M. Pleyte differs), that the remedies are considered as different from the incantations, and for the most part are described separately. This fact, if true, shows that some sound views still existed on the subject, despite of the manifest decay of the science. Perhaps indeed such a conclusion is still hazardous. Our documents are so few, that we may have accidentally recovered a higher order of treatise from the earlier, and inferior kinds from the later period of Egyptian history.[2] But the inference is sufficiently

---

[1] Cf. *Notice raisonnée*, p. 18; and *Leemans*, ii., pp. 67, 72.

[2] We may obtain more light when Mr. Smith's medical papyri are published and translated. One of them contains more than 100 pages, and the other 19. Both are in hieratic character, but as to their contents or age I have been able to ascertain nothing farther. A calendar on the back of one of them has been discussed by MM. Brugsch and Eisenlohr in *Lepsius' Zeitschr.* for 1870, where the latter ascribes them to the second century B. C., conjecturally. I think there is mentioned somewhere a medical papyrus in Mr. Harris' collection also. Dr. Birch's just published account (cf. above, p. 306, *note*) of the medical papyrus presented to the Museum by the Royal Institution

corroborated by **the general decay of the** nation in other respects to hold **its place as a** reasonable conjecture.

The next document in our list is **a demotic papyrus in** the Leyden collection, which is of course of much later date. It repeats the same technical **terms** for remedies, and shows the same small **proportion of** honest prescriptions compared with magic devices. Love philtres, in particular, play a great part in this papyrus.[1] It is remarkable that they are mostly directed **to turn** the love of women towards their husbands or lovers, and not *vice versâ*, **as in almost** all the cases told in classical authors. Here, again, **to use the remark of** Herodotus, they seem to have reversed all the laws and customs of other nations.[2]

---

is too brief. He thinks that no rational medicine existed in the days of Cheops, and holds a development of medicine between the fourth and eighteenth dynasties. He has however not yet given sufficient evidence to overthrow the view sustained above.

[1] The Greek part is described by M. Reuvens in his *Description raisonnée des Monuments égyptiens du Musée de Leide*, p. 121; and also *Lettres à M. Letronne*, *appendix*. There are prescriptions for attaining happiness, for acquiring agreeable manners, and making friends, and for succeeding in enterprises. Also prescriptions for obtaining dreams, for keeping people awake till they died for want of sleep, and for separating lovers or married people by estrangement. **The whole document bears** evidence of belonging to the Gnostic school.

[2] Cf. Herod. ii., 35, and his curious examples.

From the Coptic period there is also extant a fragment of four pages, noticed by Zoëga in his catalogue, which treats of skin diseases, one of the most prevalent and permanent plagues of Egypt. With that curious pertinacity that distinguishes the nation, the same forms and the same technical terms are used —nay, even the same invocations to the Deities— that appear in the earliest papyrus; but the ancient gods have been dethroned, and Uriel, Gabriel, and Raphael substituted in their stead. Neither M. Chabas nor M. Brugsch, both of whom are acquainted with this Coptic fragment, notice the two translations of it referred to above. A careful perusal of this treatise, written in the Theban dialect, and dating perhaps from the fifth or sixth century A. D., will impress the reader with a higher idea of Egyptian hygiene than any of the earlier treatises, although it most certainly employs no new remedies, and represents, not the intellect of the decayed Coptic Egypt, but that of the wise and great Pharaohs.[1] It is a small fragment of the original work, as the first prescriptions preserved are called the 185th chapter, and is exclusively de-

---

[1] M. Éd. Dulaurier (*Journal asiatique* for May, 1843, pp. 433) inclines to the opinion that a number of these prescriptions are not originally Egyptian, but borrowed from the school of ‚Galen. This inference rests solely upon similarities of nomenclature, and all the Coptic writings of this period are full of Greek words.

voted to eruptions and skin sores. The staple substances employed for remedies are sulphur, vinegar, oil, and some sort of alkali. These were prescribed in potions, baths, and unguents.

The prayer preserved in the second paragraph of our fragment is hardly an incantation, the possession by spirits being then a commonly received notion; but, like that at the end of the Berlin papyrus, a general supplication to accompany all remedies. It runs thus:—'I conjure thee, angel that relievest from all the diseases that afflict man, and especially from that which tormenteth him in his old age, that his healing may proceed from Uriel, Gabriel, Raphael, and Michael! May he that prayeth be delivered from all sickness!' Champollion felt that this document would afford a key to the old Egyptian medicine, and he was perfectly right.

The Greeks also had observed the unchangeable character of Egyptian medical practice. Clemens Alexandrinus, Diodorus, and Galen, all mention the ancient books. Diodorus adds that the medical men were paid by the State (as indeed they appear to have been to some extent at Athens),[1] and were consequently obliged to conform to the State notions of medicine as preserved in the ancient books. If they insisted on deviating from the estab-

---

[1] Cf. the Lexica and the Aristophanic scholia, sub. voc. δημοσιεύων.

lished treatment, they did so at the risk of their lives if the patient died. I fear such a regulation must have induced very timid practice. So it was that there was no progress in their art from the time when Moses adopted their sanitary regulations, as being characterised by the highest wisdom, till the day when Galen pronounced them mere idle folly.[1] When we see the youthful intellect of Egypt devoting all its energies to this servile and reverential cultivation of the antiquated wisdom of a bygone age, we are reminded of those sad instances, so common in our own society, where a blooming child devotes all her love and all her labour to the life-long nursing of a decrepid and exacting parent; so that the high qualities and the large self-devotion that should have expanded over a household and a family of children, are absorbed and wasted upon a sour and ungrateful hypochondriac.

§ 10. *Scientific Treatises.*—Before leaving this side of Egyptian literature, it may be well to say a word concerning their cultivation of sciences more abstract than that of medicine. The general opinion of Egyptologists is rather against the admission of an advanced state of exact science in the country. No one can doubt the great practical results attained in engineering, in architecture, and even in astro-

---

[1] πᾶσαι λῆροί εἰσιν—*de fac. simpl. med.*, iv.

nomy. The exactitude with which the pyramids face the four points of the compass, and with which their proportions are carried out, show that even in the days of the fourth dynasty the conclusions of science, if not the sciences themselves, were recognised. The general ignorance of the Greeks and Romans concerning older civilisations, and our special ignorance as to what Greek inquirers did learn from them, and embody in their own teaching—these facts make the assertion of M. Brugsch,[1] that the Egyptians had no exact science, very hazardous and premature. M. Chabas has, with his usual caution, endeavoured to qualify the statement by showing that in a document belonging to the Old Empire, and now preserved among the papyri of the Berlin museum, an oppressed peasant addresses his oppressor as the controller of *the course of the earth*, and that the expression is elsewhere used for the motion of the planets. He concludes that the Egyptians were acquainted with the earth's motion at this early epoch.[2] When he adds, however, that no scientific treatise now remains save the medical papyrus, he is inaccurate; for among the Rhind papyri, now in the British Museum, there is one called the *geometric papyrus*, of which Mr. Birch

---

[1] *Zeitschr. der Morgen. Gesell.*, ix., p. 502.
[2] Cf. *Lepsius' Zeitschr.* for 1864, pp. 97, *sq.*

has published a short description.[1] As usual, it purports to be a copy of a far older document, found in a search made for ancient writings by the scribe Aahmes; but the names of the kings which are assigned as dates for the original document and the copy are both unknown. Mr. Birch concludes from various indications, such as the colour of the papyrus, and the peculiarities of the writing, that our copy is not older than the twentieth dynasty (1100 B. C.)

The treatise proceeds in regular propositions, stating the question with 'Suppose,' and the answer with 'Therefore,' or, 'It follows.' It seems to be chiefly concerned with mensuration (the original *geometry*), the measuring of fields, and the estimating of the solid contents of pyramids, being often required by the old Egyptians. The title is as follows: 'Principle of arriving at the knowledge of quantities, and of solving all secrets which are in the nature of things.' The latter part of the title seems very ambitious indeed, and not justified by the contents. All the solutions are ultimately arithmetical, and the work may be therefore best called a treatise on applied arithmetic. There is no sign of the deductive geometry developed so perfectly by the Greeks of Alexandria.

---

[1] *Lepsius' Zeitschr.* for 1868, pp. 108-10. Lepsius had commented on a similar inscription the *Abhandlungen* of the Berlin Academy for 1855, p. 69.

The area to be measured is divided into parallelograms or isosceles triangles, and their individual areas estimated. The lengths of the sides are generally given in the statement of the question.

This brief sketch shows clearly that at the period of this papyrus the geometry of the Egyptians was experimental, not deductive, and that the profound conjecture of Kant is so far verified, when he suggested that *à priori* demonstration in mathematics was the result of a single brilliant discovery after ages of mere groping in the dark.[1]

§ 11. *Letter-writing.*—I turn with pleasure from this very imperfect and unsatisfactory sketch to a subject on whch our evidence is much more complete. Of all branches of Egyptian litera-

---

[1] Cf. *Kritik der reinen Vernunft*, p. 16 (Ed. Hartenstein). 'Vielmehr glaube ich, dass es lange mit ihr [mathematics] *vornehmlich noch unter den Aegyptern*, beym Herumtappen geblieben ist, und diese Umänderung einer Revolution zuzuschreiben sey, die der glückliche Einfall eines einzigen Mannes [war] *u. s. w.* Dem ersten, der den gleichschenklichten Triangel demonstrirte, dem ging ein Licht auf; denn er fand dass er nicht dem, was er in der Figur sehe, oder auch dem blossem Begriffe derselben *nachspüren und gleichsam davon ihre Eigenschaften ablernen müsse,*' &c. This passage, written in the last century, describes the principles of the geometrical Rhind papyrus, as well as if Kant had seen and read it. Possibly, however, it may only have been intended for common surveyors, and may not by any means contain the highest wisdom of the Egyptians—a reservation which in this most fragmentary literature we are apt to forget.

ture, epistolary correspondence may be considered, along with solar hymns, as the best known and the most perfectly understood. From the Ramessid era, undoubtedly the most literary in all Egyptian history, we have some eighty letters, on various subjects, and from various writers.[1] Some of those in the Leyden collection were even rolled up, addressed, and sealed for transmission. Others, however, appear not to have been so intended, at least in the papyri in which we now have them; for they are collected in disjointed series, and were probably intended for general circulation, like the letters of Cicero and the younger Pliny in later times. Certain moral or social tendencies are openly enough shown in them—such, for example, as the praise bestowed on a scribe's life as compared with other professions; and the eulogy of diligence and rebuke of remissness, not merely in literary matters, but also in performing other duties, such as those of steward or agent. Nevertheless, though I have already quoted one of them under the head of ethical writings, they cannot be regarded professedly as such any more than Pliny's letters. Had they been not so directly intended for publication, we should doubtless have found in them historical allusions of priceless worth.

---

[1] M. Brugsch observes (*Histoire d'Égypte*, p. 177) that the names of thirteen scribes of the literary college at this period are preserved, and that there were probably many more.

But as we have them, they are mere specimens of style and illustrations of manners, profoundly interesting as such, but not otherwise instructive.

The form employed will best be understood from the following short specimen, translated from the Leyden collection by M. Chabas.[1] The papyrus is folded flat, and tied with a string of papyrus, which is sealed with hard clay. The writer has put the address on the part turned out, as we should do, when not using an envelope. It is simply this: *The Sotem Mersuatef to his mistress, the priestess of Isis, Tanur.* Mersuatef and Tanur are proper names, and the former is equivalent to some such word as πατρόφιλος, if we might so coin it, in Greek. The exact meaning of Sotem is not certain. Some take it to mean *the obedient*, like the form with which we conclude our letters. Others think it means a

---

[1] Cf. Leeman's *Leyden papyri*, i., 360-70. There are about twenty letters in different papyri of the Leyden collection; and some of them, being prepared for transmission, and sealed, are certainly not mere literary specimens. M. Pleyte has commenced, in his *Études égyptologiques* for 1869, a treatise entitled *l'Épistolographie égyptienne*, which is full of interest. But I do not agree with his views as to the general antiquity of letter-writing, or that we have nowhere specimens of purely pictorial writing: on this point, the facts adduced and discussed in a former Essay (pp. 105-9) appear to me conclusive. Mr. Goodwin's *Cambridge Essay*, and M. Chabas' *Lettre Missive*, from the collection at Bologna, published in the third series of his *Mélanges*, are also instructive.

scribe, priest, or some other special rank.¹ It seems certainly to occur in this sense in other papyri, to be quoted hereafter.

The letter itself reads as follows:—' The Sotem *Mersuatef*, for the satisfaction of his mistress, the priestess of Isis, *Tanur*, of sound and strong life, and under the favour of Amon Ra, King of the Gods. I say to Phra-Harmachis, to Amon the god of Ramses, beloved of Amon; to Phra, the God of Ramses, beloved of Amon; to Set, the very valiant god of Ramses, beloved of Amon; to all the gods and goddesses of the temple of Ramses, beloved of Amon; and to his august personage, Phra-Harmachis (the king himself)—Mayest thou have life! Mayest thou have health! *Memorandum.*—At the present moment the military commander is well, his men are well, his children are well. Be not anxious about them; they are well to-day. What may happen to-morrow, no man can tell. Farewell!'

Several reflections are suggested by this epistle. In the first place, we have a very moderate specimen of the interminable enumeration of titles and polite greetings, which are so wearisome to Egyptologists, and so absurd, compared to our blunt practical way of writing. In all official documents, and in devotional compositions, this fulsome explicitness characterises the Egyptians. But I think we can

---

¹ Cf. Lauth, *Moses der Ebräer*, p. 20; and Ebers, *Aegypten und die Bücher Moses*, i., p. 344.

see that despite of the space these compliments occupied in the letter, the reader was supplied with means of saving time ; for the word 'advice' or 'memorandum,' being in all their correspondence written immediately after the compliments, and often in red, we may be sure the reader ran his eye down till he caught this word, and then applied his mind to the rest. Here we generally find terseness and clearness of expression, with frequent repetitions only when the injunctions are important. The moral reflection on the mutability of human life recurs in many letters, and finds, like most Egyptian moral sentiments, its counterpart in the Hebrew proverbs—' Boast not thyself of to-morrow ; for thou knowest not what a day may bring forth.' It does not, certainly, seem the sort of reflection best calculated to reassure an anxious lady about her friends ; but we know that now-a-days Oriental fatalists find peace of mind and comfort in a doctrine to us the most cruel and relentless conceivable.

By far the most important collection of letters to which we can refer is that in the Sallier and Anastasi papyri of the British Museum. It consists of fifty-eight letters, a few of which are duplicates, referring to all kinds of subjects, and collected, I have already observed, as specimens of style, with an indirect view to moral teaching.[1] The collections were

---

[1] The specimens in the text are quoted from Mr. Goodwin's

made by three different scribes, about the time of
the Exodus, and their names are Pentaour, Pinebsa,
and Enna. There are in all, I may repeat, thirteen
authors of this period known by name from different
papyri—a fact which justifies us in regarding it as
probably the most literary epoch in Egyptian history.

The papyrus Sallier I contains eleven letters,
almost all from Pentaour's master and patron, Ameneman,
to his pupil; as, for example: 'The chief
librarian, *Ameneman*, of the royal white house, says
to the scribe *Pentaour:* Whereas a letter is brought
to thee, saying—*Memorandum.* Why hast thou not
sent provisions to the palace? Yet it is the season for
calves, beasts, eggs, ducks, and vegetables. Thou
didst send a message, saying, I will send provisions.
Now, when my letter reaches thee, thou shalt send
each kind of the provisions of the very best—viz.:
calves, beasts, eggs, ducks, and vegetables, of those
which are fit for the hall of the palace. Beware lest
thou make excuse.' And after a few more directions
he ends with—' Do thou consider this'—a formula
apparently used by superiors, whereas the
pupil Pentaour concludes with—'Behold, this message
is to inform my lord.'

His replies are couched in the following terms:

Essay, now so deservedly celebrated, in the *Cambridge Essays* for
1858, pp. 245-64.

'The scribe *Pentaour* salutes his lord, the chief librarian *Ameneman*, of the royal white house. Again I salute my lord. Whereas I have executed all the commissions imposed upon me by my lord well and truly, completely and thoroughly—I have done my lord no wrong. Again I salute my lord. Whereas the house of my lord is well, his servants are well, his oxen which are in the field are well, the oxen which are in the stall are well, eating their provender daily; yea, their keepers fetch them provender. The horses of my lord are well,' &c., &c. The scribe appears to have been acting as a steward for his master. Many of the letters refer to business of this kind, and to various military and financial missions on which the scribes were employed.

The exhortations to diligence, and the recommendations of a scribe's profession, as contrasted with other pursuits, frequently recur, as might be expected, in this model correspondence. In addition to the letter quoted under the head of moral literature, the following document, which is the fourth letter in the papyrus Sallier I, is worthy of notice. The cumbrous compliments are omitted in Mr. Goodwin's translation, as they are the same in all. 'Why is thy heart volatile, like chaff before the wind? Give thy heart to something else good for a man to do. Idleness is unprofitable; it is of no service to a man in the day of account whether he be a slave, or whether he commands nobles assembled before him. His works are found wanting. He has no servants to draw water, no women to make bread. His comrades are disgusted; their services are withdrawn. Such is the man whose heart is not in his business, whose eye scorns it, who is proud of heart, malignant, violent—who obeys not when thou givest orders. The business of a scribe, there is profit in it; it exceeds all dignities of the king's nobles. Do thou consider this.'

Then follows a fuller expansion of this idea, and a description of the hardships of Egyptian husbandmen, who seem to have required a Land Act more urgently than even the Irish tenantry. 'Whereas it has been told me that thou forsakest letters, and departest from eloquence—that thou givest attention to the labour of the fields, and turnest thy back on the divine words—behold, hast thou not considered the estate of the husbandman? When he would gather in his crops, the caterpillar ravages part of the corn, and the beasts [perhaps hippopotami] devour the other things. Multitudes of rats are in the fields; the grasshoppers alight; the horned beasts consume—the sparrows steal. If the husbandman neglects the rest of the crops, thieves will rob the field. His axe [or ploughshare], which is of metal, corrodes; the horses die through the labour of ploughing. The taxgatherer is at the landing-place; he exacts the tribute; there are police officers with staves, negroes with palm branches; they demand

the corn; they will not be put off. The husbandman is carried away to the canal [to task-work]: they use him roughly; his wife is bound before him; his children are stripped; his neighbours go away to attend to their own crops. The business of the scribe excels all kinds of labours; letters are no travail to him; he pays no taxes. Do thou consider this."
'Dost thou not carry the inkhorn?' says the next letter. 'That makes a difference between thee and the rower of the oar—he is condemned to toil; thou hast not many masters. When man comes from the womb of his mother, he bows to his superiors. The youth must serve the captain, the lieutenant the superior officer. The herdsman serves the farmer, the stableboy the groom. The steward must preside over the works; his horse goes to the field; he brings vegetables for his wife and children. . . The soldier must go to war without a staff, without shoes; he knows not whether to choose life or death. His horse falls among the wild beasts. The thief [?] hides in the bushes—the enemy rushes upon him. The soldier on a march cries to his god: Deliver me.' After enumerating the ills of other professions, this letter ends, like the last, with praises of the scribe's calling.

---

[1] This version is the amended translation published in the *Rev. arch.*, N. S., vol. iv., and differs considerably from its original form in the Cambridge Essays.

I shall only quote one more fragment, which gives some sporting details of interest.[1] The writer is evidently on some mission in a remote part of the country, where he devotes most of his time to field sports. 'There are [with me] 200 great hounds, besides 300 wolfdogs—500 in all.' This seems a very large pack indeed. 'They stand ready every day at the door of the house at the hour of my rising from sleep. They make their breakfast when the barrel is opened. Let me have none of the dogs of the little breed of Ha, the king's scribe. This kind of dog is a stay-at-home; deliver me from them. Hour after hour, at the time when I go out, I have to flog him; I have to kick him, till ——. The red dog with the long tail, he goes by night into the stalls of the oxen. He is equal to the long-faced dog [greyhound?]. He makes no delay in hunting. His face is joyful, like a god; loose him, he is delighted. The kennel where he abides he returns not to it. *Postscript.*—Whereas a certain scribe of registration is staying with me, every vein of whose face is swelled—ophthalmia is in his eyes, the worm gnaws his tooth—I know not how to send him away entirely. My stores are sufficient; let him receive his rations while he remains in the neighbourhood of Kankan.'

---

[1] For the whole document cf. Goodwin, *Cambridge Essays*, p. 259.

The details about the dogs are very curious. There can be no doubt that dogs were fully as common, and as well treated then as they now are.[1] An Egyptian seems always to have had his dog with him, both at home and abroad. The numerous pictures, however, which are preserved, impress us with a low idea of Egyptian dog-breeding. The house-dogs appear to have been very worthless curs, and to have had every need of the magic formulae described above (p. 301), to give them any respectable qualities. The hunting dogs seem all of the greyhound type, but more like the lanky curs we see kept by Irish country people, that go out coursing on Sunday, than any respectable animal of our day. The Egyptian drawing of such things was so accurate, that we may safely trust the representations they have left us. No doubt we sometimes find a dog of wretched appearance endowed with a good nose and a high intelligence, and what is among us the rare exception may have been oftener the case then; but still no sportsman can now look on the dogs of the monuments with the least respect. Above all, the uniform cock and curl of the tail—a feature evidently admired by the Egyptians—is to our eyes exceedingly offensive.[2]

---

[1] They are generally alluded to by proper names, as will be seen hereafter.

[2] In addition to the letters cited, there is a very interesting

§ 12. *Works of Fiction.*—These sporting reflections are detaining us from the next division of our subject—perhaps that of most interest to the general reader. I mean the novel or fiction-writing of the ancient Egyptians. We have rescued from the sands of Africa two precious and tolerably complete relics—the *Tale of the Two Brothers*, contained in the document known as the d'Orbiney papyrus of the British Museum, first described by the Vicomte de Rougé, and the *Romance of Setna*, lately discovered in the tomb of a Coptic monk by M. Brugsch, and by him translated, though not yet perfectly.[1]

The first was composed by the scribe Enna, from whose correspondence we have above quoted, and is dedicated to three brother scribes, but was apparently intended for the edification of one of the royal princes, whose name occurs in the last pages, and fixes its date in the fourteenth century B. C. 'This relates,' says the author, 'to two brothers, children of the same father and mother—the name of the elder

---

one in the collection of Bologna, discussed by M. Chabas (*Mélanges*, iii., pp. 226-46), of the date of Ramses II.

[1] In the *Rev. archéol.* for 1867, p. 161, *sqq*. The papyrus d'Orbiney, published in the Select Papyri of the British Museum, has been carefully studied by Egyptologists. It is said to be one of the easiest of hieratic MSS. to decipher. I here quote M. de Rougé's translation in the *Rev. archéol.* of 1852, p. 385, verified by Mr. Goodwin in his *Cambridge Essay*.

was Anepou, the name of the younger was Satou.[1] Anepou, being the head of the house, married, and treated his younger brother as his son.' After stating that Satou was entrusted with the care of the flocks, he proceeds: 'When he returned from the field, he brought back all sorts of fodder; he sat down with his brother and sister to eat and drink, and then went to the stall to tend his cattle. When the earth was again illumined and the dawn appeared, the hour of going to the fields being come, he called his cattle, and led them to feed in the meadow. He followed them . . and his cattle told him where were the choicest feeding places, for he understood all their speech. And when he brought them back to the stalls they found there all the herbs which they loved. The cattle which he tended became exceeding fat, and multiplied greatly.

When the season of tillage arrived, his elder brother said to him: Let us take the teams, and go to plough; for the land appears [after the inundation], and is meet for sowing. When we have ploughed it, thou shalt fetch the seed. So the young man set himself to do what his elder brother told him. When the earth was again illumined and the day appeared,[2] they went to the fields, and they

---

[1] There is some difficulty in reading this name. M. Chabas reads it *Baïta*; M. Lauth, *Batou*.

[2] This repetition is quite Homeric.

took great delight in their work. And it came to pass after many days that they were in the fields together, and the elder brother said to the younger: Go into the town, and fetch us seed-corn. The young man [went and] found his brother's wife adorning her hair. He said to her: Give me corn— I desire to go to the fields for my brother. She answered him: Go open the garner, and take thyself what thou requirest: my hair would fall down if I went.¹ The young man went to his stable; he took a great vessel—for he wished to carry out much corn—filled it, and then went out with his load.² The young woman said to him: Thou hast at least five measures of corn on thy shoulders. The young man assented, and she answered: How strong thou art! I have observed thy might; for her heart knew him—she was wholly enamoured of him. Then she said: Stay with me an hour³— I have put on my fairest apparel. The young man's anger was greatly kindled, like a leopard, when he heard these shameful words, and she be-

---

¹ M. de Rougé notices that the contemporary monuments show enormous head dresses to have been actually in fashion.

² The recent discoveries at Therasia show that very large earthen vessels were used through the Greek islands in prehistoric times for storing and carrying grain—a habit identical with that here described.

³ M. de Rougé observes that the very words of Genesis are employed.

gan to be sore afraid. He opened his mouth, and said: Thou wert ever in mine eyes even as my mother, and thy husband was to me as a father. I cannot do so great wickedness. Ask me to do anything [honourable]. Now, I shall talk of it to no man, nor shall it be told to any living.

'Then he took up his burden, and returned to his brother in the field. When even was come, the elder returned to his house, and the younger followed his herd. Loaded with all the good things of the field, he was driving his cattle to their stalls for the night. The wife of the elder was sore afraid at what she had said. She made herself to seem as a woman that hath suffered violence, that she might say to her husband: Thy younger brother hath dealt with me violently. So her husband returned home, according to his wont; and when he came, he found his wife lying, as if violence had killed her. She came not, as was her custom, to pour water on his hands, and the house remained in darkness. She stayed lying, and stripped of her garments; and her husband said: It is I that speak to thee. Speak not to me, said she; thy younger brother did thus and thus; [and then she precisely inverts the story]. So he was afraid, and dealt violently with me, that I might not tell concerning it. Also, if thou leavest him alive, I shall cause myself to die.'

So the elder brother's wrath is kindled like a leopard, and, having sharpened his sword, he lies in wait behind the stable door to kill his brother. But when the latter arrives, after sunset, the cow that went foremost to return to the stable said to her herdsman : 'I think that thy elder brother is there with his sword to slay thee when thou shalt be at the door. He heard the words, and they were repeated by the second cow. Then he looked under the door of the stable, and saw the feet of his brother, as he stood, sword in hand. So he threw down his burden, and ran for his life, pursued by his brother. Then he called on Phra, saying: Good Lord, it is thou that showest on which side is violence, and on which justice.' Phra stopped to hear his prayer, and placed between them a great river full of crocodiles, and the younger calls to the elder to wait till morning to hear his explanation, protesting his innocence. So when the day dawned and the sun appeared they saw one another, and the younger began to say to the elder: What hast thou done in following me to slay me? He then tells the real story, and drawing a knife, and mutilating himself, he informs his afflicted brother that he will leave him and go to the valley (or the mountainous district) of the cedar,[1] in the flowers (cones?) of which

---

[1] Mr. Goodwin translates *acacia*, but M. Chabas (*Rev. archéol.*, N. S., vol. iv., pp. 47-51) has shown good reason for rendering it as *cedar*. He believes the scene from this point onward to be laid in Syria, and the sea to be the waters referred to.

he will deposit his heart, so that if the tree were cut, his heart would fall to the earth and he must die. He directs his brother how to find and revivify his heart after seven years are gone by. So he departs, and the elder brother going home in great grief, slays his wife, and casts her to the dogs.

Here the first part of the story ends. It is also this part which possesses most claim to literary beauty. The remainder seeks to interest the reader rather by wonders and by theological mysteries than by simple narrative.

Satou enjoys himself very well, hunting in the valley of the cedar, till the company of the gods, going to look after Egypt,[1] meet him one day, and tell him that it is not good for him to be alone. Commiserating him on account of his misfortune, Phra says to Noum: 'What companion wilt thou make for Satou, that he remain not alone?' So Noum makes him a young maiden of surpassing beauty. The sons of Hathor, however, prophesy her a violent end. 'Satou proceeded to love her violently,' and tells her about his heart; also, he warns her when she goes out walking, to beware of the advances of the river,[2] from which he should be un-

---

[1] This feature is very Homeric.
[2] Perhaps the *sea*. M. Chabas lays the scene of these adventures in Syria.

able to save her. On her being pursued by the river, the cedar tree at which she had taken refuge gives one of her locks to the water, and it floats down, exhaling so exquisite an odour, that when it arrives at the washermen, it excites a violent discussion as to the cause of the fragrance. On its being at last brought to the king, his wise men tell whence it came, and advise him to send and fetch the maiden for his wife. After sundry failures, caused by the resistance of Satou, the girl is carried off by an army, and installed in the favour of the king.

It appears that her former husband is felt by her to be an obstacle to her happiness, though no express reasons are assigned; but up to the end of the story we are entertained with her attempts to get rid of him, and her failures. First she persuades the king to have the cedar cut down, and Satou dies; but his brother, after a long search, finds his heart under a pod (or cone), and revivifies it. Satou then assumes the form of an Apis bull, and says to his brother—'Thou shalt sit on my back, and we will go to where my wife is, that she may hear my voice.' The white bull, being received with great honour, soon gets an opportunity of speaking to his wife. 'Behold,' he says, 'I am alive, and have taken the form of a bull.' The princess was greatly terrified; but being in favour with the king, she took the opportunity to say to him: 'Swear to me by God, saying: All that thou askest I will give thee.' The king hearkened to her, and she said: 'I desire to eat the bull's liver.' After a violent quarrel, and much grief on the part of the king, her wishes are carried out; but two drops of the bull's blood fall on either side of the great staircase, and next day two magnificent persea trees had sprung up, which all Egypt heard of and wondered. After many days, as the princess is driving out in state, one of the persea trees addresses her just as the bull had done, so having watched for a good opportunity, she persuades the king to have them also cut down. But as she is standing by, a chip flies down her throat, and she becomes the mother of a child fathered on the king, and acknowledged by him with great pomp, but who is really Satou in a new form. 'In due time the king flew up to heaven;' and then Satou, as his successor, calls together all his nobles, informs them of the story, apparently executes the princess, and lives happily with his worthy brother all the rest of their lives.

Many reflections are suggested by this curious fairy-tale. In the first place, it was intended for the edification, or perhaps rather for the amusement, of a young prince. There appears to be a very free handling of topics hardly suited, in our opinion, to the minds of young people. But this is not the only document which proves that the old Egyptians, with all their high gifts, were very blunt realists in their life and language, and sought little to hide what is in modern days carefully kept in modest concealment. The low moral tone of the women introduced is another very striking feature, the more so because the wife of Satou, an older Pandora, was procured for him by the gods, and made apparently as perfect as woman could possibly be in the eyes of the author. Yet there is not the slightest hint at any social or moral worth in either of the heroines. Other documents, and especially the bilingual Rhind Papyrus, no doubt copied from ancient precedents as to form, show that the Egyptian ladies held a far higher position than is here implied; so that we must ascribe the unpleasant portraiture of the romance either to a peculiar hatred of the sex in this author, or to a moral desire of exhibiting to the young prince the risks and dangers of life—a theme often discussed plainly enough in the moral treatises.

The details of Satou's first adventure are repeated among many ancient nations, but are rendered peculiarly remarkable by their accurate correspondence with the account of Joseph in Potiphar's house—a sufficient apology for reproducing them so fully. In such a case as this, sceptical writers would be inclined to say that both the Egyptian novelist and the author of Genesis, who was so well acquainted with Egypt, had culled a popular story from the folklore or legends of the day. But in any case, I hardly think these two stories, which may not be independent, can form an adequate basis for such a general attack on the morals of the Egyptian ladies as has been made by my learned friend, Mr. Clibborn.[1]

The ideas of justice and of moral retribution are strongly sustained throughout all the fantastic details, and there is also the most complete conviction of the absolute permanence of personal identity apart from the body, whatever changes the form of man may undergo. This adds another argument to the numerous evidences which forbid us to attribute pantheism to the old Egyptians, however a few phrases in their Ritual may seem to imply it.[2] The intimacy between the cattle and their keeper is also a peculiarly Egyptian feature, to be seen in Homer alone among Greek poets. It indicates that respect for their unerring instincts which caused them to be exalted into the most proper symbols of the various forms of the Deity.

The character of the king is remarkably weak and foolish, and appears drawn with great freedom, when we consider that the book was intended for a prince's perusal, and that the official style was so replete with fulsome adorations of royalty. The details about his court remind us of the stories of

---

[1] See his curious drama, *Bethiah or Pharaoh's Daughter*, (Williams and Norgate, 1868.)

[2] It will be seen that I do not agree with my learned friend Professor Jellett; cf. the Note to his *Moral Difficulties of the Old Testament*, pp. 103-24, which should have been quoted before.

King Xerxes in the book of Esther, and display an Asiatic despot's court with all its sensuality and all its frivolity. The same features reappear in the demotic novel now to be discussed. But the learned profession of the scribes seem ever to have enjoyed liberty of speech, and not to have refrained from satire on the defects of their rulers.[1]

The demotic *Romance of Setna*, our copy of which was written in the second or third century before Christ,[2] is not nearly so easy to understand or to criticise. M. Brugsch has promised a complete analysis of the text, and a revised translation, which have not yet appeared. We are therefore compelled to trust completely to his first, and I suppose somewhat hasty, version of it in the *Revue archéologique* for 1867. The story turns upon the danger of acquiring possession of the sacred books without a clear right and great precaution. The first two pages being unfortunately lost, the opening of the story and its date and superscription are missing, so that the plot must be guessed by inference from the remainder.

---

[1] Cf. the remarks on the origin of the name Sesostris in M. Lauth's *Moses der Ebräer*, pp. 13-15. This habit of modifying names slightly, so as to distort their signification, is common in the old Hebrew literature, and I believe also among the Chinese.

[2] This is determined by the style of the writing. The royal names mentioned in it are all effaced or illegible.

The manuscript opens in the middle of the narrative of *Ahura*, the principal lady of the story. It appears, however, from her own statements, that at the time she was telling it to the prince Setna, both she and her husband were dead, and reposing as mummies in the tomb. The easy manner in which the mummy of Setna (if he also is already dead), and also that of Ahura's husband, leave the tombs and re-enter them, is so strange that I am hardly able to comprehend the gist of the story. Doubtless additional study of the papyrus will clear up many of these difficulties. The prince Setna has been identified as one of the sons of Ramses II., so that the scene is not laid, like that of the previous work, in mythical times, but in a well-known though by-gone historical epoch.

The narrative of Ahura gives an account to Setna, who appears to be near her in the tomb, of her youth and her marriage with her brother *Ptahneferka*. There appears to have been some dispute about her marriage. The king, however, interferes in a friendly way, and asks the girl's own wishes about the matter.[1] She is accordingly married, and

---

[1] That this was an unusual proceeding in old times appears from the quaint remark of Herodotus (lib. vi., c. 122) Καλλίεω δὲ τούτου ἄξιον πολλαχοῦ μνήμην ἐστὶ πάντα τινὰ ἔχειν. τοῦτο μὲν κ. τ. λ. τοῦτο δὲ κατὰ τὰς ἑωυτοῦ θυγατέρας ἰούσας τρεῖς οἵος τις ἀνὴρ ἐγένετο. ἐπειδὴ γὰρ ἐγένοντο γάμου ὡραῖαι, ἔδωκέ σφι δωρεὴν μεγαλοπρεπεστά-ην ἐκείνῃσί τε ἐχαρίσατο· ἐκ γὰρ πάντων τῶν Ἀθηναίων τὸν ἑκάστη ἐθέλοι ἄνδρα ἑωυτῇ ἐκλέξασθαι, ἔδωκε τούτῳ τῷ ἀνδρί.

receives many presents from the king, both at the wedding and at the birth of her son *Merhu*. She proceeds to tell that her husband, whom by the way she throughout calls her brother, was very clever in reading the hieroglyphics, and that he had gone to the necropolis at Memphis, and had studied the inscriptions on the tombs of the kings, and the writings on the *stelae*.

One day, as he was going to the temple for prayer, he chanced to be walking close behind a priest called *Nesptah*, and reading (perhaps aloud) the writings on the chapels of the gods. Nesptah laughed, and Ptahneferka asked him the reason. The priest replied that he was laughing at the unimportant document on which Ptahneferka was spending his time. 'If thou wilt read,' he says, 'a writing (worth the trouble) come with me. I shall bring thee to the place where is the book that *Thoth* wrote with his own hand. There are two pages of writing on the back, with the first of which thou canst charm the sky, the earth, the abyss, the mountains, the seas. Thou shalt know all about the birds of heaven and the reptiles, and all that is said about them. Thou shalt see the fish in the water, (and bring them to the surface). Recite the second, and it shall come to pass that when thou art in *Amenti* (Hades), thou shalt be able to recover the shape that thou hadst upon earth. Thou shalt see the god *Ra*, that riseth in the sky, and the cycle of the nine gods, and the moon in the form of her rising.' Ptahneferka, eager to obtain the book, promises the priest any terms. He demands 100 pieces of silver for his burial, and is paid it at once. 'The book,' he adds, 'is in the middle of the river of *Coptos*, in a box of iron, within which is one of brass, within which is one of bronze, within which is one of ivory and ebony, within which is one of silver, within which is one of gold, containing the book.'[1] Ptahneferka immediately proceeds to obtain a state barge from the king, and starts with his wife and child for Coptos, in search of the book. He sets workmen to seek day and night for the book, and at last finds it, guarded, as he had been forewarned, by a serpent, scorpions, and other reptiles. After slaying the serpent, and securing the book, he charms the sky, the earth, the abyss, &c., &c.[2]

Ahura then describes herself as in a fainting condition—why, I know not—but insists on seeing and reading the book. She also charms everything with its power. But her brother obtains a new piece of papyrus, copies out the whole book word for word, and dissolves the new book in some liquid, which he drinks. He then knows the whole contents. But when

---

[1] M. Brugsch strangely in this passage, sects. 18-9 (p. 166, *op. cit.*), inverts this order, and makes the gold case the outermost. The repetition of the details when the book is actually found (sects. 34-5) shows that this is an oversight.

[2] In all recurrences of ideas the details are most minutely repeated throughout the whole story.

the party attempt to return home from Coptos, they suddenly encounter the god *Thoth*, who knew all that had happened concerning the book. **Without** delay **he** represented the matter to *Ra*, saying: 'Know that my law and my science are with *Ptahneferka*, son of the King *Mernebptah*. He has gone **to** my great dwelling, and plundered it. He has taken the chest, and slain the guard placed over it. It was said to him in reply by *Ra:* He is given up to thee, with all that belong **to him.**'

Accordingly a divine power came from heaven to prevent him from returning with his knowledge **to** Memphis. He was charmed, together with **all his** attendants. Then the child Merhu falls into the river, invoking Ra, and is drowned. Ptahneferka, by means of the book, makes him rise to the surface, and tell all that had happened to him, also the form of communication that *Thoth* had addressed to *Ra*. They return to Coptos, and bury the child with great pomp. Then Ptahneferka proposes to his wife to return to Memphis, lest the king should be distressed at their absence. **But** at the same place in the river Ahura meets with **the** same fate as her child; **and** after being **likewise charmed, and with the same result, she** is also **buried with her child in** Coptos. **Then** the bereaved husband **soliloquises:** 'Shall I join them again in Coptos, or **return to** Memphis? If I go to Memphis, the king will ask for his children. **How can I say, I have brought thy** children to the

Thebaid; they are dead and I am alive?' Being determined to die, he has the book bound with a belt of byssus firmly to his side. He then dies, and is brought in the barge to Memphis.[1] The king wishes to take the book from his side when he came to receive him from his barge at Memphis. 'The officers of the king and the priests of *Ptah*, and the high priest of *Ptah*, said before the king: O king, live for ever! *Ptahneferka* was a good scribe, and a very learned man.'[2] So he was embalmed and buried with great honour.

Here the narrative of Ahura ends, and the story breaks into a dialogue between *Setna*, *Ahura*, and *Ptahneferka*, who appear, strangely enough, to be in the same resting place. As the scene of the dialogue is evidently at or near Memphis, and the bodies of Ahura and Merhu are interred far south at Coptos—whither, indeed, Setna goes at the close of the story to look for them — it is clear that the mummy was regarded as apart from the soul, and not essential to its life. As to the time that is supposed to elapse between the death of the actors, and the dialogue which they carry on in

---

[1] There are obscurities about his death, which I cannot understand.

[2] As this remark settles the question, and the book is not removed, it must have been the polite official way of opposing his majesty.

their disembodied state, several generations are required ; for in the thirteenth section of the fourth page,[1] Ptahneferka, who assumes the appearance of a very old man, says that the father of the father of his father told the father of his father where the tombs of Ahura and of Merhu could be found.[2]

But—to resume our story—the lady Ahura, addressing Setna, who was most anxious to obtain the book, exclaims : ' I have passed through these misfortunes on account of the book which thou desirest. Speak not to me of it, for on account of it we have lost our span of life on the earth.' Setna replies : ' Let me have the book, which is between thee and *Ptahneferka*, or I shall take it by force. Then Ptahneferka starts up on his bed, and says : ' Art not thou *Setna*, to whom this woman has told the whole sad story? Beware of taking the book. How couldst thou hold it on account of its excellent contents?' But Setna insists upon endeavouring to obtain it, and arranges a game of fifty-two points (some sort of draughts), the winner in which is to retain the book. Ptahneferka tries to cheat, but is

---

[1] p. 177, *op. cit.*

[2] It follows from this that the king Mernebptah, father of the married pair, must be placed at a date far anterior to Setna's father, Ramses II., and that M. Brugsch's hesitation as to identifying him with Mereneptah of the royal lists is well-founded.

found out by his adversary, who in the end wins his game.

The story becomes so obscure from this onward, that I shall content myself with a very brief analysis. Setna sends his brother up on earth to obtain the talismans and magic books of his father, and by their aid he carries off the book, and reads it to everybody, in spite of the warning of Ptahneferka, and of the king, his father, that he would be forced to give it back.[1] Soon afterwards, however, as Setna is walking near the temple of Ptah, he sees a woman of resplendent beauty, attended by several girls. 'From the hour that he saw her, he knew not in what part of the world he was.' He sends his slave boy forthwith to find out who she is. The lad reports that she is *Tababu*, daughter of the priest of the goddess *Baste*, and that she had been going to the temple of Ptah to pray. The prince sends back his servant to say: '*Setna-Chamus*, son of King *Usermat* (Ramses II.), hath sent me, saying: I will give thee ten pieces of silver to make thy acquaintance for an hour; if not, take notice that violence will be used.' He also proposes to keep the interview

---

[1] I cannot make out from M. Brugsch's translation whether Setna has gone down living into the tomb on an adventure, or whether it is his mummy lying in its natural resting place. It is certain that Ahura was close to him, though her body lay in Coptos, and he was in the necropolis of Memphis.

perfectly secret. When this message is brought to Tababu's maiden, 'she appeared disconcerted, as if what had been said was disgraceful; but *Tababu* said to the boy: Cease talking to that silly girl, and speak with me.' She then sends word to Setna: 'I am holy, and no small personage;' and that if he desires to see her, he must come to the temple of *Baste*, to her house. The boy repeats all that had been said, adding (what was true) that it was a disgrace for everybody (anybody?) to be with Setna.

His visit is then described, the splendour of the house, and how he drinks wine with Tababu. She compels him to sign away all his possessions to her, and his children being announced below, compels him farther to make them sign the contract also, lest they should dispute with her own children. Finally she persuades him to murder them all, and cast them to the dogs below. But suddenly, just when he thinks he has succeeded in all his designs, he finds himself in the dark, naked and helpless. This part of the narrative is mutilated, and hopelessly obscure. Presently he sees the king standing before him, who lectures him on his conduct, and orders him to go back to Memphis, where his children, who are still alive after all, are awaiting him. I would suggest that this episode concerning Tababu is really an evil dream that Setna had on account of carrying off the sacred book from the tomb. At all events, he is obliged to restore it with apologies to Ptahneferka. When he arrives in the tombs, Ahura receives him with good wishes; her husband laughs at him, and tells him he foretold all that had happened. The story ends with Setna's journey to Coptos to look for the remains of Ahura and Merhu, apparently, so far as I can make out, as an atonement to the gods or to Ptahneferka for carrying off the book. The prince searches for three days and three nights in vain, when Ptahneferka appears to him in the form of a very old man, and tells him (on his great-grandfather's authority) where to find the mummies. They are then brought in state to Memphis, received by the king, and buried with Ptahneferka. I may add a curious point of manners, that when the old man indicates the place of the bodies to the prince, and is ordered to search for them, he *obtains a guarantee from him*, that he will suffer no harm should the bodies, by any accident, not be found there.

As to the style of this curious book, M. Brugsch observes that both grammar and form of expression are identical with the Tale of the two brothers, written probably 1000 years before it, and this would be a strong additional proof of the unchangeable nature of the Egyptian language, were we certain that it was not transcribed from an older hieratic archetype, the archaic form of which would naturally be preserved by the copyist. Considering its marked contrast to all other demotic fragments as yet found, this opinion seems probable. But it is not so easy to offer reflections on the work from the difficulty of comprehending its meaning.

As to theological notions, it proves the complete distinctness of the soul and the mummy, and that the Egyptians did not regard the one as in any way restricted by the locality of the other. Of the gods, Thoth and Ra alone appear, but they seem distinct, just as in the previous novel the company of the gods is mentioned, and also Phra and Noum. The attitude therefore of the Egyptian novels, as opposed to the hymns, is decidedly polytheistic, though it is not fair to press closely the popular statements which occur casually in a work not intended to convey theological doctrine. We might, even in the books of the New Testament, find some which speak throughout of the Persons of the Trinity as distinct, without ever once insisting on their unity ; and yet this would not be good evidence for denying that unity.

The picture drawn of the morals of prince Setna corresponds well enough with that of the king in the older romance, and shows how ruinous such arbitrary conduct must have been to Egyptian society.

No farther discoveries have yet been made in this branch of their literature, but there can be little doubt that many such treasures are still safe beneath the sand, and may yet reward the earnest seeker. How perfectly we could see into the life and manners of the old Egyptians, if we possessed a dozen such stories!

§ 13. *Epics and Biographical Sketches.* — There is however another branch of Egyptian literature which is also very precious for its details of private life. I mean the epical and biographical sketches, if I may so call them, which yet remain. Under these I do not now propose to include the sepulchral monuments which give a barren abstract of the public acts and social virtues of the deceased, but which do not in the least bring out his personality. Such documents are only valuable from an historical point of view, which is not the object of the present sketch, and from a moral point of view, in which they have already been discussed. I now refer to those narrations of special adventure, either in war or travel, which are composed with a view to the graces of style, and which are indicative both of the private character of the actor and the attitude of the writer.

Among these the most remarkable from a literary point of view, though its fulsome flattery makes it historically and also ethically worthless, is the epic of *Pentaour* on the achievements of Ramses II., in his war against the Kheta, an Asiatic tribe probably corresponding to the Hittites in southern Syria. This poem, which has been called the Egyptian Iliad, was so popular and widely known, that among the scanty remains we have recovered of Egyptian literature, at least five more or less complete copies of it have already been found: one (hieratic) on a papyrus in the British Museum,[1] of which the commencement is missing, but has been curiously supplied by a page of the same copy on a papyrus presented by M. Raifet to the Museum of the Louvre. Another (in hieroglyphics) is on the south wall of the temple of Amon at Karnak: a third and fourth (hieroglyphics) on the north and south walls of the *propylaeum* of the temple of Ramses II. at Luqsor, and a fifth on a similar temple at Abu-Simbel in Nubia.[2] These various copies are of the greatest service in supplying one another's defects, and will shortly be published *in extenso* by the Vicomte de Rougé. It appears from a comparison of them that the hieratic copies are written carelessly and with many errors, which will make Egyptologists for the future very bold in amending their texts, when they present grammatical anomalies. But although the copy on the Raifet and Sallier papyri is very negligent, it is nevertheless

---

[1] Translated by Mr. Goodwin in part (*Cambridge Essays*, p. 239, *sq.*), and completely by the Vicomte de Rougé (*Séance des cinq Académies*, August, 1856); and again in the *Recueil de Travaux*, &c. (Paris, 1870), from which I translate my quotations. Cf. also M. Naville's tract, *La Littérature de l'ancienne Égypte*, p. 14.

[2] Cf. Brugsch, *Monuments*, i., p. 46.

taken from an original superior in composition to the hieroglyphic inscriptions, or if taken from them, modified by a person of intelligence. The episode of the esquire or charioteer is put in its right place, in the middle of the conflict, and there is more of the narration in the third person than in the inscriptions, which put it almost all into the mouth of Ramses.

As the document is very long, and can easily be read either in Mr. Goodwin's or M. de Rougé's translations, it will not be necessary to make full extracts here. Considering its great antiquity, we have a good deal of independent information as to the event which it describes. The poetical account of Ramses' achievements, exaggerated as an Egyptian alone would venture to do, is curiously controlled by the actual text of the treaty made by him immediately afterwards with his enemies, which has been found inscribed on a temple at Ipsamboul. But while this latter document is far more valuable for historical purposes, the poem, which avoids all cold detail, and dwells on the episode which exhibited the king's valour, is a precious specimen of the literary taste of the most literary age in the annals of Egypt.[1]

---

[1] The treaty between Ramses II. and the Khetas or Hittites, has been fully discussed by M. Chabas in his *Voyage d'un égyptien*, pp. 335, *sq*. Cf. also Brugsch, *Histoire d'Égypte*, p. 158. We shall consider this text under the head of judicial documents.

The poem opens as follows :—' Commencement of the victories of King Ramses (I omit all the titles) over the people of Khet, Naharaim, Ilion (?), Pidasa, the Dardanians, &c., &c.'—in fact, a coalition of all Western Asia. 'The young king, who has stretched forth his hand, and has no equal; his arms are powerful, his heart is courageous; his bravery is that of (the god) *Month* in battle. He has led his soldiers to unknown regions. Lord of terrors, of great bellowings ; his heart is the greatest in all the world—like a lion raging in the valley of the flocks. Hundreds of thousands faint at his sight.' 'His heart is like a rock of iron, the King of Upper and Lower Egypt, Sun, Lord of Justice, chosen of the god Ra, offspring of the Sun, Ramses *Meriamon*, gifted with eternal life !' The poem then describes the date and outset of the expedition, and the march as far as the Orontes in Syria, and up to the city of Kadesh. There the chief of the Khetas lay in ambush. It appears that the Egyptian forces were unwisely scattered. The legion of Amon ('Amon's own') was with the king; those of Phra, Ptah, and Set were each marching independently in a northerly direction. Then the allies suddenly fell upon the legion of Phra, and discomfited it at the south of the town of Kadesh. When the king heard it he seized his armour, and dashed in amongst the perverse Khetas. 'He was alone, and no one was with him; and having thus advanced in the sight of those behind him, he was surrounded by all the warriors of the perverse Kheta and his allies. Each chariot carried three warriors, and they were all united.'

Finding himself thus deserted by his troops, and even by his staff, the king exclaims: 'Who art thou then, my father Amon; art thou a father that forgetteth his son? Have I done aught without thee? Have I not advanced and halted according to thy words? Have I not offered thee myriads of sacrifices? Have I not filled thine house with prisoners, and built thee a temple (to last) for millions of years? I have offered thee all the world. I have ordered obelisks from Elephantine, and have brought thee eternal stones. Vessels carry thee tribute from all nations. Assuredly wretched is the lot of him that resists thy counsel, blessed is he that knoweth thee, for thy deeds are the fruit of an heart full of love. Behold, I am among a multitude unknown to me! All nations are joined against me, and I am left alone without help. All my men of war have forsaken me, none of mine horsemen have regarded me, and when I called them there was none to listen to my voice. But I think that Amon is better to me than a million of soldiers—than 10000 horsemen, and myriads of brothers or of sons, were they all joined together. The work of many men is nought; Amon will conquer them. Behold, I have not transgressed thy commands, and have given thee glory to the ends of the world!'

'Then,' continues the king, 'Amon heard my prayer, he gave me his hand. I shout for joy, and he cries behind me: I am with thee, Ramses Meriamon. I succour thee. It is I, thy father; my hand is with thee, and is better than hundreds of thousands. I have found in thee a valiant heart, and am satisfied.' Then Ramses falls upon them, shooting his arrows in all directions. The 2500 chariots are broken in pieces before his mares; not one of the enemy can find heart to resist, or strength to fight. They fall into the water like crocodiles, and lie in heaps one upon the other. The Kheta chief retreats, full of terror, but orders 3000 more chariots to attack the king. 'I rushed upon them like *Month*, my hand devoured them in an instant, I slew round about amongst them. Then they said: This is no man, but the great god *Soutekh* (or Set). These are not the acts of a man, to terrify thousands without officers or soldiers. Let us haste away, that we may save the breath of life! Then I pursued them, and slew them without resistance. I called to my soldiers: See, Amon hath given me the victory, though I was alone. When *Menna*, my charioteer, saw me surrounded, his heart failed him; a great fear seized his limbs, and he said to his majesty: My good lord, just protector of Egypt in the day of battle, we are alone in the midst of the enemy, for our archers and chariots have left us. Stop, and let us save our souls alive!' But the king encourages him, and penetrates their ranks six times.

Then the poet, neglecting the conclusion of the battle and the flight, passes in the very next sentence to the moment when the king calls up and upbraids all the soldiers who had failed him in the battle. He enumerates all his own benevolences to them, and his own excellence, in truly Egyptian style. The soldiers proceed to glorify and to pacify him by hymns of praise. But he continues to upbraid them, and to insist upon his own valour in saving his army. 'I have fought; I have discomfited millions of people by myself. *Victory to Thebes* and *Noura satisfied*, even my great mares, them I found beneath my hand when I was in the midst of the raging enemy. I shall have them fed daily in my presence when I am in my palace, for I found them (true) when I was in the midst of the enemy, with the chief *Menna*, mine esquire, and with *the officers of my house*, who accompanied me, and were witnesses of the battle. Those did I find.' He is then described preparing to renew the battle next day, but the Khetas are so terrified that they send a proposal of peace. It is, of course, couched in terms of abject flattery. On the advice of his nobles, the king grants the application for peace, and returns in triumph to Egypt.

This remarkable document, the only epic poem preserved in Egyptian literature, suggests many reflections. As soon as the comparative mythologers proceed beyond the limits of Aryan nations, as they will certainly do if they continue to expand at the present rate, there will surely be found quite sufficient resemblances between the poem of Pentaour and the acts of Achilles in the 20th book of the Iliad, to regard them as one and the same. The exaggeration in the Iliad is not so glaring, but differs only in degree, not in principle, from that of the Egyptian poet. It is however far bolder of the latter to place the scene of his work in contemporary, and not in legendary history.

The nature of battles in the days of Ramses differed very little from those described in the Homeric lays. The nobles professed to do everything, and the soldiers nothing. The household troops are naïvely mentioned at the end. There appear among the Asiatics three in a chariot, but this fact is noted as a peculiarity, in opposition to the fashion of both Egyptians and Greeks of fighting in pairs. It also appears that the charioteer, as in the Iliad, was a chief of high position, and not a servant.

I notice, as peculiarly interesting, the affection with which the king speaks of his mares, which were known by proper names—I had almost said Christian names.[1] This feature is quite Homeric, but

---

[1] It appears from the Amada inscription of Amenophis II. (published in *Lepsius' Denkmäler*) that ships were similarly

is more to be expected in Egypt than elsewhere, for the Egyptians, as we have already abundantly seen, were exceedingly fond of animals, and so respected them as to use them for types of the various deities. The horse indeed being a late importation into Egypt, does not appear with this dignity, but no warlike people could fail to appreciate its high qualities. The fact that the king's favorite steeds were both mares, is also worthy of notice. The reader will observe that in the satirical representation of an Egyptian battle reproduced above (p. 214), the king's steeds are evidently intended for mares. In the 23rd book of the Iliad (to mention Homeric parallels) we find the steeds of Eumelus confessed to be by far the best in the Greek army, and they are also described as a pair of mares. So also Herodotus[2] mentions the most celebrated Olympian winners at three successive festivals, and speaks of them as mares.

---

designated by proper names. The king's ship is called *Ra-aa-kheperu-smen-to* (the *Amenophis that consolidates the two worlds*). So in the palaces and temples each hall and gate (as in the temple of Jerusalem) had its special name. Cf. for these details Chabas, *Inscriptions des mines d'or*, p. 20. The same author states (*Spoliation des Hypogées*, p. 73) that he has found the names of several dogs, besides that which is translated from the Pap. Abbott (*op. cit.*, p. 61). Cf. also, on Seti I.'s horses, Brugsch, *Monuments*, i., p. 57.

[2] Lib. vi., chap. 103.

From an artistic point of view, the most striking feature in the poem is the rapid narration of the antecedents and consequents of the great scene, which the poet desired to celebrate. The action is perfectly rounded off and complete, but like Euripides' tragedies, the beginning and end of the poem are condensed and curtailed, in order to leave room for the great central picture.[1] In other respects the style is not very striking, and abounds, like all old Egyptian documents, in repetitions many of which have been omitted in the passages above quoted. But if artistically worthless as compared with the Iliad, let us not forget that it was six centuries earlier, and for that reason, were it for no other, it must command our interest and admiration.

There are, indeed, among the strictly historical inscriptions, some of which the style is almost as epic as the poem of Pentaour. On the walls of the temple of Amon at Karnak, there are hieroglyphical texts giving an account of the victories of Tothmes III. and of Seti I., which rise far above the level of ordinary prose.[2]

In one of them (now preserved at Boulaq) Amon is represented addressing King Tothmes as follows: 'Come to me, and rejoice in beholding my favour,

---

[1] See this point (as to Euripides) well expounded in K. O. Müller's *History of Greek Literature*, vol. i., p. 478.

[2] The inscriptions of Tothmes (or Toutmes) were first translated by Dr. Birch, afterwards by M. Brugsch (*Monuments*, i., p.

O my avenger, *Ramen-Kheper*, living for ever! I shine by means of thy vows; my heart delights when thou comest to my temple. I embrace thee in my arms to give thee life and safety. Lovely are thy favours by means of the image thou hast set up in my temple; it is I that reward thee; it is I that give thee strength, and victory over all nations; it is I that cause the fear of thee to reach unto the four supports of the heavens. The terror which thou causest to all the world I increase it, &c., &c.' The god then passes to a cadenced hymn with that parallelism of phrases so common in oriental poetry.

'I am come, and I grant thee to smite the princes of Tahi; I cast them beneath thy feet when thou passest through their country. I made them see thy majesty as a lord of light; thou shinest upon them like my image.

'I am come, and I grant thee to smite the people of Asia, and to take captive the princes of the land of Assyria. I made them to see thy majesty with loins girded, in armour and fighting on thy chariot.'

In this strain the king's victories over east and

---

52), and by M. de Rougé, *Rev. archéol.* for 1861, pp. 287-312; and the hymn of Amon praising the king in M. Mariette's *Notice des principaux monuments*, &c., *à Boulaq*, pp. 78-80. The inscription of Seti is translated by Brugsch, *op. cit.*, pp. 56-9.

west, over the islands of the sea and their inhabitants are enumerated.¹

The pompous descriptions of the conquests of Seti I., which have been published and translated by M. Brugsch, are very similar in character. The Egyptians of that day seem to have preferred to write their narrative in the first person, and are therefore prone to introduce a character speaking, rather than to tell the facts from their own point of view, as we should do.

I shall mention but one more of these inscriptions.

It is an account of an invasion of Egypt from the north-west by a coalition of naval tribes in the reign of king Merenptah, son of Ramses II., and is justly celebrated as containing the earliest-known mention of the εὐκνήμιδες Ἀχαιοί, here called the *Achaians from the region of the sea*. It has been translated by M. de Rougé and Professor Lauth independently.²

---

¹ Cf. Mariette, *op. cit.*, p. 79. 'Le parfum de poésie orientale qui est repandu sur ce bel échantillon de la littérature égyptienne au xviime. siècle avant notre ère n'échappera à personne.'

² Cf. *Revue archéol.* for 1867, pp. 35 and 80, &c., and *Zeitsch. der Morgenland Gesell.* for 1867; also Lauth, *die Achiver in Aegypten*, in the *Munich Sitz. ber.* for 1867, pp. 528, *sq.* The document was found by M. de Rougé, inscribed at great length on a temple at Karnak, by the orders of Merenptah, son of Ramses II., in whose reign (about 1320 B. C.) this great invasion of maritime tribes brought Egypt into extreme danger. The names of the Sardinians, Sikels, Lykians, Tyrrhenians,

It consists of 77 columns of hieroglyphics inscribed on a wall at Karnak.

There are several salient points of similarity between this text and the epic already discussed. The king tells how he sent out scouts to observe the approach of the enemy, who, however, landed and occupied part of Egypt notwithstanding. He then bursts out into invectives against his nobles, mingled with praises of himself and his paternal government, almost identical with those of Ramses. Then comes the battle, and the terror and cowardice of the hostile leader is dwelt on, just as the terror of the ' vile

Lybians, and Achaians have been apparently discovered in the list. But this is not the place to discuss so large and interesting a subject, which promises great rewards to a special investigation. The reader will be curious to see this earliest mention of the Achaians in its original form :—

A   K   A   I   U   A   SH   A   EN NA

TEST EN   PE   I   UMA

The feather and the eagle are both signs for *a*, the former with a determinative figure pointing to its mouth added. The *sh* reminds us of the Hebrew ש. After the name follow the signs which show it to be the name of a nation, and then the sign of the plural, three down strokes. The rest of the phrase means 'of the regions of the sea.' The *pe* is the article, and the word for sea appears identical with the Hebrew.

chief of the Khetas' occupies the attention of the epic poet. There follows a catalogue of prisoners and articles of booty, suited to a strictly historical document; but the conclusion is again poetical, and contains a description of the benefits done to the Delta by the expulsion of the invaders, and of the hymns of praise offered up to the king by his grateful people. The whole inscription holds a place so intermediate between history and epic poetry that it deserves mention here, if only to show how to the Egyptians, as to the Romans, positive history afforded a more congenial theme for heroic lays than the acts of mythical or semi-mythical heroes.

We now turn to a document probably contemporaneous with the Egyptian epic, and more biographical, relating the adventures of an individual less important than Ramses, but adventures of travel and of peace, not of war. The information afforded by this document is in many respects more curious, for it gives us a glimpse into the condition of Palestine and Syria, shortly after the conclusion of the campaign of Ramses, and the re-opening of friendly communications by the treaty already mentioned. These events seem to have occurred in the middle of the fourteenth century B.C., when the Hebrews were groaning under their bondage in Egypt. If the poem of Pentaour be magnified into an Egyptian Iliad, this narrative may with equal propriety be called an Odyssey. For, after inditing the praises of his superior, and discussing some other subjects, the author gives an account of the journey of the *Mohar*, evidently a high official, through Syria and Palestine, related from the correspondence or diary which the latter had sent to him.

There are no two documents, apart from theological literature, which strike the reader so strongly by their profound contrast to modern compositions, as the Romance of Setna, and this biographical sketch of the *Mohar*. We often forget through what ages of experience human thought must have passed before its form, and consequently the form of its expression, were perfected as we see them in Greek, or even in Hebrew literature. In those older days there was no logic, no grammar, no general diffusion of accurate thinking, and the cumbrous graphic systems must have sadly thwarted the unbroken flow of expression, and so of thought. Tedious repetitions, sudden transitions, confused metaphors, all of which are to be found in the old Assyrian inscriptions, and in some of the Hebrew poets, are far more numerous still in Egyptian literature.

The document before us (Papyrus I. of the Anastasi collection in the British Museum) has been three times translated—first by Mr. Goodwin partially, then by M. Chabas in a special treatise full of acuteness and learning,[1] and lastly, in the appendix to M. Lauth's curious book called *Moses der Ebräer*, autographed at Munich in the year 1868. The latter author endeavours to establish that the personage described in the work was Moses himself. He brings to his aid passages from a papyrus in the Leyden collection, from which we have already cited a solar hymn, and constructs a most ingenious and plausible theory upon them. This is not the place to enter upon a discussion of minute points; but I must express my conviction that he has by no means proved his point, though it is unsatisfactory to make such statements without giving reasons.

A graver point of dispute has arisen concerning the document, and one which has divided the learned. Both M. Brugsch and the Vicomte de Rougé believe that the voyage described is no real, but only an imaginary sketch, conveying to the reader in a lively manner a picture of the countries with which Egypt had lately been in conflict. But in the controversy raised by M. Brugsch in the *Revue Critique*, he has been decidedly worsted, and M. Lauth has found in a Leyden papyrus the curious contemporary remark: 'Hui, the *flabellifer* in the king's train, said in accusation of the Sotem *Mesu*, namely: He bathed in the Aolath, journeying to-

---

[1] *Voyage d'un égyptien* (Berlin, 1860).

wards Char,[1] he said many things concerning *Chairebu* (Aleppo) which he dare not speak of in public.' Though we can hardly assert that these allusions apply to Moses, it seems not unlikely that they refer to the traveller called the *Mohar* in the other papyrus, and so make the reality of the voyage very probable.[2] After these explanations, we may give a short analysis of this curious treatise.

It opens with an elaborate panegyric of the Mohar, very tedious to read. He is 'a hero in courage and in the works of *Safeh*, in the house of writings, a zealous master in the chair of sciences, the first of his companions, the greatest of his relations.' He is praised for quickness in understanding writings, for his power and influence in educating the young. He is besides 'a general of courageous soldiers, a man that proveth hearts, of good merits, fulfilling promises, whose like there is not among all scribes, beloved of all, fair to behold like the flowers; a scribe in every respect, that is ignorant of nothing, rejoicing in truth, avoiding lies.' After these and other such ideas have been repeated and expounded over and over again, there comes what might be called the next section, of

---

[1] Bathing in the sea, and eating fish, were held unclean by the Egyptian priests.

[2] Cf. Lauth, *Moses der Ebräer*, chap. 6.

prayers and wishes for the Mohar's eternal welfare. All the blessings specified in the Funeral Ritual are invoked upon him in detail. 'Mayest thou see the gods favourable to thee, and not angry! Mayest thou obtain thy reward (in the next world) after a long old age! Mayest thou be richly embalmed, and enter into the halls of the West, to join the society of the elect; and mayest thou hear them say: Thy word is made good (or, Thou art justified)!' And after wishing him divine food and drink, and the pleasures of bathing in the celestial Nile, this division of the work ends with these words: 'Thou meetest the Sun god, thou enterest the circle of gods, may thy words be made good in heaven; thou raisest thyself to heaven, mayest thou not be annihilated; thou goest in peace, and standest where thou wilt in what form thou pleasest; may thy presence be altogether that of a god when thou diest!'

With the heading *new subject* in a rubric, the treatise changes to more definite and practical matters, nearly five pages out of twenty-eight having been devoted to these panegyrics and good wishes. The author observes that the written missive of the Mohar had reached him by a messenger, and he proceeds to make reflections on its style. It appears that the great man had directed his correspondent to recast and put into literary form his hasty notes; just like Sully's secretaries, who wrote for his information things which he had himself communicated.[1] 'Thou art enjoying thyself,' says the author, 'and hatest the tedium of retiring[2] to thy chamber to correct thy writing, for thou dost not find it an enjoyment. Truly thy sentences are perplexed and misleading, thy words are inverted, and do not express the meaning fully, being out of order and confused. Another man, even I, is to remedy these defects.' After some illustrations, he adds:—'When I examine thy language carefully, thy expressions are so rugged, that they frighten me. But I should not be astonished, for I know thy character and thy stumbling when thou art made to rely on thyself.' Then follow some obscure descriptions of the Mohar's conduct as a judge. Despite of his rugged style, his great knowledge of ancient history is specially praised.

The writer next proceeds to state that he has made a copy of the Mohar's work in his own style on new papyrus, which he sends back to him; and protests, on his honour, that the whole work is honestly his own; and yet he complains that on this occasion he has obtained less help than ever from his correspondent, for despite of his increased trouble, the

---

[1] I allude to the work called *Économies Royales*, very justly compared by M. Chabas, *op. cit.*, p. 73.

[2] And preparest to send me back to thy chamber.—*Chabas.*

latter has turned against him. 'By the holy essence of Ptah, the Lord of Truth, I have not spoilt thy words, but given them as they were spoken by thee; and yet thou speakest against me as if I were an enemy.' He suspects that some one had accused him to the Mohar of giving distorted accounts of the great man's doings to the public, and making a laughing-stock of him. For the Mohar has been abusing him, saying : ' Broken in arm, without strength, bestir thyself to act like a scribe. I did indeed (the writer replies) spend a moment trying to amuse thee, and acted the fool, because that fellow annoyed me. But thy reproofs affect my whole family, and the words thou hast spoken turn against thyself. I know plenty of people broken in arm, and without strength, yet they have power and riches, and nobody says a word against *them*. Let me draw a sketch of the scribe *Roi*, called *consumer of the public granary*. He bestirs not himself, nor hastens since the day of his birth. Work is his horror, and real work he does not know. Although like a dead man in *Amenti*, yet his limbs are sound; the fear of the good god does not guide him.' He proceeds to describe other characters in equally bad colours, *e. g.* : 'Thou hast heard the name of *Mai*, the profligate, that creeps about on the ground never satisfied, with his hair dishevelled, and his

---

[1] This cannot be contradicted—*Chabas*.

clothes tied round about his body. When men see him in the evening, they say a gander is better than he as he passes. He is placed over the (public) weighing office. Observe his weight! He is as heavy as twenty of them, yet he is easily put aside; blow at him as he passes, and he falls like the leaves of a tree.' And then he exclaims: 'Compare me with these, and I shall defeat them at once; institute an investigation, and they will fall without my touching them; so I hurl back upon thee thy accusations. And yet thou art great and learned. A word from thy mouth hath the weight of three; I sink back in awe when thou speakest. Thou terrifiest me as a learned man more than heaven or earth, or the nether world. And yet such an one as this attacks me and says: Thou art no true scribe, nor of the position of an officer; thou art rejected by thine own superiors, and art not on the (official) list.' The author proceeds to protest his genuine official character, and appeals to a number of public documents and rolls, on which his name is duly registered. To the charge that he was not an expert at writing, he even replies by offering to submit to Anhur[1] his own compositions, and the perplexed sentences of the Mohar; he is not afraid of the decision.

---

[1] Evidently the literary autocrat of that day; cf. M. Lauth's chapter on him, *op. cit.*, p. 29.

I have entered with some detail into these curious literary disputes of so ancient a date, though they are a mere introduction to the proper subject of the treatise, which is a biographical sketch of the Mohar's adventures. The reader will find the full translation in the works above cited.

New Subject.—The author proceeds to state that he has hitherto given a faithful account of the Mohar's deeds, without any omission. The first description alludes to the transport of a great monolith dedicated to Horus, a duty which had been entrusted to the Mohar as a superior officer, and in the performance of which he had overcome great difficulties. Then follow similar commissions for the carving and the setting up of an obelisk, and of a colossal statue of the king. The next chapter tells how the Mohar had been appointed commander of a small force of auxiliaries to crush the disturbances caused by various desert tribes. The Mohar seems to have been particularly cautious as to the commissariat department, and to have checked the ardour of the negro auxiliaries, who were anxious to march without due provision. The expedition was in the direction of Hammamat, where the Egyptians procured both their best red granite, and also gold.[1]

---

[1] Cf. F. Chabas, *Inscriptions des mines d'or*, Chalons, 1862.

We next pass to the journey of the Mohar through Syria and Palestine. Egyptologists have often longed to possess his own notes, difficult as they might be, for the sketch preserved to us is very brief, and in many cases merely enumerates a series of towns which had been visited. With these names, profoundly important in an historical point of view, I am not now concerned, but shall merely cull from the document the descriptions of nature, or the personal experiences of the traveller.

His departure is first described:—' Thou examinest thine harness, the horses are swift like leopards, with flashing eyes. Thou seekest the reins, and takest thy bow.' The journey was performed *à la voiture*, and reminds us of the travels of Telemachus in the Peloponnesus, except that there two young noblemen drove together; and here, as we shall see, the Mohar was attended by very worthless servants. The narrative proceeds in a curiously interrogative style. 'Didst thou not go to the land of the *Cheta* (Hittites), hast thou not seen the land of *Aup*, &c., &c.? Didst thou not go to the *Shasu* with the mercenaries? Didst thou not pass the road to the *Magar*, where the sky is darkened by day, (the road) being overgrown with cypresses, oaks, and cedars that reach heaven; where lions, leopards, and hyenas are pursued by the *Shasu* on their way?' After some other descriptions the writer observes: ' then thou feelest the pleasure of being a

Mohar; thy chariot is laid upon thy hands; thy strength is gone; thou reachest the inn in the evening; thy limbs are all bruised, crushed, and sore; thy bones (almost) broken. Fallen asleep with weariness, thou wakest up; it is the hour of the dolorous night; thou art quite alone. Does not a thief come to plunder the incautious (traveller)? He enters the hall, the horses strike out, the thief steals away in the night, carrying off thy garments. Thy coachman wakes up and sees what has happened; he takes the rest, and joins the villainous *Shasu;* he changes himself into a worthless Asiatic.'

The clever Egyptian, however, discovered traces of the thieves and recovered his property. After visiting many towns—among them Berytus, Zidon, Zarepta and Tyre,[1] which latter was supplied with water by boats from the mainland, and abounded in fish—another very strange adventure happens to him in some narrow defile, where he is both in danger of losing his life by tumbling over the precipice with his chariot, and also of being entrapped by his foes. His way appears to lead along the steep side of a mountain with a wall of rock on one side, and a great gulf on the other. His chariot is broken, and he is reduced to despair. The details are so obscure, that I forbear quoting from this part of the document. But no sooner have we completed the description of his woes without any *dénouement,* than

---

[1] Dr. Hincks was the first to identify these names.

the scene changes. 'Having reached *Jupu* (Joppa) thou findest the fields green in their spring season. In making an attempt (to obtain some fruit) to eat, thou findest the fair little damsel that guards the orchard, she favours thy advances, and grants all thy desires. Being caught thy speech is conclusive evidence against the *Mohar*, thou hast to pay thy sweet servitude with a fine.' We then return to another adventure with a thief, quite similar to the former, and also to one at a precipice, which ends by the *Mohar* having to order his chariot to be repaired. But these orders follow immediately upon lamentations and supplications for food and water after the accident. With some farther complaints of the author as to the abrupt style of the Mohar, the document concludes.

There can be no doubt that this work had a high reputation in its day, for M. Calliaud found an *ostracon*, on which part of the 5th chapter is repeated. It states that it was sent to the polemarch of Gournah, and appears to consist of corrections of his copy, there being many words in red, and some emendations which can be even now appreciated. The very same fragment, containing the protest of the author against the Mohar's accusations, was discovered by M. de Horrack on another *ostracon* in the Louvre.[1] Another fragment is on a

---

[1] For the former, cf. Chabas, *Voyage*, p. 29; for the latter *Lepsius' Zeitsch.* for 1868, pp. i., *sq*.

papyrus of the Turin Museum, just published by MM. Pleyte and Rossi. This latter portion is that describing the erection of an obelisk by the Mohar. What is more curious, it appears to be an independent version, copied from an archetype differing in many respects from the version of the papyrus Anastasi I., both by adding and by omitting short clauses. And yet to us the composition appears very confused and defective. It is by no means so good as the epic on Ramses II., and we have to regret that the poet Pentaour did not employ his talents on this far more fruitful subject, which (as I have suggested) corresponds to the Odyssey about as much as the former poem does to the Iliad.

One more biographical document remains to be considered, of great interest from its antiquity. It belongs to the collection of Berlin, and dates, like the Prisse Papyrus, from the days of the Old Empire, prior to the invasion of the Shepherds. It has been discussed by M. Chabas, and since more completely by the greatest of English hieratic scholars, Mr. Goodwin.[2] The loss of the first page or two has made the real scope of the work uncertain, and though the translations proposed are in structure and sense very closely alike, the gene-

---

[2] Cf. F. Chabas, *Les papyrus du Musée de Berlin*, Chalons, 1863; and Mr. Goodwin's *Story of Saneha*, in *Fraser's Mag.* for February, 1865.

ral drift is by no means so clear. It is certain that *Saneha*, the hero of the narrative, was not a native Egyptian, but of Asiatic descent. It seems also certain that he was employed by King Amenemha I. of the twelfth dynasty, and that he emigrated to a distant country, and dwelt amongst a strange nation called *Sakti*. But while M. Chabas thinks that he was sent on a mission by the king, Mr. Goodwin with more reason thinks he ran away, owing to some cause stated on the lost opening of the story.

We find Saneha making his way out of Egypt when our text begins, and after much labour and fatigue, and many perils from hunger and thirst, he is hospitably received by the Sakti, a tribe adjoining Egypt (in what direction is not known), and against whose incursions frontier fortresses had been built.[1]
' I made the journey on foot till I came to the fortress which the king had made to keep off the Sakti. An aged man, an herbseller, received me. I was in alarm, seeing the watchers on the wall in daily rotation. But when the time of darkness was gone, and the

---

[1] Though Mr. Goodwin leaves the geographical position of Tennu, the Sakti's city, a perfectly open question (*op. cit.*, p. 202), yet it seems that the mention of *Abu*, which is in other papyri contrasted with *Athou* (Elephantine), and the allusion to the 'station of Snefru,' an early king (of the third dynasty), whose inscriptions are found in the Sinai peninsula, tend strongly in favour of M. Chabas' opinion that some district near the land of the Edomites is described.

dawn come, I proceeded from place to place. Thirst overtook me in my journey, my throat was parched. I said: This is the taste of death. I lifted up my heart; I braced my limbs. I heard the pleasant voice of cattle.' One of the Sakti meets him, gives him water and milk, and brings him to the king of Tennu. After inquiries concerning the state of Egypt, and his own previous history, Saneha is comfortably settled in Tennu. He obtains the king's daughter in marriage, with a good property, and is employed in all matters of trust. He carries on many successful warlike expeditions, and, above all, defends himself victoriously against a strong man who comes to challenge him, in order to drag him from his high position. It is perhaps the most curious social feature in the story that a man in Saneha's position should be exposed to such bullying, and that all the population should have 'longed to see the fight,' and considered it high sport. The king cashiers the defeated champion, and gives all his property to Saneha. But despite of all these things, when our hero became old, and his children were grown up about him, he began to long to return into Egypt. I do not believe all the reasons are honestly stated. The only ostensible one is a desire to be buried with Egyptian funeral rites, and to enjoy the inestimable benefit of King Amenemha's favour.

'Grant me (to return) home. Permit me to show

myself? Have I not suffered anxiety? What more is there to boast? (Let me) be buried in the land where I was born. Let there be a fortunate lot hereafter; grant me pardon. He [the king] acts like a beneficent being, his heart pities him who beseeches him that he may live in the land. He is to him like the sun. He is gracious, he listens to the prayer of one at a distance. He stretches out his arm to smite the earth with it, (and him) who does not bring him oblations. My name (saith he) is King of Egypt; living in his domains, serving the Queen of the Earth in his house. I hear the complaints of her children.

'O let his streams refresh my limbs. Old age descends, infirmity overtakes me, my eyes are heavy, my hands paralysed, my legs stagger.[1] When numbness of heart comes, bring me forth; let them carry me to the eternal home, the servant of the Lord of all; yea let them say: Happy (new) birth and eternal transmigrations to me.

'Behold then, spoke his majesty King *Cheperkara*, the Blessed, to the superintendent of ———. His Majesty sent him to me with kingly gifts; yea, he accorded to me, like a ruler of all the lands, that the king's children who were in his house should cause their complaints to be heard.

---

[1] The reader will remember the reflections of Ptah-hotep, above, p. 279.

'Copy of the mandate brought to me :—

'*Amenemha*, living for ever and to eternity. A royal mandate to his servant *Saneha*. Behold there is brought unto thee this mandate from the king to inform thee. Thou hast traversed the countries, proceeding from Atma to Tennu, going from country to country as thy heart bid thee. Behold that which thou hast done, thou hast done. Thou shalt not be called to account for what thou hast said, or hast not said, in the assembly of the young men, (nor) on account of thy having devised this business. Thy heart accomplished it. Thy heart was not faint. Thou didst aspire to a name which should be in the palace, durable, flourishing, like the sun, exalting its head among the kingdoms of the earth, its offspring in the palace.

'Thou hast amassed treasures; they shall be safe and abide with thee in their fulness. If thou comest to Egypt, thou shalt see a house prepared for thee. If thou dost homage to the Great House thou shalt be numbered amongst the counsellers. That is certain. Lo! thou hast arrived at middle age, thou hast passed the flower (of youth?). Think upon the day of burial, upon the passage to Amenti. There shall be given thee jars of cedar oil, wrappings [&c., &c.], service shall be done to thee in carrying forth, in the day of burial (?). An image of gold, the head of lapis lazuli, a canopy above thee made of meska (wood), beasts for thy hunting, players on instruments before thee. The poor shall make their moan at the door of thy tomb. Prayers shall be addressed to thee . . . .

'Strong shall be thy limbs, thy nerves sound, like a lord in white amongst the king's children. There shall be none before thee in the land, no Amu shall surpass (thee). Thou shalt not be treated like the fleece of a sheep, it shall be done according to thy wish. The great ones of the land shall vie in doing honour to thee.—

'When this mandate reached me, I was standing in the midst of my people. When it was presented to me I laid myself prostrate. I touched the soil. I gave it to be read out before my chosen men, yea, I caused my household to assemble to fulfil these things, I being myself like one mad, . . yea, [said I] the good deliverer inclines his heart to deliver me. Thy majesty permits me to proceed in person home.

'Copy of the answer to the mandate which I made without (delay), saying :—

'By most gracious favour, concerning this flight of mine which I made to him that knows it not. Thy majesty is the good god, lord of both lands, loving Ra, paying homage to Mentu . . . . lord of the scimitar in both lands, son of Ra Horus, image of Athom and his society of gods . . . .

the great Prince of Abydus, the Queen Ara (Uræus) adorns thy head, the great queen of Punt (Arabia), Netpe the elder, Ra, and all the gods of the land of Egypt, and the islands of the great sea—may they bring thee life and strength, let them bring their presents, granting their durations without bounds, eternity without limits. Let thy fear increase in the lands and regions. Mayest thou chastise the waters. . .

'The message . . . . from the king's majesty unto me, it is a terror to say it, it is too great to be repeated. The great god, the equal of the sun god, is mocking me. He himself grants me to be near him to give counsel to him, to be intrusted with his affairs. Thy majesty is like Horus, the power of thy arm extends over all lands. . . .

'May it please your majesty, let not Tennu be called to account before thee, as it were thy dogs. Behold this flight which I made, Tennu sought it not, it was not of my counsel, it suggested it not to me, it distinguished not between me and any other person.

'I journeyed from Abou . . . . from the land Annui, without fear, without any one coming after me. I listened not to the counsels of sloth, my name was not heard in the voice of doubt, except for a little while, my limbs were rigid, my feet stumbled. . . . God provided me (a guide) in this flight, to lead me. Behold, I am not as one afraid, (I am as) one knowing the land. The sun god hath put thy fear throughout the land, thy dread is in the region. Before I was set as lord over this place, behold thou hadst clothed this dwelling, shining like the sun. Dost thou desire water from the river? it furnishes drink; dost thou desire rain from heaven? it gives nourishment. Thou speakest, and behold I bequeath my goods to the children which I have begotten in this place.

'When I have finished doing this, let thy majesty do as it pleases thee. I live from the breath which thou givest, loving the Sun Horus, the image of thy noble countenance, loving what is agreeable to the lord of Thebes. May he live for ever.—

'I passed a day in Aam, in distributing my goods to my children. My eldest son was over my servants. My servants, yea, all my goods, were in his hand, my men and all my cattle, my fruit-bearing trees, and all my woods of dates. When I had finished, I appointed over the regions a director, who was over the workmen, to send word home, to give an account. His majesty sent his chief steward, the controller of the royal house. There were loaded boats with him, bearing royal presents of all sorts.

'The Sakti came to (see) me setting off. I chose out one of them all, in the name of all the officers, for the office of . . . . Upon my return to visit the town again on the morrow morning, they came shouting to me their farewells. Their farewells came for a good journey to **bring me** to the palace. When I reached the **land I** was **received** by the king's children, standing on the walls to conduct me; the counsellors guided **me to** the palace, to bring me **on the way to** the **court.** I found his majesty **in the** Old Palace, **in** the pavilion of pure gold. When I **was** near him I fell prostrate, amazed, before him. The god addressed me mildly; I was as one brought **out** of the dark; my tongue was **dumb, my** limbs failed me, **my** heart **was no** longer **in my body, to** know whether I was alive or dead. His majesty said to one of **the** counsellors: Lift him **up,** that I may speak to him. His majesty said: Behold thou wentest beating **the** lands, as a runaway. Age has come upon **thee,** old age has overtaken thee. It is no small boast thou hast. **Not a** Petti surpasses thee. Be **not** silent and without words; famous is thy name. I was [at first] afraid to answer. I [then] answered in terror: Behold, I said, **my** lord, how can **I answer** these things? Behold, is not the hand of God **upon me?** It is terrible. It remains **within me as something causing** (pain). Behold **I am before thee.** Thou art powerful. **Let thy majesty do as it pleases thee.**

'When **the king's** children had **been** admitted, his majesty said **to the queen: Behold Saneha.** He went as **an Amu, he has been** made into **a Sakti.** Then arose a very great shout **from the king's children,** with one voice. They said to his majesty: **He is not in the right, O my** lord **the king!** His majesty **said: He is in the right.'**

[There follow here some sentences of which the connexion is obscure.]

'His majesty said: Let him not fear, let him cease to be in dread. He shall be a counsellor among the officers: he shall be set among the chosen ones. When ye go forth to the palace precedence shall be given to him. When he goes out of the palace the king's children shall attend him, proceeding even unto the great gates.

'I was installed in the house of a prince; there were treasures in it, there was a fountain in it, the dews of heaven watered it. From the treasury (were sent) garments of kingly attire, spices of the finest, such as the king's nobles love in every chamber. There were all sorts of liquors (?) for my limbs [and] for my hair. They were brought from the country of clothes by the Nemmasha. I was clothed with fine linen. I was anointed with the finest oil, I lay down upon a couch, there was given to me . . . oil to anoint myself with it.

'There was given me a house befitting a counsellor. There were many labourers employed to build it: all its timber was new. There was brought refreshment from the palace three or four times a day, besides what the king's sons gave. No sooner was it finished than I built myself a tomb of stone amongst the chief officers. His majesty chose its site. The chief painter designed it, the sculptors carved it, the chief purveyor who was over the upper country brought earth to it; all the decorations were made of hewn stone. When it was ready I was made superior lord of the field in which it was, near the town, as was done to the chief counsellor. My image was engraved upon its portal (?), of pure gold. His majesty caused it to be done. No other was made like unto it. I was in the favour of the king until the day of his death came.

'It is finished (from) its beginning to its end as it was found in the copy.'[1]

The reader has already seen so many specimens of old Egyptian literature in the earlier part of this Essay, that he will easily be able to compare the peculiar features of this curious narrative with parallel passages from the other papyri. Some sentences of Mr. Goodwin's translation, which is not quite complete, have been omitted, as not being of interest to any but students of old Egyptian, who should compare it with the *facsimile* of the original in Lepsius' *Denkmäler*. I shall only observe that there is a tone of reality and earnestness in the veneration of the king which all the circumlocutions and compliments cannot hide.

§ 14. *Satirical Writing and Beast Fables.*—Having now discussed the most important biographical remains as yet discovered, we shall turn to

---

[1] Cf. for the whole passage, *Fraser's Magazine* for February, 1865, pp. 202, *sqq.*

another subject, suggested by some passages of the Mohar's correspondent, where he draws satirical sketches of various personages of his acquaintance. Solemn and staid as were the old Egyptians, there are nevertheless a good many traces of their *Satirical writing* rescued from oblivion. The literary class appear to have looked with a good deal of contempt upon the condition and the foibles of others, and to have considered themselves a caste in the social, though not in the political, sense. They were evidently recruited, like the literary class in China, from all ranks; but this did not prevent a strong *esprit de corps* among them. They seem to have hardly spared even the sacred person of the king, and not to have confined themselves to writing, but actually to have drawn satirical pictures in mimicry of the Pharaohs and their courts. One such papyrus, known as the satirical papyrus of Turin, has survived, and has been published, along with the drawings which it caricatures, as the last plate in Lepsius' *Auswahl*. From this I have given two or three specimens which appear to me of interest.[1]

---

[1] Cf. frontispieces to Parts 1 and 2 of this volume. This side of Egyptian Literature has been but scantily treated. The reader may consult M. Devéria's casual description of the satirical papyrus in his discussion on the judicial report of Ramses III. in the *Journal asiatique* for August, 1865, pp. 347-8. M. Lauth has also said something on the point in his *Moses der Ebräer*, p. 14; and in his curious article on beast fables in old Egypt in

RAMSES III PLAYING CHESS WITH A GIRL OF HIS HAREEM
(From the Turin Satiric Papyrus)

These rude sketches are caricatures of the concerts depicted on the walls of the palace, also of the battles, and especially of a scene on the walls of Ramses' pavilion, where the king is depicted playing chess with a girl of the hareem. It is remarkable that the beast form is that adopted by the Egyptian artist, not the human form with a beast's head (so common in the representations of the gods), but a simple sketch of the animal best suited to indicate the object of the satire. Thus Ramses III. is drawn as a lion, his concubines as *gazelles*, perhaps (as among the Hebrews) a term of endearment, which would naturally suggest them. The sympathy which the Egyptians had for the lower animals, whose instincts they regarded as the best symbols of divine wisdom and forethought, might well account for the prominent part they play even in this department of Egyptian literature.

The beast fable appears accordingly to have made its first appearance in Egypt, to judge from the document to which we have referred, as well as from a very curious papyrus in the Leyden collection (numbered 1., 384), containing not merely ritualistic fragments in demotic character and in pure Coptic dialect, but also, according to M.

---

the *Munich Sitz. ber.* for 1868, vol. ii., p. 42, &c. Cf. also on Egyptian caricature, Sir J. G. Wilkinson, *Manners and Customs of the Ancient Egyptians*, ii., p. 385.

Lauth,[1] several fables containing dialogues between animals. The first is a conversation between the wolf and an Ethiopian cat; a second between a lion and a mouse; a third between birds. The translations he gives are very interesting. In that of the lion and the mouse it appears that the mouse was about to be devoured, when it pleads: 'O Pharaoh, if you eat me you will not be satisfied, and your hunger will remain. Give me life as I gave it to you in the day of your straits, in your evil day.' Then the lion grew reflective and the mouse proceeds: 'Remember the hunters; one had a net to catch you and the other a rope. There was also a pit dug before the lion, he fell in and was a prisoner in the pit: he was pledged by his feet; then came the little mouse opposite him and released him. Now therefore reward me: I am the little mouse.'

Though it is now the prevalent theory that such fables were first invented by the Egyptians,[2] I am

---

[1] *Op cit.*, pp. 50, *sq.*

[2] See the interesting article of J. Zündel (*Rev. archéol.*, for 1861, pp. 354, *sq.*) on the probable Egyptian origin of Aesop (is Αἴσωπος Αἰθίοψ?). I quote his remarks on the moral worth of fables.

'Il y a une solidarité trop intime entre les phénomènes du dehors et les sentiments de l'âme pour que l'homme, en voyant la chute des feuilles, ne dût faire un retour sur sa propre fragilité, pour qu'en observant les luttes, les ruses, et les misères des animaux, il ne dût pas voir comme bondir ses propres passions devant ses yeux. C'est ainsi que dans le langage primitif nous

not sure whether this people were not rather the means of conveying to Europe **an ancient instinct of** the primitive **Africans, who may** have felt **that the wisdom of the lower** animals was equal to their own, **and** who had not acquired exalted notions **of the** inherent superiority of the human race. There is strong evidence that all **negroes are fond** of beast fables. I need only here mention **the significant** fact that as soon **as the Vai-Negroes invented**

voyons éclore sur la tige d'une intuition toute matérielle le germe d'une idée morale.

'Que ce soit alors par une métaphore ou par une fable que cette idée se formule, n'importe ; le fait subsiste que la nature extérieure s'est, pour ainsi dire, chargée de l'éducation de l'âme humaine en la réveillant par son sympathique appel. Cette phase de demi-réveil de l'âme, où elle commence à se rendre compte des éléments de son être moral, est l'époque où les enfants et les peuples aiment les fables. Mais on se tromperait fort si l'on se figurait que pour cela la morale elle-même dans son ensemble soit découverte. Je comprehends très-bien le sentiment de Rousseau, qui protestait contre l'usage des fables dans l'éducation. Il y a en effet quelque chose de trop fragmentaire dans l'instinct de l'animal pour qu'il soit un digne modèle de la libre détermination de l'homme. Justement ce qui rend un animal propre à devenir le type précis d'une vertu ou d'un vice, savoir l'isolement, la spécialité de son instinct, lui ôte aussi tout le mérite du choix, tous les titres pour devenir le modèle de celui qui, portant dans son sein *tous* les instincts, est appelé à les dompter tous par un principe supérieur, celui de la conscience. Ce n'est donc pas la morale qui peut se traiter dans la fable, ce n'est que la casuistique ; la morale ne se traite que dans la tragédie, dont le héros n'est pas l'animal, mais l'homme. On peut

for themselves a system of writing,[1] their very earliest essays in composition were rude fables about beasts.

§ 15. *Judicial Documents.* — I pass from the lightest to the gravest class of Egyptian literature, and for completeness' sake notice the judicial documents preserved to us. These have naturally rather an antiquarian and historical, than a literary interest, and yet some of the papyri preserved seem to have been chiefly valued as specimens of style, especially those containing the petitions of aggrieved persons to the king or his **representatives**.[2]

---

opposer proverbe à proverbe, fable à fable, ce n'est qu'en tragédie que les problèmes de morale se jugent sans appel.'

These views are to my mind sounder than the remarkable sketch of the history of beast fables in the Emperor Julian's seventh oration (on the duties of Cynics), though there is much truth and beauty in his exposition of the gentle moral stimulus administered to infants and savages by this teaching.

[1] Cf. above, p. 118.

[2] The principal judicial papyri are: (1) that of Turin, translated and explained by Devéria, *Journal asiatique*, 1865-7, including an account of (2) the papyri called Lee and Rollin (British Museum and Paris), also treated of by M. Chabas, *Mélanges*, i., p. 9; (3) the Abbott papyrus, fully discussed, first by Dr. Birch, then by M. Chabas, *Mélanges égypt.* 3ᵐᵉ série, pp. 1-143. (4) One of the Salt papyri, explained in the same work, pp. 173-201. (5) The Berlin papyrus ii., containing the appeal of a workman, cf. F. Chabas, *le papyrus de Berlin*, pp. 5-16. (6) Two other appeals (in British Museum) discussed in his *Mélanges*, iii., pp. 203, *sq.* (7) There is a judicial papyrus in the collection of M. Harris,

The most strictly legal documents, **and therefore** most instructive as to forms **of procedure in Egypt,** are undoubtedly the Turin judicial papyrus, and the Abbott **papyrus.** The former, a manuscript **of a** remarkably large and fine writing, but with its first page mutilated, dates from the reign of Ramses III., the first king **of the twentieth dynasty, and there**fore about two generations later than the **Exodus.**[1] This information **has** been gathered **from a frag**ment relating **to the same trial in the possession** of Dr. Hartwell **Lee,** which specially describes the magic arts employed by the **chief** criminal, who **had** possessed himself **of a** magic **book belonging to** the **king, and** had used it against him. **It appears** that a conspiracy was concocted in the hareem of this king, who seems **from the satirical drawings already** mentioned **to** have **been peculiarly** addicted **to** sensual pleasures.

The accused **are divided** into three **classes. They** either (1) **spoke,** or (2) kept **secret, words**

---

not yet published. I am disposed to add (8) the treaty between Ramses II. and the Kheta (cf. *Rev. archéol.*, N. S., vol. xiii., pp. 268-75, and M. Chabas' *Voyage*, p. 345), peculiarly valuable as giving us a view of international law, and of extradition treaties in ancient times. It also supplies us with the bare results of the victory of Ramses, described in the epic of Pentaour.

[1] Cf. Devéria's articles in *Journal asiatique* for 1865, pp. 227-331, and for 1866, pp. 181, 412, criticised and corrected by F. Chabas, *Spoliation des Hypogées* (*Mél. ég.*, iii.), pp. 5-47.

dangerous to the king's safety, which they had heard from others. (3) Certain judges, who had connived at the guilt of the prisoners in a former investigation, are also severely punished. The words in question were spoken in the king's hareem, and repeated by the immediate relatives of the inmates. In the papyri Lee and Rollin certain persons are accused of the additional crime of using magic formulae in order to obtain access to the hareem.

The preamble of the document is in very large letters and contains an exhortation of the king himself to his judges, the first pronoun of majesty being employed. 'Go,' he exclaims, 'and judge them. I have no knowledge of the thing. Follow the dictates of your heart; be diligent to execute judgment on the man that deserves penalty.' There follow injunctions to mercy, if the crime be not proved, and a devout prayer which the king offers to the gods that preside over justice (by which he means his ancestors), who had established a sound judicial system. Then comes the rubric: 'Persons brought up for the great abominations which they had committed— brought into court to be tried by the treasurer M., the treasurer P., the scribe M. of the library, and the umbrella-bearer H.[1] They tried them, found

---

[1] I omit the long Egyptian names as here immaterial.

them guilty, administered their punishment, and their abominations were taken from them.'

Then follows the enumeration, viz. : 'The great criminal *Penhuiban*, who was chief steward, arraigned for his crime of conspiring with the women of the hareem. He carried out their words to their mothers and sisters, who attempted to excite men by their words to engage miscreants to injure His Majesty. He was arraigned before the High Criminal Court. They judged his villainies; they found that he had really committed them, and that his iniquities were complete in him. The judges had his punishment inflicted on him.' Such is the formula. A list of fourteen persons is first enumerated and those who omitted to lodge information as to what they had heard are apparently punished with death, just as the actual conspirators.

The next rubric heads a list of six women and two men, of whom one is an Ethiopian, to whom his sister sent suggestions of conspiracy from the hareem. He is judged by three new judges, *apparently foreigners*. Then follows a list of persons tried by a second commission, and executed forthwith; and lastly, a list of judges punished by losing their ears and noses for neglecting the evidence brought before them. Some of them are afterwards executed. Among the conspirators appear not only the king's concubines, but military officers, and apparently one of the king's sons, who is, however, arraigned under an assumed name, and though executed, is not stigmatised by a single severe epithet. The papyrus ends with a single name, probably that of the executive officer employed.[1]

Apart from historical considerations, which do not here occupy us, this document discloses to us the truly oriental complexion of the Egyptian court at this epoch. The severity of the punishments and the mutilations lead us in the same direction, and would suggest a condition of law very primitive and very summary. Fortunately, other documents bear a far different complexion, and indicate a condition of things as constitutional, as cumbrous, and as complicated as the law of our own times.

I also think that foreign Egyptologists have been misled by the constant personal reference to the king in the legal documents.[2] The king seems to take personal cognisance of every case, and even

---

[1] Cf. Devéria *op. cit.*, p. 364. 'Quoiqu 'il en soit donc du but véritable des conjurés, on doit reconnaître que le papyrus judiciaire de Turin nous met sous les yeux le plus ancien example connu de ces conspirations du harem, auxquelles se mêlent si souvent des eunuques et des grands personages, dans l'histoire de tout l'orient, et qui ne manquaient jamais d'entraîner après elles de nombreuses condemnations à la peine capitale.'

[2] M. Devéria has made many mistakes in consequence, rectified by M. Chabas. The reader should guard against the impression of Egyptian law produced by M. Devéria's version, and should not omit to compare M. Chabas' sound remarks (*Spol. des Hyp.*, pp. 3 and 12, in the third series of his *Mélanges.*)

the humblest petitioner addresses **himself directly to** him. But there is in **these** things **nothing but a** fiction still common in our own constitution, by which **the Queen is supposed to** investigate, grant, and refuse thousands **of petitions** which she never sees. Even in the law courts her name is perpetually put for**ward; and** in such a state **as** Egypt, where the king was the fountain of both **law** and religion, this tendency would exist more strongly. The systematic appointment of judges **and** commissioners, the universal **practice of** reducing all business matters **to** writing, **the** established and complicated **developments** of law **and** equity—all these things persuade us that the personal interference of the king, though theoretically universal, was really very small indeed.

We proceed **to** consider the *Abbott papyrus*, the record **of** an equally curious, but far less fatal inquiry. The crime committed had been hardly less heinous than that we have just discussed. **A number of** ancient tombs had been broken into and **rifled of** their contents by some person **or** persons unknown. **The many** valuables which the Egyptians placed **in the tomb with** the mummy made such a **piece of** sacrilege **not** uncommon, **and** this partly explains the colossal coverings over the tombs of kings **and of** great men. The theft took place in the reign **of** Ramses IX., **in** the eleventh century, B. C.

The first thing done was **to appoint a commis-**

sion to investigate the facts, and these men report the precise number of tombs rifled, and the names of the occupants: and I may here repeat that throughout all the law proceedings of the old Egyptians we find a very modern habit of appointing commissioners, and obtaining written reports on all offences and crimes. We shall also find the sound principle of taking the decision out of the hands of the individual, *even in the case of master and slave*,[1] and compelling all men to appeal to the authorised administrator of the law.

According to the inferences to be drawn from the document, informations had been lodged with the governor of Thebes, and upon his report the commissioners are sent to the tombs, of which the caretakers formed a distinct municipality under the charge of a second governor. This officer, though apparently inferior to the military governor of the city, is nevertheless independent of him, and can protect his people from any interference except a formal prosecution at the regular assizes for administering justice.

The investigation showed that the informations given were inaccurate. The tombs specified as having been rifled were found untouched; but others, four or five in number, had been plundered and profaned. On this being reported, the chief magistrates (a court of four) ordered the arrest of the persons

---

[1] Cf. Chabas' *Mélanges*, i., p. 11.

accused. Among others a workman confesses that he has been guilty of the crime, but being brought blindfold into the Necropolis, is unable to identify the queen's tomb which he had professedly plundered. He is ordered to stand aside for judgment, but was evidently not guilty of the crime of sacrilege. The inhabitants of the Necropolis, being apparently responsible for the crime of the workman, were greatly relieved, and showed the governor of the town who had brought the charge against them, by their mocking demeanour, that they bore him no good will. This so enrages him that he threatens to apply directly to the king to have a special commission issued to try them, seeing that the ordinary course of justice had failed. Thereupon their own governor retorts by laying a report of this occurrence before the Poliarch, or chief magistrate of the city, demanding that the false informers shall be tried and punished. There follows in conclusion a formal trial of the persons accused of sacrilege, and an acquittal for want of evidence. This takes place at a public assize, held in the outskirts of the town. I refer the reader for minuter details to M. Chabas' excellent analysis.[1]

The courts of justice appear to have been composed not of judges set apart for the purpose, but of various high officials, whose business it was to

---

[1] *Spoliation des Hypogées* (*Mélanges*, iii.).

undertake judicial duties at times—just as our courts-martial are formed. But it must be particularly noticed that various professions are represented; military and civil officers are combined with prophets and priests, so that whatever the nature of the case, there were some of the judges specially qualified to decide it. This I conceive to have been the intention of the arrangement. The trial before us also shows a laudable promptitude, the whole proceedings having only occupied four days. There is also, in the acquittal of the accused, a distinct censure appended of the magistrate who had obtruded his false informations. All these details, as well as the systematic procedure throughout the whole inquiry, establish thoroughly the reports of the Greeks, that the Egyptians were among all men the most attached to law and order, and that the power of the kings was constitutionally defined and limited.[1]

When we turn from this papyrus to other judicial documents, our estimate is modified but not changed. We find that the great delays of our own system had their place in Egypt also, and that noted offenders could evade punishment by legal devices, and by the connivance of their neighbours, like Meidias, in the days of Demosthenes, and those who commit murders *on principle* in this country at the present time. There is in the Salt collection a com-

---

[1] Cf. the passages from Diodorus and Plutarch, cited by M. Chabas, *op. cit.*, p. 4.

plaint lodged by the young son of a chief workman against an audacious miscreant for a series of the worst crimes.[1] The document dates from the time of Seti II. (fourteenth century B. C.) The accused was a relation of the plaintiff, having access to his property, and had murdered his brother, violated several women, plundered sepulchres, &c., &c. He had escaped punishment on one occasion by transferring to the magistrate five slaves belonging to the plaintiff's family. He had, besides bribery, also used intimidation, for he had accused one magistrate to his superior for having had him beaten. It appears that such punishment was unconstitutional, and that by this complication he escaped for a time. The results of the accusation are unknown.

It appears from another document, noticed by M. Chabas,[2] that a master could not even recover his runaway slaves without having recourse to legal proceedings. Several petitions for legal recovery of lost property have survived.[3]

But a still more curious document is preserved at Berlin among the papyri of the old Empire, and published in Lepsius' *Denkmäler*. The loss of the first few pages of the papyrus makes it difficult to

---

[1] Cf. Birch and Chabas' article, *Mélanges*, iii., pp. 4-16, 201.
[2] *Mélanges*, i., pp. 11, 12.
[3] Cf. Chabas' *Mélanges*, passim.
[4] Cf. F. Chabas, *Les papyrus hiératiques de Berlin*, pp. 4-16.

comprehend the relations of the parties. There was a dispute between a workman and a superintendent, who seems to have caught the workman in the act of decamping from a salt mine with property not belonging to him. He charges him with feeding his ass upon stolen dates, and forthwith appropriates the animal. The workman apologises, but threatens to appeal to the governor of the salt mines in which he has been employed, and to complain of being ill-treated on his property; upon this the superintendent at once gives him a sound flogging, and sends the ass to his own stables. The workman supplicates for the length of a day, and then departs for *Soutensinen*, to complain to the great man, as he had threatened. This person, called *Meruitens*, sends some of his servants to inquire into the complaint. They state the case rather against the workman, but Meruitens holds his peace in order to draw from the wretched man an interminable series of flatteries, and supplications for mercy. Then the matter is referred to the king, and the workman brought before him.[1] The king directs

---

[1] Nebkera, of the xi. dynasty. So M. Chabas, *op. cit.*, p. 13. M. Pleyte, on the contrary, *Étude sur le chap.* 125 *du Rituel*, refers it to Ka-neb-ra, the last king of the third dynasty I think he is wrong, and that the very expression (maâ-xeru) which he quotes is evidence against him. Cf. Mariette's *Notice, &c., du musée à Boulaq*, (third ed.,) p. 27. He shows that this expression was not common before the vi. dynasty.

a written report to be made, meanwhile appropriating the wife and children of the accused, according to a law in force against vagrants, and orders him to be properly fed till the matter is decided. The rest of the document, and of its duplicate, papyrus iv. of Berlin, occupied with additional supplications. The result of the affair is lost.

So large is the part occupied by descriptions of the justice and mercy of the great man, that some critics[1] have thought the whole composition to be one of moral purpose, and that these supplications are indirect descriptions of the ideal governor. 'Thou that art the father of the wretched, the husband of the widow, the father of the orphan (girl), the clothing of him that has no mother. May thy name be like a law in the land.' Such is the style. But whatever may be the intention, the state of things even under the old Empire presupposes fixed forms of law, appeals to higher authorities, written reports, in fact all the conditions attained only under a long-established and fully-developed civilisation.

The international treaty of peace between Ramses II. and the Kheta, with whom he had carried on war in Syria, will fitly conclude this

---

[1] E. S. Pleyte, *Étude sur le chap. 125 du Rituel*, pp. 10-11.

part of the subject. The historical bearings of this very interesting text have already been pointed out.[1]

The treaty appears to have been made on perfectly equal terms, though solicited by the enemy, and of course all offensive epithets towards them, with which the epic poem on the preceding battle teems, are carefully avoided. It was drawn up on a silver plate, and in both languages. Our inscription is a copy of the Egyptian version. It establishes a close offensive and defensive alliance between the nations, and even provides for the extradition of all emigrants, deserters, and *skilled artificers* who may escape from one country to the other. It specially provides that on condition of such extradition, no penalties for desertion are to be exacted from persons brought back to their own country. 'His crime shall not be raised up against him, nor shall his home be destroyed, nor his wives, nor his children. His mother is not to be slain, nor is he to lose his eyes, his mouth (tongue?), or his legs, and no crime is to be brought up against him.' This provision shows what barbarous vengeance had been wreaked in former days, and although M. Chabas thinks[2] that the mention of murdering the deserter's family was necessitated by Kheta manners,

---

[1] Above, p. 354, where the authorities are also cited.
[2] *Voyage d'un égyptien*, p. 346.

as Egyptian lawgivers constantly insisted upon the principle of *personal responsibility* in crime, yet when mutilation is openly practised, it is but a step in cruelty to the murder of innocent relatives.[1] The laws of Moses also inculcated personal responsibility, and deprecated the punishment of innocent relatives; yet how constantly in Jewish history are we shocked by this hideous travesty of justice! I rather think, therefore, that these details are added by the Khetas, who drew up the treaty, in order to satisfy their consciences in giving up such suppliants as claimed from them the protection of their hearth and hospitality.

§ 16. *Official Lists, Accounts, &c.*—The many lists of operatives employed, and the many accounts and official registers which have been preserved, can hardly take their place as a portion of Egyptian literature, but are in themselves interesting, as showing the business habits of the nation, and their uniform practice of reducing all such things to writing.[2] The votive inscriptions indeed, of the

---

[1] The extraordinary delight of Saneha (above, pp. 382-3) at being allowed to return in safety and honour to Egypt seems to point in the same direction.

[2] For details the reader may consult the Summary of the Leyden Papyri in Leemans' *Monuments*, &c., ii., p. 69, supplemented in Chabas' *Mélanges*. The Turin papyri of this nature have been partly published by J. Lieblein (*deux papyrus hiératiques*, Christiania, 1868), and in the first three numbers of

kings, commemorating their victories, are full of statistical details, in which the names of conquered nations, the catalogues of tributes and spoils, and other such practical evidences of their success occupy no small space. These inscriptions are referred to by Tacitus, when he describes the Egyptian priests expounding to Germanicus the painted writings on their temples and obelisks.[1]

But apart from these public monuments, the discovered papyri abound with similar lists, made by private individuals, or by subordinate government officers. Many valuable facts as to the economy of old Egyptian life are disclosed to us on this indirect, and therefore undeniable, evidence. I have abstained systematically from historical inferences, yet I cannot avoid mentioning that in these documents, and in these alone, a distinct mention of the Hebrews in Egypt has been first found.[2] But apart

---

Pleyte and Rossi's *papyrus du musée de Turin*. The Rollin collection of the Bibliothèque Impériale at Paris has been described by M. Chabas in *Lepsius' Zeitschr.* for 1869, pp. 85, *sq.* M. de Rougé (*Zeitschr.* for 1868, p. 130) has noticed similar entries on the back of Pap. Sallier IV.

[1] Tac. Ann, ii., 60. Legebantur et indicta gentibus tributa, pondus argenti et auri, numerus armorum equorumque et dona templis ebur atque odores, quasque copias frumenti et omnium utensilium quaeque natio penderet.

[2] Cf. Chabas, *Mélanges*, i., pp. 42, *sq.*, and with it cf. Brugsch, *Histoire d'Égypte*, p. 174.

from this, the statement in the books of Moses, that the children of Israel longed for the fleshpots of Egypt, is corroborated by the care and benevolence shown in the papyri as regards feeding the labourers engaged in public works. Their holydays, too, as might be expected from so religious a people, were not fewer in number than those claimed by Irish Roman Catholic workmen as saints' days. The Turin papyri published by M. Lieblein speak clearly on these points. There seems also to have been provision made for the support of sick labourers.[1]

The detail with which all these tasks were copied down by clerks and scribes seems to have been as irksome to them as it would be to us; and so we find these papyri covered with scrawls and flourishes such as any man now-a-days is sure to make on paper, if he is kept scoring slowly, and obliged to idle over this task alone. I know no documents, among all those left us by the Egyptians, which produce a more strangely modern impression.[2] Here, as elsewhere, the more we study antiquity, the more clearly we see that the main differences between the oldest historical times and our own were in the material appliances of civilisation, but that in moral

---

[1] *Op cit.*, pp. 12, 27.
[2] Cf. *Lepsius' Zeitschr.* for 1868, p. 130, and for 1869, p. 90; also *Select papyri of the Brit. Mus.*, vol. ii., p. 1.

and social development men were then, as now, ennobled by honour and piety, degraded by selfishness, passion, and idleness. Empires may decay, and culture change hands; human nature has been, and will perhaps ever be, the same.

§ 17. *General Remarks.* — It remains to offer some concluding remarks on the general features of the varied documents which have been described in this Essay. In doing so, we must endeavour to free ourselves from all favouring prejudices, caused either by their immense antiquity, or the labour required for their interpretation. But we must avoid disparaging this truly original development as contrasted with the maturer products of other nations, who in succeeding ages profited by the genius of older Egypt. Even the Assyrians cannot be said to have produced an original literature, when we know that their cuneiform graphic system was borrowed from an older race. The Hebrews and the Greeks started with all the greatest difficulties overcome, and with models placed before them to rival and to surpass.

But, nevertheless, these later nations appear to have been gifted with a love of beauty for its own sake, and hence of artistic perfection *in literature*, quite strange to the Egyptians. No doubt many of the Egyptian material monuments, especially those of the Old Empire, possess the greatest beauty and majesty; but it is the unconscious and unintentional perfection attending successful efforts to represent nature and to secure permanence. Our materials have of late so increased, that we can express an opinion on the character of the ancient Egyptians without presumption. The most prominent feature was assuredly plain practical realism. The grossest features in human nature are reproduced with the same naïve bluntness, and with the same calmness as the noblest and most divine characteristics. The grandeur of their monuments, so far as it arose from magnitude, appears to have been rather the result of a desire for permanence—an instinct which they had gained from the prehistoric traditions of an old established empire, and the teaching of a spiritual religion. The enormous structures of the kings were no mere ostentatious display, but rather the clear evidence of a strong conviction that the immortal soul required its earthly tabernacle to be immortal also.[1]

I shall, however, not deny that beyond this majesty of size, there was much real beauty in the architectural productions of the old Egyptians. Their use of colour has never been excelled, and the grace and delicacy of their floral designs are still the models of our best patterns. The use of the lotus flower, for example, in borders, apart from its religious suggestion of a re-opening future life, is

---

[1] Cf. Mariette, *Notice*, &c., p. 46, above quoted.

for all time beautiful.¹ Still more, their bold inaccuracy in imitating nature, their contempt of lesser details, in order to produce broad and true effects—these qualities, most perfectly displayed in their earliest statues, show us a nation whose realism was tempered by strictly artistic considerations.²

But human speech is a far more resisting material than granite, and the perfect harmony of a poem a far subtler structure than the massive temple. It may require centuries upon centuries of use before men can command their words, and not be led and trammelled by material difficulties in writing, and hence by interruptions to continuous and harmonious thought. The symmetry of a logical discourse is a far higher and more complex product than the mere harmony of architectural details.

These reflections are suggested by the great artistic contrast between the material structures of the Egyptians and their literary remains. I do not believe that the cumbrousness of the graphic system accounts for it. Hieratic writing was sufficiently cursive for a style more glowing than the monumental style, and was certainly discovered and used

---

¹ The reopening of this flower every morning aptly symbolised the resurrection after the night—the valley of the Shadow of Death. Cf. Mariette, *Notice*, &c., p. 129, &c.

² I allude to such statues as that of Shafra in the museum at Boulaq, and the wooden statues of the iv. and v. dynasties generally.

in the early days of Egypt's real greatness. But if the language and its awkward grammar are called in to bear the burden, the answer is obvious, that these are the truest expression of a nation's genius, and that a people with formally beautiful thoughts to be expressed, will never fail to find a beautiful expression wherein to clothe them.

An honest critic must therefore confess that a sense of *form* in literature, such as the Greeks possessed so perfectly, is almost totally absent from Egyptian writing. Its symmetry consists in wearisome repetitions of formulae, while the poetry is a clumsy parallelism, which so frequently wearies us in Hebrew, but which is often there, though seldom in Egyptian writings, the vehicle for striking effects. This absence of form does not shock us in the every-day correspondences, or in the judicial documents, which are for the most part clearly, and (if we except the ceremonious titles) concisely expressed; but when we turn to those compositions which are properly poetical, and more especially to those which treat of the noblest subjects, we feel a very great inadequacy in the expression, as compared with the thought.

It is impossible that the solar hymns, or the epic poems on the exploits of kings, should not contain both majesty and beauty. The adoration of the Unseen and Uncreate, the contemplation of external nature as the emanation from the Eternal substance, and the effect of the Divine benevolence—these great conceptions cannot be expressed without infusing their majesty into the words that portray them.[1] Again the thrilling crisis of the battle of Ramses II. with his countless enemies must necessarily inspire the poetical historian with vividness, and so far with eloquence.[2] But beyond this necessary beauty of style, if I may use the expression, we see hardly a trace of artistic composition. Even when the Egyptian author stumbles upon a fine thought, he casts it in among his ordinary materials without recognising its value. When, for example, the teacher writes to reprove his erring pupil for idleness and drunkenness, and tells him that a man in such a condition is 'like a shrine without its god,'[3] this very noble metaphor is associated with others so ordinary, that we can hardly believe the author to have appreciated it fully.[4]

---

[1] Cf. above, pp. 265-6.   [2] Cf. above, pp. 356-9.
[3] Cf. above, p. 293.
[4] Cf. E. Lefébure's remarks (*chap.* 15 *du Rituel*, p. 15). 'Je ferai remarquer seulement, au sujet de la forme de ces hymnes, que les Égyptiens songeaient peu à composer leur poëmes ; au lieu d'en grouper les détails de manière à produire un effet voulu, ils ne faisaient guère que les réunir, sans beaucoup d'ordre, suivants les hazards de la verve et de la mémoire.'

Their poetry, in fact, consists of parallelisms, and not verses. We see in their compositions, as in those of the Hebrews, the first steps towards a loose blank verse, with irregular *caesuras*,

It is then in its *matter* that we must look for the main interest of Egyptian literature. *Historically*, there can be no question that it stands in the first rank among the remains of antiquity. Here, if anywhere, we may hope to attain a glimpse of the first gradual origin of civilisation, and of the uncertain stages by which a growing national mind essays to attain Light and Truth. This aspect, however, of the subject, though constantly before us, has been necessarily avoided in the present discourse, as the intricate controversies and wide extent of Egyptian history make it a separate study.

But nothing has hitherto been said of a large class of historical documents, and that the most peculiar and characteristic of all, I mean *chronological* documents. Their past history being computed after the manner of early nations, not from a fixed era, but by the succession of a list of kings and priests, there have been found official catalogues of these dignitaries, of the greatest value in determining the antiquity of Egyptian civilisation and the various dynasties and capitals that successively

---

and guided by antithesis and repetitions often feeble. These cadences are not necessary, but only occur when the author warms to his subject, just as the Hebrew authors pass from prose to poetry—a feature common to the Indian and Chinese plays also. Besides this sort of verse, the Egyptians also used assonances and refrains, especially at the opening of phrases.

held empire in the valley of the Nile. And where these catalogues have been defaced, they have been to some extent supplemented by curious sepulchral monuments, where a king or priest is represented entering in another world the happy resting-place of his ancestors, who sit in great ranks on the walls, marked by their names and titles, ready to receive him. To the casual observer, no literary monument seems so dull and idle as a long list of barren names, and yet of all the documents left us by ancient nations, these have been perhaps the most fruitful. I shall not insist upon the obvious value of determining not only the chronology of a nation, and of fixing the dates of the several monuments, which bear the names of the builders engraved upon them; I shall merely reiterate the fact that but for these lists of names, neither the hieroglyphics nor the cuneiform inscriptions would ever have been deciphered. Proper names gave the first clue to the sound of the strange character, and led learned men upon the right track.

May we not add that from another point of view, though such lists are neither eloquence nor poetry, yet in eloquence and poetry there is nothing which can excite the emotions with greater power, than the associations that cling to these venerated names? In our very devotions, how much is due to the mere recital of different titles for the object of our adoration? In history do not proper names stand out like points of light, to fasten the attention and excite the sympathy of the great mass of readers?

And to the sober, pious, conservative Egyptian, who lived on the even tenor of his life, venerating all that was ancient as if it were divine, we can conceive these series of names to have been no common statistics, no dry compendium of chronology, but each to have suggested the great days of old, and reminded him of his ancient parentage and descent from the older gods. Even in the most prosaic age and the most degenerate and denationalised country, among a people whose political life has been almost annihilated, and whose patriotism were long since choked but for the strong hand of nature—even in such a nation and such an age, there are memories clustering about proper names that make the pulse beat high, and the heart glow, and there is not an assembly even in such a country, which could not be inflamed by the mere mention of the men that strove to secure them their forgotten liberty.

Theologically, the earliest spiritual religion of the world has found its vehicle in the hieroglyphics; and the close relation in which the Semites stood to Egypt makes every detail about her faith of the last importance. When we are told that the earliest reputed lawgiver and author of Jewish records 'was learned in all the wisdom of the Egyptians,' we cannot fail to see that the Hebrews were deeply impressed with the debt they owed in spiritual things to their ancient oppressors. How far the details of Hebrew religion can be traced to Egyptian influences is an open question, and will in due time give rise to bitter controversies, but even now the solar hymns astonish us with the discovery that none of the surrounding nations, and succeeding civilisations, attained to the height and majesty of Egyptian religion, till the matured philosophy of Greece mastered the threadbare theosophy of Alexandria, and that Neo-Platonism arose, which proved the most dangerous ally and foe of Christianity.[1] There is indeed hardly a great and fruitful idea in the Jewish or Christian systems, which has not its analogy in the Egyptian faith. The development of the one God into a Trinity;[2] the incarnation of the Mediating Deity in a virgin, and without a father;[3] his conflict and his momentary defeat by the powers of darkness; his partial victory (for the enemy is not destroyed); his resurrection and reign

---

[1] This last form of Egyptian theology will be best seen in Hermes Trismegistus, and Iamblichus.

[2] Cf. Mariette, *op. cit.*, p. 113.

[3] Cf. Mariette, *Notice, &c.*, p. 104. 'La mère d'Apis passait pour vierge, même après l'enfantement. Apis, en effet, n'était pas conçu dans le sein de sa mère par le contact du mâle. Phtah, la sagesse divine personnifiée, prenait la forme d'un feu céleste et fécondait la vache. Apis était ainsi une incarnation d'Osiris par la vertu de Phtah.'

over an eternal kingdom with his justified saints;
his distinction from, and yet identity with, the
uncreate, incomprehensible Father, whose form is
unknown, and who dwelleth not in temples made
with hands—all these theological conceptions pervade the oldest religion of Egypt. So too the contrast, and even the apparent inconsistencies between
our moral and theological beliefs—the vacillating
attribution of sin and guilt partly to moral weakness, partly to the interference of evil spirits, and
likewise of righteousness to moral worth, and again
to the help of good genii or angels; the immortality
of the soul and its final judgment, the purgatorial
fire, the tortures of the damned—all these things
have met us in the Egyptian Ritual and moral treatises. So, too, the purely human side of morals,
and the catalogue of virtues and vices, are by natural
consequence as like as are the theoretical systems.
But I recoil from opening this great subject now;
it is enough to have lifted the veil and shown the
scene of many a future contest.

Lastly, the indications of *social* life and manners
in Egyptian literature, though in themselves less
complete, and less interesting psychologically, than
those left us by David and by Aeschylus, are yet
worthy of serious study and increased research.
Here it is fair to lay stress on mere antiquity. The
footprints on the sand of yesterday are of little moment; the footprints on the sand 3700 years ago

affect the mind with a strange emotion.[1] Be it remembered that our documents are not the tenth hand copies of monks, centuries removed from the real authors, but for the most part either original inscriptions, or copies taken by contemporaries and fellows of the writers. We often have them prepared, not in special books, but on papyri of which the backs are covered with rough accounts, with exercises in calligraphy, with random scrawls and vagaries of penmanship. We have surprised old Egyptian literature, as we surprised Roman life at Pompeii, not in its full dress and studied elegance, but just as it existed among the people in their everyday work. We hear it not in the faint echo of late and garbled copies, but speaking its own tongue, and answering for itself to our inquiries.

Beyond this feature, I need not recapitulate the details suggested by the extracts which have been brought before the reader. They show plainly enough that the old Egyptians were men of like passions with ourselves. Even the vices and tastes of effete civilisations are to be found among them. La Rochefoucauld had probably no wider experience than the authors of the Prisse papyrus. Pru-

---

[1] Cf. Mariette, *Notice*, &c., p. 66. He describes the discovery of an untouched Apis tomb: 'Quand j'y entrai pour la première fois, je trouvai, marquée sur la couche mince de sable dont le sol était couvert, l'empreinte des pieds des ouvriers qui, 3700 ans avant, avaient couché le dieu dans sa tombe.'

dence, Passion, and Principle contended then, as they have ever since done, with varying success for the command of society, and the conflict is not now nearer to its solution than it was 4000 years ago. Let these facts lead the reader, not merely to reflect on the uniformity of human nature in all ages; but rather to consider that the perfection of Egyptian civilisation may have been not an early blossom, but a late and ripe fruit, perhaps in the autumn of the world's existence.

INDEX.

NOTE.—In this Index the page only has been indicated, without distinguishing text and foot-notes. References here first mentioned are marked with an asterisk.

Abbott papyrus, 396, *sq.*
Abhandlungen (*Transactions*), quoted:
  ,,   of Berlin, 319.
  ,,   of Copenhagen, 190.
  ,,   of Göttingen, 13, (Sauppe on Plutarch's *Perikles*).
Abou and Athou, 237, 378.
Academy, the, quoted, 82, 233.
  ,,   the Royal Irish, *Transactions* of, 190.
Achaians in Egypt, 87 (first mention of, 363-4.)
Achaemenid, 179, 199.
Achilleus, discussed, 50-4, 84, 359.
Accounts, Egyptian, 405-6.
Aeschylus, quoted, 48.
Ahalyâ and Achilleus, 50.
Amenemha I., king of the 12th dynasty, 291, 294, 381.
Anaglyphs, 143-5.
Anastasi papyri, collection of, in British Museum, 231, 324.
Anastasy,   ,,   ,,   Leyden   ,,   262-5.
Anatomical theory, an Egyptian, 307.
Ancestors, worship of, 275, 392.
Animals, treatment of, in Egypt, 330, 340.
Asia, Upper, historical importance of, 192.
Aspasia, silence of Thukydides on, 12-14.
Assa, king of the 5th dynasty, 277.

Assyrian language, 195, *sqq.* Semitic character of, 209-10.
,, and Phoenician inscription, 212.
,, graphic system, 198, *sqq.*
Athanas, 134-5.
Auramazda, deciphering of, 183.
Avesta, the, 173, 179.

Balance of power, not a wholly modern principle, 27.
,, ,, ancient examples of, *ibid.*
Bashmuric, a disputed dialect, 135-6.
[* Zoëga (*Catalogus*, 140-4) has a good discussion on the probable situation of the district.]
Beer, 181.
Behistun inscription, the, 185-6, 197.
Benfey, Th., *die Persischen Keilinschriften*, 184.
Birch, Dr. Samuel,
,, in vol. v. of Bunsen's *Egypt's place in History*, 246, *sqq.*, 259, 261.
,, in Wilkinson's *Manners of the ancient Egyptians*, (Introduction to the study of hieroglyphics), 102, 111, 126-7, 144, 151.
,, in the *Archaeologia*.
,, in Chabas' *Mélanges*, 232.
,, in *Lepsius' Zeitschrift*, 306, 314, 318-20.
,, in *Revue archéologique*, 231.
,, in *Transactions of Royal Society of Literature*, 152.
Blackie, Prof., referred to, 51.
Body, future of, 254-7.
[* Add de Rougé in *Rev. archéol.*, n. s., vol. i., p. 364, and Mariette's *Notice, &c.*, pp. 108, 112.]
Botta, M., 195-7.
Boulaq, papyri of, now being published by M. Mariette, 233.
,, Museum of, see *Mariette.*
Broad views, when desirable, 25.

Brugsch, Dr. H., his following works are quoted :—
,,   *Histoire d'Égypte*, 224, 227, 270, 301, 321, 354, 406.
,,   *Recueil de Monuments*, 353, 360-1.
,,   in *Göttingen Transactions*, 144, 260.
,,   in *Revue archéologique*, 331, 341, *sqq*.
,,   in *Lepsius' Zeitschrift*, 101, 276.
,,   referred to 244, 309, 318, 344, &c., 367.
         [* *Über Bildung u. Entwicklung der Schrift*, Berlin, 1868.]
,,   *Grammaire démotique*, 102, 119, 127, 237, 247.
,,   *Zwei bilingue* (Rhind) *papyri*, 232, 253.
Bunsen, Baron, *Egypt's place in universal History*, 123, 166, 219, 275.
Burnouf, E., 179.
Byron, Lord, referred to, 39.

Caricatures, Egyptian, 389.
Chabas, M. F., his following works are quoted :—
         Mélanges égyptologiques (first series), 100, 120, 150, 222, 269, 310, 391.
         [* The second series has been out of print for the last two years, and to me inaccessible.]
,,   ,,   ,,   (third series), 231, 233, 322, 331, 360, 401.
,,   *Voyage d'un Égyptien* (Berlin, 1860), 100, 163, 231,
,,   243, 354.
,,   *les papyrus hiératiques de Berlin* (Chalons sur Saône, 1863), 156, 230, 391, 377, 400, *sq*.
,,   *Inscriptions des Mines d'or* (Chalons, 1862), 229, 269, 360, 373.
,,   *Papyrus magique Harris*, 233, 268, 296, *sqq*.
,,   in *Revue archéologique*, 232, 262-3, 273, 277, 335.
,,   in *Lepsius' Zeitschrift*, 99, 156, 274, 277, 406.
Chalouf, *stele* of, 154.

Chambers, his *Popular Rhymes of Scotland*, 92.
Champollion (le jeune).
   ,,   *Précis du système hiéroglyphique* (Paris, 1828),
           referred to, 112, 117, 120-2, 126, *sqq.*, 136,
           140-8, 154, 167, 237, 306.
           quoted, 113, 127, 148-9.
   ,,   *Grammaire égyptienne*, 114.
Champollion-Figéac, 126.
Charlemagne, crusade of, explained, 39, 40.
   ,,   referred to, 42.
Chinese, graphic systems of, discussed, 108, 117, 121, 207, 341.
Chorene, Moses of, *Armenian History*, 117.
Christianity, its effects on Egypt, 129, 234.
Chronicon Benedicti, referred to, 40.
Chronological documents, Egyptian, 413.

> [* The best authorities on early Egyptian chronology are (1) Lepsius, *die Chronologie der alten Aegypter*; (2) Brugsch, *Histoire d'Égypte*, vol. i.; (3) Bunsen, *Egypt's place in Universal History*, vol i.; (4) Max Duncker, *Geschichte des Alterthums*, vol. i., chap. i.; (5) F. Chabas' *Aperçus chronologiques*, in his *papyrus hiératiques de Berlin*; (6) Goodwin's Introduction to the *Story of Saneha* in *Fraser's Magazine*; (7) Lauth, *die geschichtlichen Ergebnisse der Aegyptologie*.]

Clemens Alexandrinus, 123, 144, 310.
Cleopatra, cf. Kleopatra.
Clibborn, Mr., his drama of *Bethiah*, 340.
Coptic alphabet, 119, 131, 235.
   ,,   literature of, 131, *sq.*, 315-16.
   ,,   dialects, 134, *sq.*; analogy to old Egyptian, 160-3.
Coreans, their alphabet, 117.
   ,,   signs, borrowed from Chinese, 207.
Cox, Rev. F. W., *Mythology of the Aryan nations*, discussed, 42-95.
   ,,   in particular, linguistically, 42-63.

Cox, in particular, geographically, 63-5.
,,   ,,   psychologically, 65-75.
,,   ,,   logically, Essay ii., *passim*.
Creasy, Sir E., his *The Old Love and the New*, referred to, 19.
Culture, national, discussed, 24.
,,   antiquity of, 284, 289, 418.
Cuneiform inscriptions, Essay iv., *passim*.
,,   specimens, 169, 171, 175-9, 181, 192, 197, 199.
,,   characters, origin of, 193.
,,   list of works on, 169, 184, 196.
Curtius, Professor E., referred to, 38, 39, 81.
Cyrus, referred to, 42, 46, 89, 187.
Czermak, Professor, on Egyptian mummies, 224.

Darius I., 153, 185.
Decius, probably the last royal name in hieroglyphics, 129, 230.
Dedications, Egyptian, 271-2.
Delaware language, its antiquity, 161.
Demotic character described, 100-2, 234.
,,   literature, 102, 236.
Determinative ideographs, 114, 120, 143, 236.
Devéria, M., 234, 243, 245-6 (on *maá xeru*), 253, 301, 388, *sq*.
Diligence, exhortations to, 292-4.
Diodorus Siculus, 245, 316, 399.
Dioskuri, apparitions of, 47.
Doalu, inventor of the Vei-negro alphabet, 118.
Dogs, Egyptian, 302, 329-30.
Dublin, funeral Rituals in, 245.
Dulaurier M.S., in *Journal asiatique*, 306, 315.
Dümichen, M. J., 144 (in *Lepsius' Zeitschrift*).
,,   *Tempelanlage von Dendera*, 260.
,,   *Felsentempel von Abusimbel*, 273, 279.

Ebers, Professor G., '*Aegypten und die Bücher Moses*,' vol. i., (Leipzig, 1868), 151, 220, 222-4, 323.

[* His work, *An Egyptian princess* (Leipzig, 1871), containing much accurate information, should also have been cited.]

Ecclesiastes, quoted 280-1.
Eginhard, his *Vita Karoli Magni*, referred to, 40.
Egyptian graphic systems, 100, 119, &c., chronology of, 228, *sqq.*, 235.
,, language, 114, 215, *sqq.*
,, literature, stability of, 238.
Egyptians, physical type of, 223-4.
Epics, Egyptian, 352, *sqq.*
Esther, book of, 174, 185.
Ethics, Egyptian, 278, *sqq.*
Euripides, 280, 361.
Evidence, historical, peculiarities of, 7.
Extradition, Egyptian treaty of, 404.

Fables, Egyptian, 389-90.
Fatalism, consolations of, 324.
Firdusi, 173, 295.
Fou-hi, inventor of one of the Chinese graphic systems, 108.
Freytag, L., his Essay on *Tiberius und Tacitus*, 5.
Funeral inscriptions, Egyptian, 271-3.
   [* Brugsch's *Aegyptische Gräberwelt*, and É. Naville's *la Littérature de l'ancienne Égypte*, should also have been cited.]
Future life, Egyptian notions of, 274, 369.

Galen, 315, 317.
Gautier, M. Léon, his *Épopées Françaises*, quoted, 40.
Genesis, book of, 339.
Gobineau, Comte de, *Histoire des Perses*, 9, 173, 194.
God, names of, 191, 203, 266.
,, self-creation of, 263, *sqq.*, 416.
   [* Cf. also Mariette's *Notice, &c.*, 113-4, 124, and de Rougé in *Rev. archéol.*, n. s., vol. iii., p. 420.]

Index. 427

Goodwin, Mr. C. W., *The Story of Saneha*, 101, 164, 231, 377-387.
,, referred to, 228.
,, in *Cambridge Essays*, 231, 273, 293, 325, *sqq.*, 335, 353.
,, in *Revue archéologique*, 154, 236.
,, in *Lepsius' Zeitschrift*, 138, 244.
Graphic pictures, contrasted with pictorial writing, 105-9.
[* Cf. also Steinthal, *Entwicklung der Schrift.*, 62, *sqq.*, and H. Brugsch, *über Bildung &c., der Schrift*, Berlin, 1868].
Greeks, their evidence on Egyptian writing, 123, 159.
,, ,, ,, medicine, 316, and cf. *Medicine.*
Grote, George, his *History of Greece*, quoted, 17, referred to, 21, 26, 34, 37, *sqq.*, 78.
,, his scepticism on legends considered, 11, 37, *sqq.*
Grotefend, 154, 175-8, 211-12.

Handbooks, historical, 18.
Harits and χάριτες, 49.
Harris, Mr., of Alexandria, his papyri, 233, 301, 391.
Heath, Mr., 277-8.
Heeren, *Ideen über die Politik der alten Welt*, 179.
Herakleidae, return of, discussed, 37, *sq.*
Hermippus (comicus), quoted, 12.
Herodotus criticised, 2, *sqq.*
,, his historical theory, 9.
,, referred to, 31-3, 35, 100, 172-4, 304-6, 342, 360.
Hieroglyphics, Essay iii.
,, specimens of, 109-10, 120, 125, 128, 140, 364.
,, list of some translated inscriptions, 229.
Hieratic writing, 127.
,, papyri, list of translated, 230-2.
Hincks, Dr. E., referred to, 168, 182, 190, 197, 208-9, 243, 375.
Histology, science of, used as an illustration, 29.
History, origin and growth of, 1-3.
,, critical, 2, 17, *sqq.*

History, ancient, its claims, 23, 26.
„   „   modern complexion of, 26-8, 418.
„   „   probable conclusions in, 75-9.
„   contemporary, what it means, 31.
Hitzig, Dr. F., on *Ecclesiastes*, 281.
Homer, Sir G. Lewis on, 35.
„   Grote on, 37.
„   referred to, 43, 79, *sqq.*, 303, 332, 336, 340, 359-60.
Homophones, 120, 146-7, 191, 197, 200.
Horace, quoted, 264, 281.
Horapollo, 121, 139, 145.
Horrack, M. de, 376.
Horses, Egyptian, 359-60.
Huet, *Demonstratio evangelica*, quoted, 58.
Humboldt, A. Von, *Vues des Cordillères*, 106, 108.
Humility, exhortations to, 273.
Husbandmen, Egyptian, hardships of, 327.
Hymn of Amon to Tothmes III., 362.
Hymns, solar, of the Egyptians, enumeration of, 262, *sqq.*
„   quoted, 263-71, 411.

[* The remarkable specimens given in M. Mariette's *Notice des principaux Monuments du Musée à Boulaq*, 46, 85-7, should have been added.]

Ideographs, 108, 191.
„   Egyptian and Assyrian, compared, 201.
„   illustration concerning, 203-6.
Iliad, probable historical basis of, 79-84.
Inscriptions, Italic, 157,
„   Lykian, *ibid.*
„   Etruscan, 120, 158.
„   Egyptian hieroglyphic, 229, &c.
„   Persian cuneiform, 169, *sqq.*
„   Scythian   „   190, *sqq.*
„   Assyrian   „   195, *sqq.*
„   Chinese, 108.

Invention, pure, scarcity of, 41.
Irish Protestants, their bigotry, 133.
,, Catholics, ,, 249.

Jamblichus, *de mysteriis Aegyptiorum*, 225, 266-8, 276.
Japanese, their syllabic graphic system (borrowed from the Chinese), used to illustrate the Assyrian, 207.
  [* I should have added greater details concerning the Annamite graphic system, for which see the article of W. Schott, in the *Transactions of the Berlin Academy* for 1855, 115-30.]
Jaquet, 181.
Jellett, Rev. J. H., *Moral Difficulties of the Old Testament*, 240.
Journal des Savants for 1859, 209; for 1870, 81.
  ,, *asiatique* [the special articles are referred to under their author's names.]
Judicial papyri, list of, 391.
  ,, papyrus of Turin, 392-5; papyrus Abbott, 396-8.
Julian, the Emperor, on the moral use of fables, 391.
Justice, Egyptian, 395-6.

Kant, quoted on Egyptian geometry, 320.
Khetas, war with, 355.
Kirchhoff, Prof., *Composition der Odyssee*, referred to, 85.
Klaproth, *Aperçu sur les diverses écritures de l'ancien monde*, 108.
Kleopatra, name of, 128.
Knapp, *Lectures on American Literature* (Boston, 1829), 118.
  [* Out of print; there is a copy in the British Museum.]
Koelle, S. W., *Grammar of the Vei Language*, 118.
Kottabos (the Dublin University periodical), referred to, 57.
Kuhn, Dr. A., referred to, 44, 73.
Kumârila, referred to, 51.

Language, stability of, 160.
Lassen, Dr. C., 180, *sqq.*, 188.
Lauth, Dr. F. J. *Moses der Ebräer* (Munich, 1868), 231, 262, 264-6, 323, 341, 367, *sq.*, 372, 388.

Lauth, Dr. F. J., in *Sitzungsberichte der. kön. Akad. zu München*, 123, 159, 232, 244, 255, 277, *sqq.*, 289, 291, 363, 388-90.
,, in *Lepsius' Zeitschrift*, 144.
,, *die geschichtlichen Ergebnisse der Aegyptologie*, 151.
Layard, W. A., 195.
Lee papyrus, 301.
Leemans, Dr., *Monuments du Musée des Pays bas*, 137, 262-3, 267, 291, 297, 322, 405.
Lefébure, M. E., 243, 262-3, 274-5, 412.
Legends, Slavonian, referred to, 43.
,, Turanian, ,, 40, 91.
,, Aryan, ,, 43, *sq*.
,, Semitic, ,, 91.
,, coincidence of, not trustworthy, 90, 93.
,, contrasted with inscriptions, 97.
Lenormant, M. F., 129, 132, 230.
Lepsius, Prof. R., *Denkmäler*, 231, 235, 359, 387, 400, 401.
,, *Zwei sprachvergleichende Abhandlungen*, 217.
,, *Auswahl*, 388.
,, *Königsbuch*, 233.
,, *Todtenbuch*, 244-5.
,, in *Lepsius' Zeitschrift*, 112, 129, 217-9, 230.
,, in *Berlin Transactions*, 319.
,, referred to, 289.
Letronne, M., 123, 128.
Letters, Egyptian, 291-3, 320, *sqq*.
Lewis, Sir G. C., *Credibility of early Roman History*, 36, 75.
,, *Astronomy of the Ancients*, 155, 166.
,, criticised, 36, 98, 155, *sqq*.
,, quoted, 5-7, 75, 166.
Leyden papyri, see under Leemans.
Lieblein, M., *deux papyrus hiératiques*, 233, 405.
Lithuanian language, its stability, 161.
Logographers, modern, 19.

Lottner, Dr. Carl, on sister families of language, 218, 221, 225.
,, on the discoverers of cuneiform writing, 193.
Löwenstern, 196.
Lubbock, Sir J., *Origin of Civilisation*, 71, 105.
Lucretius, quoted, 70.
Luzzato, 209-1.
Lytton, Lord, his *Last of the Barons*, referred to, 19.

Maâ-xeru, 246-71, 402.
Magic, Egyptian, 295, *sqq.*, 343, *sqq.*
 [* I should have added to the references Dr. Birch's article on one of the Salt papyri, *Rev. archéol.* for 1861, 119, *sqq.*]
Manetho, 150-1.
Mariette, M. A., in *Revue archéol.*, 153.
 ,, *Notice des principaux monuments du Musée à Boulaq*, 233, 256, 260, 305, 309, 362, 402, 418.
Maspero, M. G., 102, 232, 269.
 ,, His article on Mariette's *Boulaq papyri*, 233.
Medicine, Egyptian, 303, *sqq.*
 ,, ,, authorities on, 305-6.
 ,, Greek, sketch of, 311-2
Menander, quoted, 286.
Ménant, M. J., 170, 175, 196, 200, 227.
Menkera, king of the 4th dynasty, 244.
Mexican graphic system, 106-7.
Misfortunes, the thirty-two, of the Irish Catholics, 250.
Misrob, inventor of the Armenian alphabet, 117.
Moland, M. Louis, his article on Charlemagne's crusade, 40.
Mommsen, Dr. Theod., *History of Rome*, quoted, 26, 27, 33, 38, 77.
Monosyllabic languages, their need of ideography, 114.
Monotheism, Egyptian, 241, 263, 266-71, 340.
 [*And Mariette's *Notice*, &c., 19-22.]
Monument, the oldest known, 229.
Moral treatises, Egyptian, 274, *sqq.*, 403.

Moses, Egyptian culture of, 269, 339, 367.
Mountain chains, importance of their direction, 64.
Müller, Prof. Max., referred to, 44-61, *passim*, quoted 61, 216.
   „   „   identified with Polyphemus, 57.
   „   K. O.,   quoted, 73-4, 361.
   „   Wilhelm,   referred to, 72.
   „   Dr. Friedrich, 221 (*Cruise of the Novara*), 225.
Münter, Bishop, 135, 171.
Murghâb, site of, 187.
Mutilation, in Egyptian laws, 404.
Mythology, comparative, discussed, 43, *sqq.*
   „   „   scientific basis of, 44-5.
Myths, uniformity of, in nations *not* related, 91, *sqq.*, 359.

Naville, M. É., *Textes relatifs au mythe d'Horus*, 107, 223, 260.
   „   *La Littérature de l'ancienne Égypte* (Geneva, 1871), p. 353.
Nebuchadnezzar, the name, 202.
Nibelungenlied, its legends discussed, 88-9.
Niebuhr, B. G., referred to, 33.
Niebuhr, Carsten, 170, 175, 181.
Novels, Egyptian, 335-52.

Obedience, filial, 282-4.
Odyssey, of Homer, 47, 303, the Egyptian, 365.
Odysseus, character of, 53-55.
Old age, miseries of, 279-81, 380.
Oppert, Dr. J., 153, 170-1, 196, 209.
Orbiney, Mde. d', papyrus of, 331, *sqq.*
Osiris, identified with the soul, 246, 298.
   „   Hymns to, 252-3.

Paṇis, compared with Paris, 50, 58.
Pantheism, Egyptian, 274-6, 340.
    [* The notes to Prof. Jellett's *Moral Difficulties of the Old Testament* should have been more fully quoted. The most remarkable pantheistic statements in the Ritual are mentioned by de Rougé in *Rev. archéol.*, N. S., vol. i., 237-40, and 261.]

Papyri, select, of the British Museum, 407.
Pehlvi language, 174, 216.
Pentaour, 325; epic of, 352, *sqq.*
Persians, old, 171, *sq.*
Phonetic notation, origin of, 110, *sqq.*
  ,,   ,,   detected in the hieroglyphics, 126-7.
Physicians, Egyptian, 305-17.
  ,,   Greek, 311-12.
Pichard, M., *Moïse de Khoren*, 118.
Pickering, Essay on the North American languages, 118.
Pierret, M. P., 243, 289-91.
Pleyte, M., *Études égyptologiques*, 228, 243, 251, 306, 322, 402.
Plato, quoted, 239, 268, 311-12.
Pliny, the younger, 321.
Plutarch, *de Iside*, 140, 399.
Poetry, Egyptian, nature of, 412.
Polyphemus, legend of, 57, 91.
Polyphony, 199.
Prisse papyrus, 255, 277-90.
Pronouns, Semitic character of Egyptian, 220-1.
Proverbs, Egyptian, 291.
Proverbs, the Book of, quoted, 287-8.
Psamtik I. (660, B. C.), 233, 245.
Psychology, ignorance of, among comparative mythologers, 68-70.
Ptah-hotep, moral treatise of, 273, 277, *sqq.*
Ptolemy, name of, in hieroglyphics, 125.

Quadrilingual inscriptions, 153.
Quatremère, M., 131, 134.
Quippus, Peruvian and other described, 107-8.
  [* Add as reference Juan de Perez' article on the subject in the *Revue Orientale et Americaine*, vol. ii., and Von Tschudi, *Travels in Peru*, p. 492.]

Raifet papyrus, 353.

Ramses II., 331, 342, 352, *sqq.*, 403.
,, III., 389, 392.
,, IX., 396.
,, XII., 300.
Rask, Professor, 179, 183.
Rawlinson, Sir H., 170, 182, 197-8, 212.
Recueil de travaux relatifs à la philologie égyptienne et assyrienne, (Livraison 1re, Paris, 1870), quoted, 102, 231, 247, 289, 353.
Rémusat, A., *Grammaire chinoise*, 108, 112.
Renan, E., referred to, 34, 132, 209, 222-3.
Reuvens, C. J., *Lettres à M. Letronne*, referred to, 102, 297, 302, 314.
Rhind bilingual papyri, 253, 259, 274, 339.
Rillier, M. A., referred to, 6, 81.
Ritual, the funeral, of the Egyptians, 146, 200, 238, 241, *sqq.*, 275, 296.
,, commentaries on, 243.
,, analysis of, 246-9; 64th chapter, 244, 247; 89th chapter, 253-4; 125th chapter, 251; 155th chapter, 252.
Review, Edinburgh, for October, 1870, 45, 59, 71-2.
,, *Westminster*, for 1843, quoted, 39.
,, *Saturday*, for July 31, 1870, quoted, 92-3.
Revue archéologique (old series, vols. i.-xvi.; new series, vols. i.-xxii.). [The articles quoted are classed under the names of their respective authors.]
,, *critique*, 367.
Romans, narrow spirit of, 164-5.
Rougé, De, Vicomte É.
,, *Chrestomathie égyptienne*, 146-8.
,, *Rituel Funéraire*, 246, *sqq.*, 258.
,, *Inscription du Tombeau d'Ahmès*, 220, 229.
,, *les Monuments des* vi. *premières dynasties*.
,, *poème de Pentaour*, 353, *sqq.*
,, in *Journal asiatique*, 229.

Rougé, De, in *Revue archéologique*, 87, 229, 268, 331, *sqq.*, 363-4.
,,   in *Lepsius' Zeitschrift*, 406.
Rosetta stone, the, 112, 124, *sqq.*
Rosny, M. Léon de, *Archives paléographiques*, 105, 207.

Sacy, M. de, 126, 174.
Sahou, meaning of, 255.
Saidic, the Theban dialect, 134, *sqq.*
Sallier papyri, in the British Museum, 293, 324.
Salt   ,,   ,,   399.
Saneha, story of, 378-87, 405.
Saramâ, not certainly identical with Ἑλίνη, 49.
Saranyu and Ἐρινύς, 49.
Sassanids, 174-6, 217.
Satirical writings of the Egyptians, 371, 387, *sq.*
Saulcy, M. F. de, 197.
Scepticism, historical, sketch of, 33-43, where the school of Grote and Lewis is compared with that of Max Müller and Cox.
,,   ignorant, 151, 155.
Schoolcraft, *Report on the Red Indians*, 68, 105.
Schröder, *Thesaurus linguae Armenicae*, 117.
Schwartze, M. G., *das alte Aegypten*, 134-5, 217.
Science, Egyptian, 317, *sqq.*
Scott, Sir W., his *Anne of Geierstein*, referred to, 19.
Scribes, advantages of Egyptian, 326-8, 388.
Scripture metaphors, in Egyptian literature, 293, 299.
Scythian (?) inscriptions, 154, 211.
Semitic languages, 217, 221.
Sent, king of the 2nd dynasty, 229, 306-7.
Sequoya, discoverer of the Cherokee alphabet, 118.
Seti II., king of the 18th dynasty, 399, 401.
Setna (or Setnau), Romance of, 138, 235, 254, 341-52.
Shafra, king of the 4th dynasty, 309.
Sins, the 42 mortal, of the Egyptians, 245.

Sister families of languages, 225.
Sitzungsberichte (Proceedings) of Munich Academy. See under the heading *Lauth*, and 229.
Smith, Mr. Edwin, of Luqsor, his medical papyri, 233, 306, 313.
Snefru, king of the 3rd dynasty, 289, 378.
Society, *Royal Asiatic, Transactions of*, cf. Rawlinson.
Sophokles, quoted, 280.
Soul, the immortality of, among the Egyptians, 256-7.
Spiegel, Dr. Fr., *Altbaktrische Grammatik*, 117.
,, *Persische Keilinschriften*, 169-70, 179-80, 184, 188.
,, *Eranische Alterthumskunde*, 193.
,, *Avesta*, 194.
Steinthal, Dr. H., his *Entwicklung der Schrift*, 105, 114.
,, *Mande Neger Sprachen*, 118.
Style, Egyptian, 411, *sqq*.
Suez canal undertaken by Darius I. (from Nile to Red Sea), 153.
Sun-worship, Egyptian, its real nature, 262, *sqq*.

[* The reader will find the best exposition of its ideal aspect in Julian's 4th oration on Helios ; cf. Mücke's *C. Flavius Julianus*, 165, *sq*.]

Syllabaria, Assyrian, 209.
Syllabic notation, 115, 190.
Syria, in the 14th cent. B. C., 374-6.

Tacitus, criticised, 5.
,, object of his historical writing, *ibid*.
,, referred to, 31-2, 406.
Tanis, inscription of, 152.
Tell, William, legend of, 40, 81-2, 91.
Temper, regulation of, 285-6.
Thukydides criticised, 2, *sqq.*, 161.
,, compared with Herodotus, 3-4, 16, 31-2.
,, his historical theory, 11-14.

Theology, Egyptian, 415.
Tothmes III., king (18th dynasty), 361.
Transactions, *Edinburgh*, 62.
   „   of *Royal Irish Academy*, 190.
Travels, Egyptian, 365, *sqq*.
Turin, Museum of, 233, 388.
Two Brothers, Tale of, 331, *sqq*.
    [* I should have also cited M. Maspero's version in the *Revue des Cours Littéraires*, for Feb. 28, 1871.]

Ushas, compared to 'Ηώς, 49.
Utilitarianism, old Egyptian, 274, 285.

Vei Negroes, their graphic system, 118.
  „   „   their beast fables, 390.
Valle, Pietro della, 168.

Westergaard, Prof. N. L., 182, 184, 189-90, 194.
Wilkinson, Sir J. G., 389.
Women, treatment of, in Egypt, 287, 332, *sq.*, 336, 339.
Writing, origin and first developments of, 104-17.
    [* I should have also referred to Dr. Brugsch's tract, *Über Bildung und Entwicklung der Schrift* (Berlin, 1868), which corroborates the views of my Essay.]

Xerxes, 154, 187-8, 341.

Young, Dr. Thomas, 126-7.

Zend language (old Bactrian), compared with old Persian, 183, 211.
  „ alphabet, its richness in vowel signs, a proof of its late origin, 180.
    [* On this point, cf. also J. Oppert, in *Journal asiatique* for Feb. 1851, p. 281.]

Zeitschrift, Dr. Lepsius' and Brugsch's, *für Aegyptische Sprache*, &c. (Berlin, 1863-71). [The articles are referred to under the names of their respective authors.]
Zeitschrift für die Kunde des Morgenlandes, 181.
,, *der Morgenländischen Gesellschaft*, 318.
Zoëga, *de usu obeliscorum*, quoted, 106, 126.
,, *Catalogus codicum copticorum*, 134, 235, 306.
Zündel, Prof. J. (of Zürich), 390.

THE END.

www.ingramcontent.com/pod-product-compliance
Lightning Source LLC
Chambersburg PA
CBHW022133300426
44115CB00006B/169